MW01258504

FOUR DAYS A WEEK

ALSO BY JULIET B. SCHOR

After the Gig

True Wealth

Born to Buy

The Overspent American

The Overworked American

FOUR DAYS A WEEK

The Life-Changing Solution for
Reducing Employee Stress,
Improving Well-Being,
and Working Smarter

JULIET B. SCHOR

HARPER
BUSINESS
An Imprint of HarperCollins*Publishers*

HarperCollins books may be purchased for educational, business, or sales promotional use. For information, please email the Special Markets Department at SPsales@harpercollins.com.

FIRST EDITION

Library of Congress Cataloging-in-Publication Data has been applied for.

ISBN 978-0-06-338243-5

25 26 27 28 29 LBC 5 4 3 2 1

For Prasannan

CONTENTS

AUTHOR'S NOTE

This book is based on a collaborative effort among a team of researchers. In the introduction, I discuss the origins of our work and how the team came together. Its core members are Wen Fan, Guolin Gu, Ami Campbell, and Orla Kelly. Together we designed the research plan and survey instruments and have analyzed the data and written academic papers. Guolin handled all the survey administration in the first two years, and she has carried out the statistical modeling. After joining the team, Ami took over much of the survey administration and has led the qualitative data collection. However, we have all participated in most parts of the research. Phyllis Moen and Youngmin Chu of the University of Minnesota joined the team in 2022 and have collaborated on the interviews, analysis, and paper writing. Others are named in the acknowledgments. I alone wrote this book, so my colleagues should not be held responsible for its content. However, if there is any credit to be had, it should be fully shared.

INTRODUCTION

The origins of this book go back forty years. At the time, I was an assistant professor in the Harvard economics department, specializing in labor economics. I published a book called *The Overworked American: The Unexpected Decline of Leisure*. Working hours was an orphan topic in those days, but my interest had been piqued by a distinguished scholar's (faulty) argument about it. First, I wrote a little model to highlight his error. Then I started looking at the data. In contrast to what many scholars were arguing, I found that working hours were not declining. Richard Nixon's 1956 promise of a four-day week in the "not too distant future" was nowhere on the horizon. There was no crisis of leisure time, as many predicted would be the case by the 1970s. It looked as if hours were actually going up. Subjective data on the time squeeze revealed that people felt they were busier and more harried than ever.

The book, published in 1992, hit a nerve. It landed on *The New York Times'* bestseller list. I was getting media attention and was invited to speak to CEOs of major American corporations. I was even getting calls from people in Washington, D.C. Bill Clinton's presidential campaign frequently referenced the fact that "most people were working harder for less." And it wasn't only liberals who were concerned. Conservatives who cared about "family values" were also critical of excessive working hours. The "overworked

American" was later identified as one of the country's most influential social science ideas since the 1990s.

And then . . . nothing. Despite widespread agreement that Americans were working too much, the issue died. I had conversations with some large companies to encourage them to experiment with work-time reduction, but none panned out. Neoliberal economics was on the ascendancy. September 11 happened, and the United States invaded Iraq. Attention turned to the worsening income distribution. Not only was work time no longer on the agenda, but a kind of amnesia took hold. Keynesian economists, who resurfaced after the 2008 global financial crisis, forgot that Keynes himself was a strong advocate of using productivity growth to reduce work time. I even encountered some hostility to the idea of working less.

So I wrote books on other topics and mostly directed my research on working hours to academic articles. And then the pandemic of 2020 hit. Almost overnight, it transformed the conversation. The four-day week took off—in the form of a thirty-two-hour workweek with a full day off and no reduction in pay. The movement went viral, and I was invited to lead a global research effort studying companies that were piloting these schedules. This book tells the story of those organizations, their phenomenal success with this innovation, and what it means for management, employees, and society.

In sharing the findings from our research, I hope to ignite interest in the four-day week among business, labor, and political leaders, as well as human resource executives, entrepreneurs, nonprofit and public sector employers, and individual employees. In all these quarters, people are aware that the old way of working is no longer working. This book was written with all of you in mind. If you are an employer, I hope that the extensive research we have done will interest you in trying out this model at your company. If you are in government, there's an opportunity for your employees to work less and also for legislation to spread this model. Labor union leaders can bargain for more time off. If you are an employee who feels that "two days is not enough," there's plenty of evidence here you can bring to management. This book is my analysis of how and why it's time to work four days a week.

THE CRISIS OF OVERWORK

All is not well in the global workplace. Workers are burned out and demoralized. They were already struggling before the pandemic. Then things got worse. We've been witnessing quiet quitting, loud quitting, labor shortages, employees refusing to return to the office despite corporate dictates, labor force dropouts, unfilled positions, and an uptick in strikes and unionization. Gallup's 2024 report on the global workplace found that two-thirds of all employees fall into the "struggling" or "suffering" category. In the United States and Canada, about half of all respondents were stressed "a lot of" the previous day, were "not engaged," and were watching for or actively seeking a new job. Microsoft's 2024 global survey of knowledge workers discovered that 68 percent are struggling with the pace and volume of work and 46 percent feel burned out.

Overwork is at the center of these problems, especially in the United States. The country has not only failed to reduce its workweek; its hours have gotten longer and have diverged from other wealthy countries. Americans log ten or more weeks of work per year (that is, four hundred plus hours) than the Germans, Danes, and Dutch, and seven or eight weeks more than many western European countries. Americans now spend more time at work than even the Japanese, whose government's 2021 annual economic policy guidelines included encouragement for a four-day week. That said, overwork is not exclusively an American problem. Hours are long in other places too, such as East Asia and other Anglophone countries. The latter are the places where we've collected data, and they all have similar findings. Our collaborators running trials in other countries have comparably positive results.

Back to the United States. The conventional view is that American overwork is cultural, part of the national character. So it's a surprise to many that the United States led the world in work-time reduction until after World War II. In the 1970s, annual hours began to rise, and although they haven't followed a straight-line pattern, they've increased in subsequent decades. But if culture isn't the reason the United States lost that leading role and fell off its century-long path of declining hours, what is? It's a puzzling history.

One part of the answer is that new technologies haven't given Americans more free time, despite repeated expectations that they would. A hundred years ago, Keynes predicted that if productivity trends continued, we'd have a fifteen-hour week by now. In the immediate post–World War II period, labor unions revived demands for shorter hours, including the Depression-era goal of a thirty-hour week. In the 1960s, what was quaintly termed automation was expected to create a crisis of excessive leisure time. The early 1990s were another moment when "overwork" and "work-family conflict" produced a flurry of interest in work-time reduction, as I described above. But hours continued to climb. Now, as the digital revolution has given way to the age of galloping artificial intelligence (AI), work time is back on the agenda. People are terrified that AI is coming for middle-class jobs. Finally, we have a solution with momentum.

THE FOUR-DAY-WEEK TRIALS

The idea of a four-day week had been around for a long time, but the movement had limited traction. When companies, such as Microsoft Japan, which tried it out in 2019, implemented it, it got plenty of press coverage. But individual company experiences didn't move the needle. In the U.K., campaigners have been active for years. They got a big boost in 2018 when John McDonnell, shadow chancellor of the exchequer, announced steps to institute a four-day week when Labour came to power. But that effort stalled because the Conservative Party, which is hostile to the idea, stayed in control of government. Pre-pandemic, momentum came from the private sector and was propelled in large part by a man named Andrew Barnes.

Barnes is a British-born, New Zealand–based entrepreneur who owns a successful financial services company called Perpetual Guardian. He got the idea for moving his company to a four-day week after reading about a survey that found U.K. office workers were productive for only one and a half to two and a half hours a day. That got Andrew thinking: If his employees were working well below their capacity, he could offer them a full day off in exchange for ramping up their effort on the other four—what he came to call the 100-80-100™ model. It was a brilliant idea because it was designed to maintain business performance without reducing pay or expanding daily hours. Andrew fired off an email to his HR officer and in early 2018 began planning an eight-week trial, enlisting local academics to study outcomes. The results were outstanding. Employee engagement, productivity, and work-family balance improved. As they publicized the results, interest poured in from around the globe. Andrew and his partner, Charlotte Lockhart, began devoting their efforts to spreading the word. In 2019 they founded 4 Day Week Global (4DWG), an NGO dedicated to expanding the movement. Soon enough, the pandemic scrambled normal life. But it turbocharged progress on the four-day week.

For employees, the pandemic led to a reassessment of priorities. When existence can be snatched away at any moment, it feels more important to spend each day doing what matters. For employers, it broke down resistance to change. As Adam Husney, CEO of the first company to join the U.S. trials, told me, "The pandemic taught us that we could trust our workers about where they work, so now we're trusting them about how much time they put in." Tinkering with flextime, wellness classes, or small pay increases would no longer cut it. Employers needed something dramatic. That something has come in the form of a full day off with no loss in pay. And when they give this shocking "gift," it has a truly transformative effect.

During the depths of lockdown I was mostly toiling away in my third-floor home office, teaching, and giving Zoom talks. Europeans were becoming more interested in shorter work time, and I was getting a lot of early morning invitations. After a February 2021 talk on work-time reduction to the European Trade Union Institute, a man named Joe O'Connor approached me. Joe worked for Fórsa, the largest public sector trade union in Ireland. The union was interested in a four-day week but recognized it would need private sector proof of concept before getting buy-in from the government. Joe had put together a coalition of civil society organizations, including women's groups, environmentalists, and employers, to run a four-day-week trial. He asked me if I'd be interested in doing the research. We reached out to Orla Kelly, a former student from my department who taught at University College Dublin, and the three of us began working on what would become the first of many global trials on the four-day week—the Irish pilot. Before long Joe was collaborating with Andrew and Charlotte and became CEO of 4DWG. They started planning a U.S. trial to follow the Irish one, and I signed on as lead researcher. I expanded the research team, bringing on my colleague Wen Fan, who is a specialist in work and family, well-being, and remote work, and our PhD student Guolin Gu, and we got moving. Two thousand twenty-two would prove to be the coming-out year for the four-day week.

Company trials (or pilots, I'll use the terms interchangeably) began in early 2022 and are continuing today. By the summer of 2024, 245 organizations and more than eighty-seven hundred employees have been part of our research. We've done trials in the United States, Canada, Ireland, the U.K., Australia, New Zealand, and South Africa. Our collaborators have led the research for trials in Portugal, Brazil, and Germany, with more countries on the way. Reports from the completed trials are available on the 4 Day Week Global website (www.4dayweek.com), and for the U.K., on the Autonomy Institute website (autonomy.work), under their research tabs.

The results have been outstanding. For many employees, it's a "life-changing" innovation. We track twenty well-being metrics—everything from burnout to sleep—and all show statistically significant and often large improvements.

- Sixty-nine percent of participants experience reduced burnout, and nearly 40 percent are less stressed and anxious.
- More than half experience fewer negative emotions, and nearly two-thirds feel more positive emotions.
- Forty-two percent have better mental health, and 37 percent see improvements in physical health.
- People also score much higher on work-family and work-life balance.

These aren't retrospective answers. We survey people before the trial begins and track their individual responses at three, six, twelve, and twenty-four months. We've done statistical modeling on why people are so much better off as they work less, and find that it's a combination of inside- and outside-of-work factors (details in chapter 2). Thirteen percent of our sample say they wouldn't go back to a five-day schedule for any amount of money. "Thank you for a glimpse into what life can be like," one person tells us.

These findings may not surprise you. Who wouldn't prefer less work time at the same pay? But what may be unexpected is how much success *organizations* are seeing with this model. We have fewer metrics from them, because we wanted common yardsticks across a diverse group. However, one figure stands out: twenty. That's the number of companies that have discontinued their four-day week by the one-year mark. They represent just 10 percent of the total. And a few of those put their four-day weeks on hiatus and plan to restart at some point. We also have excellent results from their organizational performance metrics: revenue, absenteeism, and res-ignations. The bottom line is that the four-day week has been a huge win for the companies. We ask them to rate the trials, and they give consistently high scores—an average of 8.2 out of 10. Employers are mindful of the fact that their employees are thriving. As one wrote, "We've just done our annual happy check, and it's our best employee engagement result in twenty-seven years (across twenty questions). And I think a lot of that is down to the four-day week."

These great results don't happen automatically. There's a strong focus in the trials on maintaining or improving productivity, and the expectation for many organizations is that they will get five days' work done in four. To that end, the trials begin with a two-month period of "work reorganization" to eliminate time-wasting and low-value activities. As one participant commented, "In busi-ness, we plan better, utilize our time wisely. More productive. Ev-eryone pulls their weight." That's a common experience. However, in some organizations, it's less about productivity and more about reductions in turnover. Jon Leland, who introduced the schedule at Kickstarter, explains, "Losing one or two key employees every six months is just so disruptive. And if you stopped doing that, it just changes everything." Retention is especially valuable in a tight labor market. On the two-year anniversary of its trial, our contact at a small U.K. start-up was effusive: "Yes, not had a single leaver and it helped massively with recruitment. I have not had to use a single recruiter!" While much of the media coverage has focused on productivity hacks such as shorter meetings and eliminating distractions, in our research we find multiple pathways to success. The companies differ a lot; so do their experiences.

We also find that some things we feared don't materialize. Positive features of work, such as people's sense of autonomy and control of their schedules, are stable or improve. The productivity results aren't mainly due to speedup. People are not taking on second jobs. A measure of workplace sociability does not decline. In another, perhaps unexpected result, customers seem to be fine with it. A senior customer-facing employee told me that when she informed her main client she wouldn't be working on Fridays, their reaction was "That's great" and they would respect it. The four-day week now feels like common sense.

BEYOND THE KNOWLEDGE ECONOMY

Contrary to what many assume, this schedule doesn't only work for white-collar knowledge workers. While professional services and tech are overrepresented among companies adopting four-day schedules, with well-known examples such as Bolt and Wanderlust, there are also successful cases in manufacturing, construction, health care, and other services. Our trial participants include hundreds of white-collar organizations, but also entities such as the Platten's fish and chips shop in the U.K. and Advanced RV, a motor-home manufacturer in Ohio. We have surveyors, engineers, and bankers. We've got social service agencies, mental health providers, a police department, and a hospital chain. Nurses are getting four-day weeks. Law firms are going to four. Lots of nonprofits and even a few local governments are adopting this model. So far, it's successful in almost all the industries we have data from.

This book dives into the stories of organizations across that wide range of industries. They include the following:

- Kickstarter, a Brooklyn-based medium-sized tech company supporting crowdfunded creative projects that dramatically improved its performance metrics
- Praxis, a marketing and communications company in Toronto that found a solution to Parkinson's law
- Pressure Drop Brewing, a small craft beer producer in London that reengineered its workflow
- M'tucci's, a New Mexico–based restaurant chain with four locations, whose chefs and managers work four days
- The Canadian team at a large global digital-first marketing, advertising, and tech firm that achieved remarkable retention results
- A thirty-five-thousand-person New Jersey hospital chain that addressed nurse manager burnout by giving an extra day off
- Grand Challenges Canada, a social service agency solving global problems, whose employees were emotionally drained before their four-day week
- ArtLifting, a small Boston-based company representing disabled and unhoused artists that has achieved remarkable growth as it reduced working hours
- And more . . .

Our sample includes people working remotely, in the office, and hybrid. And while most of the companies in our trials are small, that's also true of 99.9 percent of U.S. businesses, which together employ just under half of all employees. We have one organization that trialed with 999 employees and is now rolling out to its other 4,000. We've also got global companies. Simpro, a private SaaS customizer with employees around the world, joined our first trial in 2022. Our results are consistent across the variations in our sample: countries and regions; for-profits and nonprofits; large and small organizations; whether the company is remote, hybrid, or in person; how they manage the off day; as well as industry, occupation, gender, race, age, and most every other distinction we can think of. That said, our sample is disproportionately white-collar. Only 4 percent are manufacturing and construction firms. And it's mostly made up of relatively privileged workers—not the low-wage end of the labor market.

It's important to note that the four-day week doesn't magically cure all that ails the modern workplace. There can be complicated aspects to this schedule. The workload in professions that experience strong seasonality, such as accountancy, is harder to control during the busy season. Some of the very senior people in our trials have too much work to take a day off, but use it for catch-up, which eases their nights and weekends. One participant explained, "I'm the boss so it's harder for me to take a day off every week than it is for everybody else, but I do usually manage it."

While we haven't seen evidence that the four-day week works only in certain industries or for some kinds of employees, the organizations we've been studying do seem to share one characteristic: They care about their people. As you read their stories, I think that theme comes through. It's an important part of their success.

HOLD ON A MINUTE

By this point, I'm sure your head is bursting with questions. I've just addressed one of the most common: Isn't this just a white-collar thing? But that's only one of many that people have asked. You may also be wondering about others:

- How are these organizations getting five days of productivity in only four days? Addressing meetings and distractions can take you only so far.

- If companies can raise productivity via work reorganization, why don't they just do that, without giving a day off? Then they can be more profitable by either laying some people off or asking everyone to do more for a full five days.
- Aren't people in four-day-week companies paid less? After all, it's a valuable perk, and maybe employers will think they can get away with lower salaries.
- Are these six-month results durable? Sure, people feel better when they get a benefit like a four-day week. But over time, they adapt and revert to their earlier state. Won't they eventually just get burned out and stressed once again?
- This might work for nine-to-five organizations. But what about health care or services where they're operating 24/7?
- And here's another variant of "how is this feasible for everyone?" This is a self-selected group of companies. Sure they can make it work. That's because they're different from those that haven't tried it.
- Won't this fail because Americans are workaholics?

Or you might just agree with Christian Lindner, the German finance minister who in the fall of 2023 claimed, "Never in history has a society increased its prosperity by working less. The key to our prosperity remains hard work." Lindner was commenting on the fact that in early 2024 fifty German companies signed up for a four-day-week trial. It's an odd perspective from a person whose workers are some of the most productive in the world, despite an annual average workweek of just twenty-six hours.

Whether you're curious about objections like these or skeptical of the whole idea, you'll find answers to them and many others in the pages that follow.

THE FOUR-DAY WEEK IS COMING

It is a little-appreciated fact that it has been eighty-five years since the United States last reduced its workweek. That happened in 1940, through an amendment to the New Deal–era Fair Labor Standards Act (FLSA). Yet over these eighty-five years, the productivity of the American worker has increased more than fourfold. Getting a two-day weekend wasn't an easy lift. That fight took more than twenty years. So far, the four-day-week effort is unfolding with uncanny similarity to the movement from six days to five. At that time, it started with small employers, as it is today. Then unions came on board. The next big development was a major employer taking the plunge; in the 1920s it was Henry Ford. Finally, the government passed legislation. I don't know if it'll be Ford again, although the 2023 demand by the United Auto Workers (UAW) for a thirty-two-hour week suggests it's possible that history will repeat. And 2023 and 2024 also saw a flurry of legislative activity to reduce the workweek, although no major bills have yet passed.

But even if those last two stages take a while to materialize, there's growing evidence of an organic shift. Fridays are becoming a different kind of day. There are No Meeting Fridays, Work from Home Fridays, alternating Fridays off, and Fridays off or early Friday closing times in the summer. There's also a hint of change at the beginning of the week, with Bare Minimum Mondays, a twenty-first-century version of the early modern practice of observing St. Monday, an informal nonwork holiday. These are all signs that we are evolving away from Monday through Friday to a workweek that is more in tune with the needs of a knowledge-based, technologically sophisticated, high-productivity economy. People are struggling with current work patterns.

There's also a certain urgency to this moment, which wasn't a factor eighty-five years ago. We are facing a high degree of uncertainty about jobs as a result of the rapid introduction of artificial intelligence. The ability of large language models like ChatGPT to wipe out millions of good-paying positions means we need to be intentional about how we adjust to that technology. Reducing hours per job is a powerful way to keep more people employed.

Shortening hours is also a potent climate policy. There are multiple pathways through which work time affects carbon emissions. Commuting is the most obvious, but just slowing down, which tends to happen when people have more time off, also has carbon benefits. There's plenty of evidence that countries that work less also pollute less. We're at the point in the climate breakdown process that any changes we make to the world of work must also contribute to the process of decarbonization.

PLAN OF THE BOOK

At this point I'm hoping you're eager to hear more about how and why the four-day week has been such a success. In chapter 1, I set the stage, explaining the problems this schedule solves and how we studied these trials. Then it's on to employees and their life-changing stories (chapter 2). The next three chapters (3–5) detail the experiences of the companies—what motivated them to take the plunge, how they prepared, what they achieved, and the problems they encountered. If you're interested in how a four-day week might work for your organization, this is where you'll find answers. This is also the part of the book where I pose and discuss common questions and address skepticism about whether this model can work. Those discussions will be useful if you're trying to persuade colleagues to give it a try. The next two chapters of the book (6 and 7) zoom back out to situate the four-day week in the context of artificial intelligence and the climate crisis. The final chapter (8) is about why I think the four-day week is on its way. Each of the chapters can be read as a stand-alone. I've tried to keep the text free from jargon, excessive details, and technical issues. Those are confined to the notes, appendix, and in some cases references to our academic papers. Now let's get started!

FOUR DAYS A WEEK

1

TWO DAYS IS NOT ENOUGH

Our story begins in Toronto, in 2020, during the early weeks of the pandemic. The city is in extreme lockdown. Millions have been laid off. Schools are shuttered. The border is closed. Even outdoor spaces, like public parks and playing fields, are off-limits. There are long lines at the grocery stores, and once inside shelves are often bare. People are stressed.

Tessa Ohlendorf, a highly awarded advertising industry veteran and managing director at a global media company, was having a particularly rough time. She was one of the very first COVID cases and had been sick for weeks. A single parent, she was struggling to care for her six-year-old daughter. The week the closures started, headquarters asked managers to wait before acting. She defied the policy and sent people home a few days early, knowing what awaited them.

The next few months were brutal. Tessa was waking at 4:30 to log a few hours of work before her daughter woke. Seven thirty to 9:00 was kid time, then 9:00–3:00 and 3:00–6:00 were a mix of work, homeschooling, and play. Six to 9:00 she spent with her daughter. She knew her team was going through something similar, with full-time work and full-time childcare, plus endless hours spent provisioning for basic needs. Tessa was ordering coffee from the shop down the road and begging them to add rolls of toilet paper to her delivery. She had been studying for a graduate degree, which she had to put on hold, delaying further career advancement. All told, life was a nightmare.

Tessa had a history of being responsive to her team's needs. In 2019, she'd noticed people rushing out at 4:59 to get to an exercise class or trying to squeeze a trip to the gym into their lunch hour. When someone with a health issue asked for permission to swim mid-morning, she just gave everyone three hours a week of exercise time, to be taken whenever they wanted. Exercise was good, she felt.

Now, with the pandemic, she wasn't sure what would help. Counseling? Money? As she started asking her team what they needed, the answer became obvious: time. So in July 2020, she announced that everyone could have Friday afternoons off. Eventually, a team member came to her with the observation that four plus three (Friday afternoons plus exercise time) is seven hours off. That's a four-day week. So, after months of planning, and hearing about a trial we were starting in June 2022, Tessa pulled the trigger. She was bringing in a lot of money for the company and knew that protected her. Once again she didn't ask her bosses; she just forged ahead. It was the beginning of a life-changing experience for her team—and for Tessa.

As with so many of the companies in our trials, the team's experiences were great. People described the trial as "amazing," "phenomenal," "incredible," "awesome," "life-changing." Their well-being measures improved. One person reported, "I've been living with a health issue that I never felt was serious enough to take the time off work to address, so I suffered for years instead. Having this extra day meant that I could finally prioritize what I felt I didn't have time for, which is *me*." Many reported marked improvements in their lives. They also talked about being more productive, motivated, and willing to "go the extra mile" for the company. One person noted that they were no longer "trying to pour from an empty cup."

I met Tessa about a year after her trial had started. She wanted advice about how to expand the four-day week within Canada, and throughout the company's nearly ten-thousand-person global workforce. Most of the messaging around the four-day week, especially in the press, had focused on "productivity hacks" that compressed five days' work into four days. Getting more efficient with meetings, reducing distractions, and improving focus were the bread and butter of the program. These are real gains. But as Tessa talked about her team's experience, I started to question whether it had benefited much from the usual productivity hacks. She seemed so talented and professional that I doubted she'd run a shop with much inefficiency to begin with. When I raised this point, she largely concurred. They did introduce some tweaks to meetings, she said. However, the secret to their success lay in the well-being benefits for employees. Advertising is a notoriously high-turnover industry, and the teams Tessa worked with were seeing annual rates of resignation of 30 to 40 percent. Her group of fifty-seven had lost only one person since the trial began. That not only yielded obvious cost savings but led to better work and additional business. Another exciting part of the story for Tessa was that she was discovering new ways to monetize the benefits of the four-day week. It wasn't just a boon for employees; it had morphed into a business strategy.

I'll return to Tessa's story in chapter 4, with more detail on how creating team stability works. For now, let's zoom out to the big picture—why workers are struggling, the importance of time, and how the pandemic led to soaring burnout and spurred hundreds of companies to take the plunge.

THE FOUR-DAY WEEK WORKS FOR EMPLOYEES *AND* EMPLOYERS

It might seem obvious that employees would benefit from a four-day week. What may be less obvious, but also true, is that companies benefit too, as our research shows. To a large extent, company success results from employees being better off.

To see why, consider that workers face dueling economies of time—inside and outside the workplace. Even pre-pandemic there was too much time *in* work and not enough time *out* of it. The pandemic exacerbated that imbalance.

Outside their paying jobs, people face what the sociologist Arlie Hochschild has memorably called the "second shift"—the unpaid household labor that reproduces families and communities. When women were full-time homemakers or part-time workers, most of this household and community reproductive labor was done during the week. Now, with two-thirds of U.S. women workers holding full-time, full-year jobs, much of it has to be done on the weekend. And as we hear over and over, two days is not enough.

Meanwhile, inside many workplaces, a perverse dynamic is at play. With the standard workweek stuck at five days and forty hours, there isn't much incentive to save time and make people more efficient. When hours don't fall, work expands to fill the available time, in what is popularly known as Parkinson's law. This is the context for what 4 Day Week Global has called the 100-80-100 model. (It stands for 100 percent of the pay in 80 percent of the work time, but with 100 percent of prior productivity.) This model succeeds in many white-collar organizations whose work intensity is low or inefficient enough that they can find timesaving innovations that allow staff to complete all their work in four days. We see this in finance, marketing, and other professional services, for example. Employees are grateful and loyal to their employers, feel empowered by their newfound higher productivity, and give their all. The company reaps those benefits.

Of course, not all workplaces suffer from this level of inefficiency. Some have already engineered out wasted time. However, in this efficient group many put heavy demands on their employees, who then become overwhelmed at their "high-intensity" jobs. (Think nurses or restaurant workers.) The four-day week can work for these companies too, but with what I call the 100-80-80 approach. (A hundred percent of the pay in 80 percent of the work time, but with only 80 percent of the productivity.) These employers can't ask for more per hour. They just need to reduce work time, to solve burnout and loss of personnel. Companies that follow 100-80-80 may have to add staff. But they stanch the bleeding. Extra costs, in salary or other adjustments, can be less than what they save in retention, talent attraction, and better quality of product and service.

This was the world pre-pandemic. When COVID hit, these problems intensified. People were experiencing more stress outside work and, in many cases, inside the workplace too. At the beginning of the trials, we saw many 100-80-100 companies. As time went on, and pandemic burnout accelerated, there seemed to be more whose main motivation was stemming the tide of resignations. Many of these are in the 100-80-80 group. And of course, there are plenty that have elements of both.

So that's the argument in a nutshell. Employees have a time problem that the four-day week solves. They become more productive and loyal. This in turn helps the businesses they work for. Let's unpack each step in this chain of explanation.

THE LONG-HOURS ECONOMY

In *The Overworked American*, I called it the time squeeze. Other terms are "time crunch," "time poverty," and "overwhelm." There aren't enough hours in the day—or week—to combine job work and household work.

The salient point about paid working hours in the United States is that despite amazing technological advances they are stubbornly long. They're long in comparison to similar countries, and they're long in historical terms. As I noted in the introduction, the historical trajectory is what originally got me interested in this topic. When I started looking at the post–World War II trends, I was struck by the fact that after many decades of steady decline, hours of work had stopped falling. As I dug into the data, I realized that in the 1970s hours had begun to rise. Measuring from the peak of each business cycle to the next—because hours of work move up and down with the strength of the economy—and correcting for unemployment and involuntary part-time work, I calculated that from 1969 to 1989 the average worker was putting in an additional month of work each year. One hundred sixty-two additional hours, to be precise. Most of this was due to changes in women's patterns of paid work. Their weekly hours rose by about two and the number of weeks they worked each year grew by six. (Think fewer mothers opting out during the summer to care for children.) Total paid hours rose by 305 a year. Men's paid hours rose too, by just under 100. I didn't continue with my calculations, but the Economic Policy Institute did, although without the correction for involuntary part-time work. Its data show that hours continued their upward climb through the 1990s and 2000s. Between 1989 and 2016, work time rose from 1,783 hours to 1,883, exactly an additional 100 a year.

The severity of the time squeeze is even more pronounced from the vantage point of families. In the United States, half of households with married couples have two earners, and many of these have two full-time earners. A pre-pandemic estimate of the increase in households' annual work time found that the average middle-class couple with children worked a combined schedule of 3,446 hours. That's 600 hours more than in 1975.

Because annual hours is not the most intuitive metric, it may also be useful to consider what's happened to weekly hours. Here there are more readily available data, over a longer period of time. In January 1950, according to the Current Population Survey, average weekly hours of paid work were 41.2. By 2023, that figure, which includes part-timers, had fallen to 38.5. That's a bit of progress. However, for full-timers, the 40-hour workweek hasn't yet arrived; it sits at 41.9.

As I pored over these numbers, I remembered another one: 39.4. That's the average workweek of U.S. and Canadian participants in our trials (before they start their shorter schedules). It's not much lower than the amount of time U.S. employees were on the job in 1950. After seventy years of automation, digitization, and a bit of AI, hours are still stubbornly high.

U.S. hours are long in another way—in comparison to other wealthy countries, such as those in western Europe. These nations stayed on the path of hours reductions when the United States fell off. Germany is the star here; between 1950 and 2023, it reduced annual hours by 1,086, or about as much as a half-time job on a 40-hour week. Other countries also logged impressive reductions—850 for France, 670 for Denmark, 575 for Spain. In contrast, the U.S. decline has been a meager 216, and most of that came by 1980. Since then hours have fallen only 34, or about four days.

By 2023, the average American worked 460 more hours than counterparts in Germany; 400 plus more than in Denmark and the Netherlands; 300-plus more than in France and Sweden; 286 more than in the U.K.; 150-plus than Spaniards; and 72 more than in Italy. Even Japan, which a few decades ago was thought of as a workaholic country like Korea or China, where people were suffering from *karoshi*, or death by overwork, now has lower annual hours than the United States, by about 155.

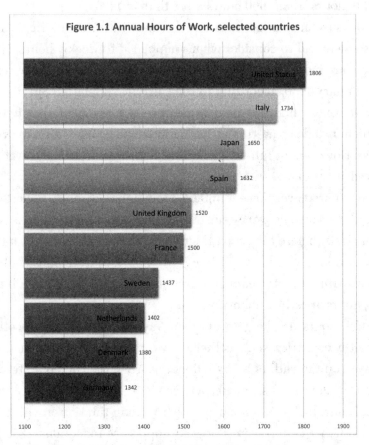

Figure 1.1 Annual Hours of Work, selected countries

Country	Hours
United States	1806
Italy	1734
Japan	1650
Spain	1632
United Kingdom	1520
France	1500
Sweden	1437
Netherlands	1402
Denmark	1380
Germany	1342

Note: Average Annual Hours per Worker. 2023. Total Economy Database, The Conference Board.

And lest you think that short work hours are a bad thing, it's worth noting that they go along with high hourly productivity. Yes, high productivity can fund work-time reduction, which partly accounts for the connection. But as we'll see throughout our company stories, reductions in working hours can also boost hourly output. France and Germany, two of the biggest economies in the list above, have seen enormous increases in hourly productivity since 1950. This measure grew about eightfold. They've just about caught up to the United States, whose productivity growth during that time was about half as large.

Why are U.S. hours so high? And why didn't the United States continue to reduce hours after World War II, as it had done in the prior seventy years? I'll get into this question in more detail in chapter 6. The distorting effect of tying health insurance to jobs has been a major factor because it creates a de facto tax that discourages hiring and encourages long hours. Weak unions and high inequality have also played roles. To understand the time squeeze, however, a key factor is the prevalence of what has been called the "ideal worker norm." It's a cultural construct reinforcing the idea that to be a successful employee, one must work long hours, show unlimited dedication to the job, and not let family or personal responsibilities intrude. Adherence to this norm obviously disadvantages parents and especially women, who still bear more responsibility for child and eldercare, and other household labor. And it's a big part of why the outside-of-work dynamics of the time squeeze are so constraining.

HOUSEHOLD PRODUCTION

If people had only one site of work—the market—the time demands of most jobs would be manageable. But few of us are in that situation. We're not only working for pay; we're also doing unpaid labor in the household and community. These sites of social life have their own economies, and they are not trivial. According to the economist Nancy Folbre's analysis of data from the American Time

Use Survey, across the population, weekly hours of unpaid labor on childcare, household work, and volunteering are larger than time spent in paid employment—29.4 hours versus 24.5. In high-income countries as a whole, paid and unpaid work are just about equal.

The dual demands from these two sites of production have resulted in persistent shortages of time. Here's an eye-popping statistic, albeit about one of the most time-stressed groups— middle-class full-time dual-earner families with children. They spend a combined 139 hours a week doing paid and unpaid work. Divided evenly, that's a seventy-hour workweek for each. American families are straining under the growth in structured activities for children, the increased burden of eldercare, bigger houses to maintain, long commutes, and high demands from everyday life.

One of the most striking findings in the literature on U.S. time use is that contrary to expectations, as women's paid work increased, they didn't cut back on childcare. In *The Overworked American*, I included estimates of how increases in paid work affect household labor. My models found that for every additional hour a woman worked in the market, she cut back nearly half an hour at home. I didn't parse the different types of household work, because I was focusing on total work time. A decade after my book was published, the U.S. government began administering time-use surveys regularly, which led to much better coverage and quality of data for household activities. The trends in housework were as expected. Women were doing less of it, particularly when it came to cooking. One study, covering the period when market hours rose substantially, found a daily reduction of twenty-nine minutes per day for women in the labor force. As expected from previous research, men's housework time didn't go up by much to compensate—just six minutes.

However, as researchers crunched the numbers, they found very different trends for childcare. Even as their paid working hours were rising substantially, American women were spending more time caring for children. Leading researchers found that weekly childcare hours doubled between 1975 and 2010. Men tripled their time in childcare over the same period. These are underestimates because they don't always include care that it is done in conjunction with something else, and it's likely that kind of multitasking has been rising. American mothers spend a lot more time caring for their children than Europeans do, in part because they are less likely to use out-of-home care. But another factor has also led to the counterintuitive trend of longer hours of both paid work and parenting, which is the increasing importance of what scholars have called "intensive mothering." It's a norm in which the mother needs to be a constant presence, expert at all facets of childcare, from psychological and physical health to education, nutrition, sports, cultural activities, and social life. This "ideal mother" is the counterpart of the ideal worker. Intensive mothering has always been rooted in middle- and upper-middle-class white culture but has oozed out into other communities. It's a problematic ideal— both for the children it oppresses and for the women who can never live up to its norms. And it has spawned even more excessive parenting styles, such as helicopter and Velcro parenting.

The combination of long hours at home and at work has produced a chronic condition of time squeeze. It has been hard to shake because employers have been rigid about not reducing hours and have held to the ideal worker norm. Parenting expectations and pressure have risen, both for cultural reasons and because competition for college entrance and good jobs has intensified. Housework has been cut to the bone. Across our whole sample, at baseline, total weekly paid and unpaid hours were 56.8 for men and 59.3 for women. For parents living with children under age eighteen, the average is a whopping 70.9. This is why we so often hear the weekend lament that "two days is not enough."

And then the pandemic hit.

PANDEMIC STRESS AND BURNOUT

The pandemic had an almost instantaneous disruptive impact on work. More than fifteen million people lost their jobs. Tens of millions of white-collar employees were suddenly relocated to their homes. One estimate finds that by June 2020, 42 percent of U.S. employees were full-time remote. Essential workers continued in person, of course, with high levels of COVID risk and its accompanying anxiety. For many, especially mothers, the pandemic added a third shift to their day at work and home—composed of online schooling and managing the added burdens of the pandemic. That precipitated the first-ever "she-cession," in which women exited the labor force at unprecedented speed, with mothers, single mothers, low-wage mothers, and Black and Latina mothers most likely to have left their jobs.

These developments resulted in high levels of stress, burnout, and labor market dissatisfaction. It was all chronicled in the popular culture as labor market trends appeared on TikTok before they showed up in the statistics. The first year of the pandemic featured "take this job and shove it" vids, with people complaining loudly about being unwilling to stay in their bad jobs. r/antiwork, a subreddit that had been around since 2013 and was devoted to "Unemployment for all, not just the rich," soared in popularity, eventually gaining 2.8 million subscribers, up from a few thousand in 2019. Users posted about the many indignities they were suffering in their jobs and the failings of work under capitalism.

By 2022, the big trend, especially for white-collar jobs, was quiet quitting, the idea that you didn't leave, but dialed down the effort. The year 2023 was a succession of quiet quitting variants. We had Bare Minimum Mondays, Lazy Girls, and then Lazy Girl Jobs—the kind you can keep even if you're quiet quitting. In late

2023, @Briellybelly123 went viral, complaining about the nine-to-five job she took after college. Between hours in the office, commuting, cooking, and grooming, she had no time for life. Needless to say, Brielle incited vigorous responses—both sarcastic and empathetic. The productivity expert Cal Newport dubbed this moment the "Great Exhaustion." He believes that pre-pandemic most knowledge workers were managing workloads that were just short of unsustainable. The pandemic put them over the edge. I suspect that was also true for many other kinds of workers.

These pop culture trends were confirmed in survey data. Less than a year into the pandemic (January 2021), a global study by Microsoft of more than 30,000 workers found that 41 percent were considering leaving their employer within the year. In the United States they followed through and created what was called the Great Resignation, a historically unprecedented mass exodus from work. In 2022, 50.5 million Americans, or almost a third of all employees, left their jobs. At its peak from late 2021 to early 2022, 4.5 million were quitting each month. Most didn't permanently drop out, leaving some economists to talk of a Great Reshuffle rather than Resignation. While quits came back to earth by late 2023, the topsy-turviness of the labor market left employers sitting with unusually high numbers of empty positions. In early 2022, there were just over 11 million unfilled vacancies, almost twice pre-pandemic levels. Those open slots would turn out to be important in prompting organizations to pilot the four-day week.

The popular culture phenomenon of Lazy Girls and Bare Minimum Mondays also shows up in the data. Gallup reports that in 2022, 50 percent of U.S. workers were quiet quitters. Among the rest, only about a third were actively engaged at their jobs. Almost 20 percent were what Gallup calls "actively disengaged," that is, loud quitters. Rates of quiet quitting and disengagement were higher among younger workers.

While some interpreted these trends as entitlement or laziness, particularly among the young, the reality is that people were having a very hard time. The Microsoft study found that with one exception, in all the groups they surveyed, more than half the respondents were "struggling," rather than "thriving." (The exception was "business leaders.") The highest levels of struggling were found among single people (67 percent), new employees (64 percent), frontline workers (61 percent), Gen Z (60 percent), and working mothers (56 percent). This study also found that 17 percent of respondents reported that they had cried with a co-worker, with higher levels in some of the most stressed industries, such as health care, travel and tourism, and education. Burnout among nurses, waitstaff in restaurants, and other service sector jobs reached crisis proportions. Interview studies of how people, especially women, fared through the pandemic paint a grim picture. They describe it being "crazy," having to manage emergency situations at work, sacrificing sleep and self-care, feeling guilty. Among the fifty-three mothers in one study, all reported having more anxiety and stress than pre-pandemic.

Soon, researchers began to refer to a new phenomenon: pandemic-related burnout, or PRB. PRB is more widespread and severe than what workers had been experiencing pre-COVID. And for many, the problems go beyond burnout. The Centers for Disease Control reported that in 2020, 41 percent of all Americans were suffering from some type of adverse mental- or behavioral-health-related condition, a large increase from before the pandemic. These included depression, anxiety, substance abuse disorders, suicidal ideation, and trauma disorder symptoms. Rates were higher among the young, racial minorities, essential workers, and unpaid adult caregivers.

The collapse of the boundary between work and home was particularly difficult for employed mothers, and especially in families that relied on traditional gender roles. Schools and day cares were closed, and many private caregivers and housecleaners were no longer on-site. A McKinsey study found that 75 percent of mothers were spending more time on household responsibilities. More parents were finding it difficult to balance remote and household work as the pandemic wore on. A growing body of literature finds that the pandemic exacerbated existing gender and racial inequalities in the workforce.

My colleague Wen Fan and her co-author Yue Qian researched the impact of the pandemic on well-being. One of their studies found that only 12 percent of respondents did not experience a "stressful life event" during the pandemic. The most common type was health related, but events related to paid work ranked second. Women were more stressed than men, and more stressed by work. In a second paper, they used a clever design that exploited the fact that infection rates, COVID-containment measures, and layoffs happened at different times across U.S. states. They found significant negative impacts on mental health and life satisfaction, not only as a result of individual factors but also from the larger macro-environment at the state level, and especially from heightened levels of job insecurity. The pandemic labor market had itself become an adverse life event for millions.

While some employers attempted to ease the stress occasioned by the pandemic, others embarked on work intensification. Plenty of companies were in crisis mode. One qualitative study found the large majority of mothers were experiencing impossible demands, because the pull of the ideal worker norm led to increased work expectations while they also had to take care of their children. Many companies paid lip service to flexibility, but didn't follow through. In companies that went through layoffs, the employees who remained had more work than ever.

Hours of work plummeted at the beginning of the pandemic but quickly began to recover. They then started a steep upward climb, peaking in January 2021, returning to pre-pandemic levels after two years. White-collar workers appear to have had especially big increases, according to data from people logged onto Microsoft Teams. By that measure the span of the workday expanded by forty-six minutes, although some remote workers had flexibility to jump on and off their machines (as Tessa did). These data also show big increases in after-hours and weekend work, and that the amount of time people were spending in meetings rose. On the other hand, some studies find that people were working fewer hours. One in-depth analysis found a marked decline in hours worked between 2019 and 2022, with prime-age, college-educated men showing the largest drop. Other research suggests that most of the reduction has been voluntary and that at least some of it is temporary.

These pandemic-driven changes in labor force participation and desired hours of work partly reflect the ways in which people were reevaluating how their jobs fit into their larger life choices. One reason is that the pandemic forced people to reckon with the precarity and in some cases the brevity of life. Seeing people die before their time was a wake-up call for many. The popular press was full of surveys and stories about how people's attitudes to work had changed. For some, the experience of spending more time with family changed what they were looking for in a job. This isn't something that our surveys captured, but it did come up in one of my interviews. Tracy Smith had been employed in advertising and on workdays barely saw her daughter. When she decided to find a new job, she said that "flexibility, which had never really been a high motivating factor for me, now came to the top of my list." She ended up at one of the organizations in our research, "because there are certain things that I will not give up on now, that I didn't even know that I was missing before. I used to drop my child off very early and pick her up very late. And I will never have that again."

While there is some uncertainty about exactly how average work time changed over the pandemic, and a lot depends on the time period, there's no doubt that work demands resulted in intensified stress and burnout in the United States, and around the globe. Among participants in our pilots, satisfaction with time ranked lowest among our satisfaction questions. The pandemic meant that people needed more time. A lot more.

This is the context that led to the four-day-week trials. Many people were already suffering a time squeeze due to having long hours on the job and facing the same situation at home. When COVID hit, demands became unbearable, especially for parents. Both employees and employers needed a solution to an impossible situation. The four-day week proved to be their salvation.

THE HISTORIC NATURE OF THE TRIALS

The four-day-week trials, or pilots, were historic in many ways. They were the largest ever to take place. As of this writing, 245 organizations and eighty-seven hundred employees have participated. (See table A.1 in the appendix for details.) They have included many countries; we've had trials in North and South America, Europe, Africa, and Australasia. Most prior workplace interventions have involved one company, not hundreds. And while there was one large experiment with a shorter workweek in Iceland from 2015 to 2019, it featured smaller reductions in hours and involved only public sector employees. Numerous Scandinavian shorter work-time trials also covered the public sector. The 4 Day Week Global pilots were pathbreaking, and ambitious, for enrolling a wide range of private sector organizations. We had participants across all the major industrial categories, not just in professional services, IT, finance, and other white-collar sectors, but also hospitality and health care, manufacturing and construction. We had small and medium-sized companies. (There were a few large companies of five thousand or more employees, but only smaller groups within them did the pilots.) The trials, and our research efforts, have stretched over multiple years, demonstrating viability in a variety of macroeconomic contexts. And because we've kept the research effort going, we've been able to track the companies over time—two years at this writing. Every one of the pilots in the first two years has been successful, with very little attrition and great employee outcomes. This effort has blazed a path that led not only to tremendous interest in the four-day week from private sector organizations but also to a number of governments sponsoring their own trials.

TRIAL RESEARCH DESIGN

Our research design was straightforward, and consisted of employee surveys, data uploads from the companies, plus employee interviews. (See the appendix for details.) The trials began with two months of planning, coordinated by 4 Day Week Global, followed by a six-month period of a four-day week. 4 Day Week Global handled all recruitment. Participants were required to maintain pay and cut working hours by at least four hours a week; however, all but a handful implemented an eight-hour reduction. The employee surveys followed the same individuals over time—from before the trial started (that is, at baseline), then at three, six, twelve, and twenty-four months. The surveys varied in length, with the baseline and six-month versions being the longest, with approximately 150 questions about work experiences, time-use patterns, energy use, and twenty well-being outcomes, plus open-ended comments. By 2023, our survey instrument, as well as translated versions, was being used by researchers around the world, including in official national trials in Portugal and Scotland.

For the company data, it was important to keep things simple because there are so many different kinds of organizations participating and so many are small. We decided that revenue would be the most practical overall success measure. While people often ask about productivity, many companies don't have straightforward productivity metrics, and where they do, they aren't common across trial participants. (We did ask organizations to rate the trial on productivity and performance.) We also asked for data on resignations, sick days, new hires, and energy use. The trials varied in size, with the third (U.K.) being the largest. We collaborated on that one with the 4 Day Week Campaign (U.K.) and the Autonomy Institute. When I decided to write this book, I began interviewing CEOs and others at participating companies to get their stories.

It's also worth noting that from the beginning we set up the research team to be independent of the NGOs we were working with. They were all absolutely respectful of that independence. We raised our own funding, controlled all the research and the data, and were prepared for whatever the numbers showed. As it turned out, our findings offered strong validation for the mission of 4DWG and our other collaborators—that the four-day week can work for employers and workers.

The research was designed to assess the impact of the four-day week on employees and businesses. Because there are so many different types of impact, we collected many kinds of outcome variables. And because we went into the research with an open mind and not to "prove" that the four-day week would work, we made sure to include questions that would capture unexpected adverse consequences. Did work reorganization lead to speedup and a higher intensity of work? Did the reduction to four days mean people lost control over their schedules? What happened to their feelings of connection with co-workers? Were they more tired at the end of the workday? Were participants taking on second jobs on their off day, which would reduce the well-being benefits? Surprisingly, few of these possible blowback effects occurred.

DESCRIBING THE COMPANIES

So who are these companies? I've already talked about the range of countries, industries, size, and other features, but only in general terms. First up is country. The U.K. trial was the largest, with 29 percent of the companies. The United States was second at 23 percent. With respect to size, as I've already noted, most of the organizations in the trial are small. Twenty-eight percent are really small (one to ten employees), 35 percent are in the range of eleven to twenty-five, 17 percent are twenty-six to fifty, 9 percent are fifty-one to a hundred, and 11 percent have more than a hundred employees. This is partly an artifact of the trial setup. Big companies don't need to partner with an NGO to change their schedules. They can do it on their own. In terms of industry, the biggest group is professional services and marketing, which make up 45 percent of the sample. Next come civil, social, and other services at 18 percent. Administration and IT are 9 percent. Health care and education are 5 percent each. Finance and insurance are 4 percent, as are construction and manufacturing. Retail is 3 percent. The remaining companies are a mix. In terms of in-person versus remote, the biggest category is hybrid at 69 percent, with 25 percent fully remote and only 5 percent fully in person.

And finally, how did they implement their four-day week? One day off per week is the most common arrangement, with 81 percent of the companies doing that, plus another 14 percent with a mixed

Table 1.1 Describing the companies

Country		Industry	
Australia	10%	Professional services and marketing	45%
Canada	9%	Civil and social services	18%
European Union	4%	Administration and IT	9%
Ireland	6%	Other	6%
New Zealand	4%	Health care	5%
South Africa	13%	Education	5%
United Kingdom	29%	Finance and insurance	4%
United States	23%	Manufacturing and construction	4%
Other	0%	Retail	3%

Size		In-person v. remote	
1-10	28%	Fully in-person	5%
11-25	35%	Fully remote	25%
26-50	17%	Hybrid	69%
51-100	9%		
101+	11%		

arrangement, allowing employees to choose between the four-day week and shorter daily hours. Five percent had an alternative arrangement. Fridays off was the most popular option, with 43 percent choosing it. Another 17 percent have a Monday and/or Friday arrangement. Thirty-seven percent have something different (rotating, personal choice, and so on).

Table 1.2 How the companies arranged their four-day weeks		
		Percentage of companies
Four-day week arrangement	One day off per week (4DW)	81%
	Other arrangements	5%
	Mixed 4DW and other arrangements	14%
Choice of day off	Monday	1%
	Wednesday	2%
	Friday	43%
	Monday or Friday	17%
	Other or no designated day off	37%

THINKING LIKE A RESEARCHER

If you follow research findings, especially in fields like medicine and economics, you'll know that the gold standard in design is the randomized controlled trial (RCT). Participants are randomly assigned to two groups. Some get the "treatment" (or intervention)—in this case a four-day-week schedule with no reduction in pay—and the others continue with business as usual. The RCT model comes from medicine, where half the patients are given a new drug and the other half get a placebo. It's a robust way of figuring out whether the drug works, although strong placebo effects do complicate things. About twenty-five years ago, development economists and other social scientists began using RCTs to figure out whether interventions meant to reduce poverty or improve public health worked. But we had a more complicated situation. We were dealing with organizations, not individuals, which created two reasons why an RCT wasn't feasible. First, how could we get companies that wanted to shift to a four-day week to agree to hold off for six months? No sane management who thought this would help their organization would tie its hands in this way. Some had an urgent need for change. But even if they didn't, we had no leverage over them. In drug trials, people are often eager, even desperate, to get a new drug, and the trials are the only way to get access. They join even though they have only a 50 percent chance of receiving it. In many of the RCTs run by economists, poverty creates that willingness. A four-day week is not a commodity we had exclusive access to. Any company could institute it.

The second reason is that the four-day week is an organization-wide change. Many previous workplace intervention studies have involved only a subset of employees, which allowed researchers to add a control group for comparison. But in our case the "treatment" is not at the individual level. The idea is that the whole company undergoes a work reorganization to change culture, practices, and policies. An important part of the impact is that the stigma of individual accommodation—which has doomed many prior flexibility initiatives—is eliminated. People aren't disadvantaged by working less. While it might have been possible to run control groups in large organizations with some separated divisions or locations, our trials were attracting smaller employers where this wasn't an option. They had to be all in.

One way around this would be to recruit some control companies—organizations that had interest in the four-day week but weren't jumping in yet. Of course, they wouldn't be a random group, but they'd add some power to the findings. In the Irish trial we were able to get a few, and the differences with the treatment group were striking. However, the number of survey respondents was small. Our colleagues who conducted the Portuguese government–sponsored trial included a control group and found that well-being increased significantly in the four-day-week companies and declined on many of the same measures in the control group. In 2022, our recruitment of control companies fell short, but in 2023 we ramped up our efforts and succeeded. I report on those findings in the next chapter. Short version: Well-being and self-reported productivity go up significantly in the four-day-week companies but not in the control organizations.

While it would have been ideal to conduct an RCT, and we're hoping that some of the government trials that may be forthcoming will have enough leverage over companies to do that, there are features of our research design that mitigate its absence. In particular, because we are collecting data over a long time span, there is less concern about "period" effects. Those occur when the results are due to something else happening over the same time frame that is driving results. In early 2022, when we started, a potential period effect was that countries were emerging from the pandemic. That would be an obvious factor that would improve well-being. It would likely affect company performance as well. But our results have held up throughout 2022, 2023, and 2024, long after nations had opened up. And they haven't changed much over that period. A second feature of our design is that the sample varies on dimensions other than timing. These include national context, industry, size of organization, and whether it's a for-profit or nonprofit entity. We even have a couple of public sector employers. The more types of organizations that are included, the more robust the findings. And of course, the large size of our sample matters. The more we replicate findings, the more confidence we can have in them.

Finally, there's the issue of what's called selection bias, which is why randomization into treatment and control conditions is so important. Selection bias occurs when the people who are selected for a study, or who select into a treatment, are different from those who don't. This type of bias is serious in many studies. For our companies, there's no question it's an important consideration. Companies that have decided to try a four-day week are almost certainly different from those that haven't. If we assume that senior managements know their companies, it's likely they'll be more successful than those who are reluctant to try it.

This is why we never claim that our research shows that *any* company can profitably institute a four-day week right now. *What our findings show is that some companies can benefit.* However, they also show that it's not just a certain type of company, or country, for which success is possible. Over time, as we have results from more and more companies, we see that success is being achieved in multiple ways, and for multiple reasons. That suggests that more companies can achieve it and that the selection bias in our sample is likely getting less severe. Because we have many more white-collar firms, it's also likely that there's less selection bias in those industries. I return to this issue in the final chapter, where I explain why I believe this model can work quite generally.

The other type of selection bias involves employees. Are the people in our trial different from other employees? The selection bias in this case would not mostly be because the employees are selecting into the four-day week, because in nearly all cases the impetus for participating has come from senior management. But perhaps the managers are motivated because their people are more over-worked, stressed, and burned out than other workers. In that case, these companies might benefit more from the four-day week.

These research issues notwithstanding, the trials have been a revolutionary intervention that has succeeded beyond expectations. That has been the experience of the companies and the people who participated in them. I turn now to those employees.

2

A LIFE-CHANGING
INNOVATION

For decades, employers have been instituting programs and policies designed to improve workers' well-being. They've offered flextime, stress reduction, yoga classes, wellness apps, mommy tracks, and more. Almost none of these interventions, which target individuals rather than organizational practices, solve the problems they are ostensibly aimed at. A recent analysis that included more than forty thousand U.K. employees found no positive well-being impacts of these programs, echoing previous findings. Some of these efforts are just ways to get people to work more. Others end up stigmatizing the people who use them or reducing pay without changing workloads—a common mommy track complaint. One of the conclusions from scores of studies is that interventions that put the onus on individuals will fail. Another finding from this literature is that until recently almost no companies were designing interventions that let people work less with no loss in pay.

That's what's different about the four-day week. It focuses on the organization, rather than the individual. It addresses the big problem people have: They need time. It doesn't reduce their income.

And there's another thing. It's not tinkering or baby steps. It's a big, bold change.

WELL-BEING IMPROVES, SOMETIMES DRAMATICALLY

As I went through our data, I kept seeing words like "lifesaving," "life-changing," "brilliant," "amazing." Some called it revolutionary or transformational. We got comments such as these:

- "Love the pilot. All great!"
- "Everyone should do it!"
- "I have been so grateful for this trial. My life has changed drastically."
- "I loved this trial because it improved my life in every possible way."
- "My life is materially improved and I would be hard pressed to give it up."
- "Oh my goodness. What an amazing project."

Sam Smith, the co-founder of Pressure Drop Brewing, said, "I feel like I'm twenty-three again." That's not to say there are no naysayers. There are a few. But as one employee from a U.S. company said, "This 4DWW is the best thing that's ever happened to me and my family (since the birth of our children)."

These sentiments make sense given what we have learned about the impact of a third day off. We ask about subjective well-being with questions about job and life satisfaction as well as behavioral practices such as exercise and sleep. On every one of our twenty metrics we find statistically significant improvement from the beginning of the trial to the end point. We find reductions in burnout and stress. People are less anxious. They experience fewer negative and more positive emotions. Their subjective assessments of their mental and physical health improve. After a year on this schedule, one employee told us, "This past year my mental health has improved so much and I now enjoy my time off work (before I would be too tired on weekends to enjoy my time off work!). I have autonomy which feels unique and new." One reason is that people are sleeping better and are less fatigued. They exercise more. These aren't retrospective results. We ask people how they're doing at different points in time and track those findings—when the trial begins, and then at three, six, twelve, and twenty-four months. We find that these improvements are sustained, even at the two-year mark. Ninety-six percent of the employees in our sample want to retain this schedule, and 13 percent of those who prefer it say that no amount of money could induce them to take a position where they'd have to return to five days.

Sometimes the response to these findings is a shrug of the shoulders. Sure, people feel better when they work less. That's a no-brainer. But is it really? They might be more stressed on the job. And then there's the question of *why* things improve. Our modeling suggests it's not as obvious as one might assume. When we dug into why people are better off, we identified two main pathways. The first is the one that has probably already occurred to you. People have more time for their families and friends, sleep, hobbies, exercising, and communities. Those dimensions of life enhance well-being. While the direction of change is what we expected, we did not think these results would be so large, universal, or durable. The data reveal improvements for all types of people, across all the industries, countries, time periods, size of company, business model, length of time on the new schedule, and type of schedule change.

The other pathway was the unexpected one. The four-day week

makes people feel much more effective at work. "I feel more organized, efficient, productive both in my professional and personal life." Some no longer wonder if they can get through the week. The "Sunday scaries" disappear, as people feel refreshed and ready to get back to work. Overall, we find a large increase in self-reported productivity. And that turns out to be an unexpected factor driving well-being improvements.

In subsequent chapters I'll explain how changes in well-being affect the bottom line for companies. But first, let's explore how people's lives—in and out of work—change when they get the extra day.

GETTING HEALTHIER

Many employees shared stories about how the four-day week has improved their health. My favorite is from someone who credits it with saving their life. "Had it not been for the pilot I wouldn't have had the time or the availability to get medical appointments and procedures which ultimately led to the early detection of something that might've proved fatal. Thanks to just those few extra days off, I can type this email knowing I'm healthy." That "something" was cancer, and this person felt that if he hadn't had his Fridays off, he might not have made that initial appointment. Many of us know that feeling. If we are busy, we might not make the call. Or we're relieved that we weren't too busy, and averted disaster. Having a job that leaves us so little time that we put our life, or those we care about, in jeopardy is not something anyone should have to experience.

Less dramatic stories chronicle major changes to physical and mental health as well. One participant reported being able to stop taking so many painkillers because their headaches have subsided. They're less "angry and tense," because they've got one less day with a long and, for them, excruciating commute. (They also like saving money with less driving.) Another participant explained that having more available time slots meant they could get into counseling sooner, which has had an enormous impact on their life. "Emotionally I feel a lot less burnt out, before it felt like two days just wasn't enough time out of work to be able to give myself an emotional break from the continuous emotional strain of the job. The four day week has made it much easier to bounce back from life struggles/ life events as it gives me so much extra time to sort out problems."

One employee reported that they suffered their first episode of psychosis and were able to keep their job, which they didn't think would have been possible with a five-day schedule. We've also heard that for people with disabilities, including invisible ones, the schedule is what makes it possible for them to hold a regular job. An employee with a generalized anxiety disorder reports, "Time pressures are a trigger for my symptoms." The relief from the extra day off means that their symptoms have gone down "appreciably."

A South African participant told us they've weaned off one of their antidepressants and their "calming tablets." (Others report this as well, but with different terminology.) They explained that the four-day week had become essential to their life. "I am feeling heart palpitations by just thinking that we may not carry on with this. It took me out of such a bad spot in my life, where I felt that all I do is work, eat, sleep, repeat. I am 60 years old and have been working all my life, this is like being on pension but still working and in SA we will never be able to take pension as life costs are too high."

A U.K. participant also connected mental and physical health and told us that the trial had changed her life. "At the start of the trial i soon realised i was not dealing with a few mental health issues very well. This made the first month hard to deal with. The extra day has allowed me to overcome a lot of these challenges, i have changed my diet and i dropped 13KG during the trail [*sic*]* and got promoted at work. If the 4 day week continues or not i think i will come out of it a different person." The person who reported getting into counseling explained that since starting, "I've found it really impactful on every aspect of my home and work life. I've signed up for the gym again, I've found it easier to do housework, and I have started returning to old hobbies that I didn't have the energy or motivation for." In their study of a custom manufacturing company, which they call BldWrk, that went to four days, our collaborators Phyllis Moen and Youngmin Chu interviewed someone who reported that they have needed physical therapy "literally for years," but hadn't been able to take time off. With Fridays off they now had "the freedom to do that."

One European participant reported big improvements on multiple dimensions. She suffered from type 2 diabetes, but adjustments to her lifestyle have put her in remission. Her doctors consider this development "astounding, remarkable, significant." She has lost forty pounds and is less stressed, and her sleep apnea has improved. Her polycystic ovary syndrome has improved enough that she might even be able to get pregnant. In fact, being able to get pregnant now— either because of health or for time pressure reasons—is something that a number of participants wrote about.

Our survey data confirm the validity of these individual experiences. Mental health improves and anxiety declines. Burnout falls for 69 percent of participants. Stress declines. So do anxiety and negative emotions. Positive emotions increase. Physical health also improves, in some cases because it's closely tied to mental health. Every one of these changes is statistically significant at the most stringent probability level, meaning these are not random changes. These findings are detailed in table 2.1.

---

* I have kept comments as people wrote them, even where there are typos or grammatical or spelling mistakes.

Table 2.1 Well-being improves

	Baseline	Endpoint	Change	% Decrease	% No change	% Increase
Work stress	3.2	2.9	-0.3	38%	47%	14%
Burnout	2.8	2.4	-0.4	69%	9%	23%
Job satisfaction	7.1	7.6	0.5	24%	29%	48%
Physical health	3.0	3.3	0.3	17%	46%	37%
Mental health	2.9	3.3	0.4	16%	41%	42%
Anxiety	2.4	2.1	-0.3	38%	47%	15%
Positive emotions	3.1	3.6	0.5	25%	11%	64%
Negative emotions	2.3	2.0	-0.3	54%	21%	24%

Note. Decrease, no change, and increase are fraction of the sample whose scores went down, up, or did not change. Stress: frequency of work stress over the past four weeks (1-5 scale). Burnout: 7-items (1-5 scale). Job satisfaction: (0-10). Physical health: (1-5). Mental health: (1-5). Anxiety: (1-4). Positive emotions: 5-items (1-5). Negative emotions: 3-items (1-5). Where reported, significance levels are based on paired-sample t tests to determine whether baseline and endpoint values are significantly different: +p<.1, *p<0.05, **<0.01, ***p<0.001. Where there are no significance indicators, as above, all baseline to endpoint changes are significant at the p<0.001level.

The table also includes the fraction of people for whom each outcome improves, does not change, or worsens. You may be wondering why some people have worse scores. It's important to remember that employees are affected by factors other than the work schedule. Over the six months of the trial all sorts of things are happening to people that affect their health and well-being, some good, some bad. Looking over one person's survey results, I noticed that their sleep and exercise had plummeted, their anxiety had climbed, and other well-being indicators fell. In sum, their experience didn't support the general pattern of findings. "Aha," I thought, "this person must be a new parent." Sure enough, he was. We heard something similar in the comments, as one person noted, "Some notes on why my health may not be 'excellent' at the moment and/or why my answers may seem skewed. I have a 10-month-old baby that I care for at times during the workday. While having a 4-day work week has helped me and my family tremendously, having a baby and learning to be a mom is taxing. ha! Also, I was recently (within the last 4 months) diagnosed with an autoimmune disorder and have had a flare up within the past 4 weeks that affects my physical, mental, and emotional health as well as my work."

These kinds of life events are happening over the course of the trial, and they are one reason that about a quarter of the sample has worse physical health and fewer positive emotions at the end of the trial than at the beginning. For some, it may be the case that the new schedule isn't working, but since we find that 96 percent of people want the four-day-week trial to continue, negative outcomes are more likely due to unrelated random factors such as a diagnosis or an adverse life event. (Early in the research, people were writing into our open-ended comment box to criticize the survey instrument on the grounds that it didn't factor in a bad thing that happened to them that was unrelated to the four-day week. They were concerned that their answers would mistakenly suggest the new schedule wasn't working for them. We started offering a separate comment box to criticize the survey. We knew that these events were both positive and negative and, in a large sample like ours, would likely cancel each other out.)

A second set of outcomes helps explain why people are scoring so much better on anxiety, health, and burnout. These are behavioral changes such as exercise, sleep, and fatigue. All improve over the trial period. More and better sleep is a major change. Thirty-nine percent of the sample report fewer sleep problems, and sleep hours inch up by twelve minutes a day. By the end of the trial, people are sleeping 6.9 hours a night, almost achieving experts' recommended seven. Some people catch up on sleep during the off day. A Canadian employee explained, "I have taken the opportunity to catch up on lots of needed sleep during the trial. I find that when I go back to work on Mondays I actually feel like I had a chance to disconnect over the weekend. Before I never got rest on the weekend as there is always too much to do. . . . I think I will need to continue working on selfcare to be able to fully feel rested. . . . I have many years of burn-out to get over!" Another Canadian employee, at a high-intensity start-up, explained, "During the trial, my mental health improved significantly. My sleep routine has also improved; I usually sleep all night and wake up feeling energized." Another, from the U.K.: "The flexibility of having an extra day a week to manage my own mental health, my own sleep cycle and my own practical life tasks, as well as into which to fit fulfilling personal life activities and activities pertaining to my own self-development—has been invaluable."

Trial participants are also more physically active. We see increases in the frequency of exercise. Going to the gym more is one of the most common things mentioned in the comments. And quite a few people report joining or rejoining a gym. "I've had such a positive experience being a part of this pilot program. Not only has it enabled me to improve my time management skills at work and at home, but it has allowed me to spend more time with my family and feel less stressed about life in general. I find myself more productive at work and at home. My son actually looks forward to playdates with me. . . . I'm able to join the gym again and going 2–3 times a week. This is huge for my health which I've been battling, little things here and there. . . . [I] hope this will be the new norm for all companies! I think this world will be a better place, with happier people."

Given that participants are sleeping and exercising more, it's not surprising that fatigue declines quite a bit, and for 44 percent of the sample. (Only 13 percent experience a rise in fatigue.) One participant noted how exhausting the old schedule was: "I found it mind opening discovering how tired I am on Thursdays and how we could keep up with a five day work week for so long. During this trial, having an extra day became essential in my life routine, to do personal things sure, but most important to actually rest and be prepared for the next work week ahead." Fatigue is associated with workplace stress and the demands of family and life. The four-day week helps with both.

Table 2.2 More sleep and exercise, less fatigue

	Baseline	Endpoint	Change	% Decrease	% No change	% Increase
Sleep hours	6.7	6.9	0.2	17%	18%	35%
Sleep problems	2.3	2.0	-0.3	39%	46%	15%
Exercise frequency	2.4	2.7	0.3	18%	50%	32%
Fatigue	2.7	2.2	-0.5	44%	43%	13%

Note. Fatigue: (1-4). Sleep hours: number of hours per day. Sleep problems: (1-4). Exercise frequency: times per week (0-7+). All baseline to endpoint changes are significant at the p<0.001 level.

Another change we hear about is that people have more time to cook and are eating more healthfully. This isn't reflected in the average hours people report cooking, but 29 percent of respondents do log increases in cooking time. As one person said, "One of the biggest changes is that I could spend a decent amount of time on Fridays to do groceries (while it's not crowded), take appointments, and meal prep. I just feel a lot healthier as a result, and doing more meal prep helps me save money too. With inflation being so high lately, it's essential. Before, I would feel too tired and busy to do groceries and meal prep properly, so I would end up having to eat out more. It's more expensive, less satisfying, and less healthy, and I would feel more sluggish and frustrated at work too." The open-ended comments are filled with people reporting that they are cooking more, whether it's batch cooking for the week ahead, ordinary daily cooking, healthier cooking, or more ambitious, complex cooking.

WHO ARE OUR PARTICIPANTS?

Before going on to talk about other well-being outcomes, I want to pause a moment to say something about who the people in the trials are—demographically and socioeconomically. (The appendix contains a table if you prefer to look at the information that way.) The feature that stands out most obviously is that our sample skews female; 64 percent check that box, while 34 percent are males and 2 percent are other/nonbinary. It's also a predominantly white group, with 72 percent choosing white and 28 percent opting for all the other racial/ethnic options. (Those vary a lot because the countries in our sample use different terms and categories. Since some of the groups are small, we have collapsed them into white and nonwhite for our analyses.) We have people of all ages, with 43 percent in the eighteen-to-thirty-four group, 28.5 percent in thirty-five-to-forty-four, and 28.5 percent at forty-five and over. Almost three-quarters (74 percent) have a bachelor's degree; 26 percent have some or no college; and 31 percent have a postgraduate degree. More than half identify as professionals, and managers and senior officers are 16 percent of the sample. A third have children under eighteen living at home. They come from a variety of countries. The biggest group is from the U.K. and Ireland at 42 percent. The United States and Canada are next, at 32 percent. Australia and New Zealand are 13 percent; South Africa is 5 percent; and 8 percent are "other." (There was a mixed-country trial in early 2023 that enrolled companies from a few European nations.) And in the United States, the median salary for the group is $60,000–$75,000. In the last few trials we added questions about disability and union status. Fifteen percent identified as having a disability; 11.5 percent are in unionized workplaces.

FAMILY AND DAILY LIFE

Only some participants told us dramatic health stories. But nearly everyone described life-changing experiences, because they could finally manage the demands of family and daily life. For some, it was about coping with the time demands of toddlers or special-needs children. For many more it was about the reduction of garden-variety time stress. As one respondent noted, "The experience has been completely transformational. My work-life balance is better than I ever thought possible. I feel like I'm finally able to manage the many competing priorities in my life (work, self-care, relationship, social life, family, hobbies, education, etc.). I am so grateful to my organization for participating in this trial and valuing employee well-being in this way. It has really made my life feel much more balanced, fulfilled and enjoyable."

People report improvements in their relationships. "My home life is better in terms of my relationships and the quality of time I spend with my partner and our children. I am more connected to them than I have ever been." One person reports being more "present" with their children. Parents are able to spend more time with children, whether it's doing routine things like picking them up from school or special activities on the off day. As one employee who now has time for children on the weekends says, "It has been life changing for us as a family." Our data show that for those who use the time off to be with children, the savings in childcare costs can be significant. One U.K. employee reports saving £12,000.

The four-day week also helps when partners have heavy work schedules, as this mother explains: "This summer my husband started a job that requires him to work long hours and is often gone for a week at a time. With a rambunctious two year old, having one day off a week was the only way I survived this summer. It gave me time to practice selfcare and take care of household tasks." And we've heard from fathers who say the four-day week enabled their being in their children's lives. "Being a new father, and having an extra day in the week to be with her, is invaluable. It's changed my life and I am forever grateful for this bonus time."

Some report spending time with other family members. Liz Powers, a CEO we'll meet in the next chapter, usually visits her mother and grandmother on her off day. One U.K. participant also told us that in addition to spending more time with children (school sports day, matches, assemblies), they met their "Mum" for a birthday lunch and trained for a twenty-six-mile marathon hike. We're also hearing about potential future families. One person told us that they "feel more relaxed knowing that I have time to build a family and find my partner." Being able to socialize and have friends is another frequent theme. The South African who weaned off antianxiety medication explained that they were no longer too tired to engage. "I am delighted with the extra off day. I did so many different things from just being lazy too doing arts and crafts, having coffee with friends and decluttering my home. Having friends over for the weekend and many more, and I was actually prepared for that, usually I am tired and do not feel like socializing. Since the 4day work week I want to do more fun things."

Our survey results support what we're hearing in the comments. More than half (57 percent and 59 percent, respectively) report improvements in work-family and work-life balance. These scores go up a lot—0.7 and 0.8 on a 1–5 scale, a 25 percent increase. And when we ask about conflicts between housework and jobs, we find fewer problems in both directions. Family matters are less likely to impinge on work performance, and there's an even bigger decline in people saying that they're too tired from their job to do household work. Just over half the sample report less of that on the new schedule.

And there's one other finding that's worth noting. While for large majorities of both men and women, the four-day week doesn't change the amount of household labor they do compared with their partner, about 20 percent of men do increase their share of both housework and childcare. Women, on the other hand, don't take on a larger share of either, as some feared might happen.

Table 2.3 Family and work life are more in balance

	Baseline	Endpoint	Change	% Decrease	% No change	% Increase
Work-family balance	2.8	3.5	0.7	11%	32%	57%
Work-life balance	2.9	3.7	0.8	10%	31%	59%
Family-to-work conflict	1.5	1.2	-0.3	42%	44%	14%
Work-to-family conflict	2.1	1.5	-0.6	52%	39%	9%

Note. Work-family balance: ability to combine (1-5). Work-life balance: ability to combine (1-5). Family-to-work conflict: difficulty concentrating on work due to family (0-3). Work-to-family conflict: too tired from work to do household jobs (0-3). All baseline to endpoint changes are significant at the $p<0.001$ level.

ME TIME

Then there's "me" time. For many of our participants, their weeks were so busy between paid and unpaid work plus time with family that they didn't have time for themselves. One of my first interviewees talked about being able to get a pedicure "guilt free." In fact, we find that feelings of time inadequacy are highest in the "me" category. At baseline, 87 percent of respondents report that they wished they had more time for their own hobbies, and 78 percent wanted more time for self-care such as sleeping and relaxing. Those numbers fell to 59 percent and 53 percent, respectively.

"The three-day weekend feels like I have plenty of time to manage family and household while still having some time to myself. I can't imagine returning to a 5 day week." One respondent sums it up enthusiastically: "Overall, this has been an incredible experience and has contributed significantly to work-life balance. Personally, I have found it difficult to disconnect from work, but only because I have been so used to being connected all the time. I have had to force myself to NOT work on our reward days, and have also tried to figure out what hobbies I actually have. . . . Historically I spent so much time on work and household/children, that I NEVER had time for anything else. So I am rediscovering what I actually like to do in the free time that I finally have!"

Table 2.4 Finding enough time

	Percentage who want more time for selected activities		
	Baseline	Endpoint	Change
Housework	28%	16%	-12%
Cooking	36%	20%	-16%
Caring for others	40%	25%	-15%
Volunteering	60%	52%	-8%
Hobbies	87%	59%	-28%
Contact with family members	64%	39%	-25%
Other social contact	75%	53%	-22%
Self-care	78%	53%	-25%

Note. Percentage who would like to spend more time compared to time spent last week. All baseline to endpoint changes are significant at the $p<0.001$ level.

MORE PRODUCTIVE AT WORK TOO

I've been focusing on how an extra day off transforms life outside people's jobs. We also find large impacts on people's work experiences, as self-reported productivity and effectiveness soar.

When we started our data collection, we included a variable called "current work ability," which asks people to compare their ability at work in that moment with their "lifetime best." We've seen dramatic increases in that measure in all the trials. Across the whole sample, it goes up by 0.9, nearly a whole point on a 0–10 point scale. More than half the sample (56 percent) experiences a rise in this measure from the beginning of the trial to when they report six months later. The size of this change surprised us, although perhaps it shouldn't have. After all, getting more productive in a shorter amount of time is the premise of the trial. But this is a big impact. We added a direct question about productivity to make sure this was a robust finding. And it is. We have similar findings for the direct productivity metric—at 0.8, and it also rises for 56 percent of the sample. So what's going on?

Table 2.5 More productive at work

	Baseline	Endpoint	Change	% Decrease	% No change	% Increase
Current work ability	7.0	7.9	0.9	19%	26%	56%
Productivity	7.3	8.1	0.8	15%	29%	56%

Note. Current work ability: compared to lifetime best (0-10). Productivity: self-rated productivity (0-10). Baseline to endpoint changes are significant at the $p<0.001$ level.

Intentionality is an important part of the story: "This trial has been life changing (not to be overly dramatic.) I've felt more productive at work in smaller quantities of time, more intentional about what I do and when I do it, and saying no to items that don't drive the business forward or make sense right now." A Canadian participant noted being more efficient: "4 day work week has been the best thing that happened to me in my professional life. . . . I feel more organized, efficient, productive both in my professional and personal life."

Monday through Thursday feels manageable; people don't suffer as much from Sunday scaries. Reflecting on whether they were able to do as much in four days as they had in five, one participant explained that "work productivity remained the same but felt easier to achieve." This person expressed optimism about whether they could keep it up. "I'm confident productivity can be further increased in the year ahead too. The 4DW has been a complete game changer. I feel much more grounded and engaged with work week to week and don't have the burn out and living for the weekend."

There were mixed views on how workload and pace changed—on which more later—but even for those who said it had increased, only a small percentage prefer the five-day schedule. Over and over we hear it's a trade-off that people prefer. "I wake up happy on a Friday when I have the day off. It just feels different and special. I absolutely love having Friday's off and I hope it continues. Although we work harder and Faster in the 4 days, it is worth it to be able to have Friday off."

IT'S JUST BETTER, OVERALL

Our global measures of well-being also show improvements. A commonly used metric is life satisfaction. That rises a lot, by eight-tenths of a point (0.8). Satisfaction with the job also goes up, although by less, 0.5. We suspect this is partly an artifact of timing. When employees get the baseline survey, they already know they're about to start on a four-day week. Job satisfaction has probably already risen. Other aspects of life also improve—finances and relationships. And not surprisingly, satisfaction levels with time increase a whopping two points. This comes out clearly in the comments as well as in our other measures of how much people like the four-day week.

Table 2.6 Overall, more satisfied.

Satisfaction	Baseline	Endpoint	Change	% Decrease	% No change	% Increase
Life	6.7	7.5	0.8	19%	26%	54%
Job	7.1	7.6	0.5	24%	29%	48%
Time	5.3	7.3	2.0	12%	16%	72%
Finances	6.1	6.6	0.5	26%	27%	46%
Relationships	7.2	7.8	0.6	23%	31%	45%

Note. Level of satisfaction with these realms. All measures are (0-10). All baseline to endpoint changes are significant at the $p<0.001$ level.

"I will never go back to working a 5-day week. If my company expands the standard work week, I will leave." One European, who works for an advertising firm, explained that it has become essential to their relationship with the company. "Since we started this trial my physical & mental health became better, I feel more motivated at work, more productive as I've learnt to manage my time better and I don't need to stress that much about taking care of personal responsibilities because I have time on Friday to do them." They then contrasted this with what would happen if their company reverted to a five-day workweek. "[That] would be terrible for me, I would be exhausted, both mentally and physically, and less motivated to work. It would also decrease my trust in my employer, as me and my team expressed how much better the 4-day week is, so if they decide to go back to a 5-day week, it would suggest that they don't actually take into consideration our opinions."

And one American, from a small marketing firm, put the whole story together—health, work, relationships, hobbies, plus the need for social change: "During this 4-day work week trial period, for the last 6 months—everything from my mental health, to physical health, to my working relationships and personal relationships—has significantly improved that it's quite undeniable at this point to state that the 4-day work week should and NEEDS to be the new normal. It has benefited me in quite literally [every] area and aspect of my life. I have time to actually take care of myself, my partner, my animals, my home, and my family. I have time to learn new things, enjoy my hobbies and interests, and most of all be PRESENT in my day-to-day life. I no longer get constant anxiety once Sunday rolls around—I know that the week is going to fly by. It makes work that much more enjoyable. There is such a healthy balance of work and personal life now. My stress has reduced greatly. I can sleep better!!"

While we expected well-being to improve, we did not anticipate the magnitude and universality of results that we have gotten. We're seeing improvements for all types of people, meaning men, women, parents, nonparents, across age groups, education levels, race, and ethnicity. We're also finding that the well-being results hold across all the types of companies in the sample: across size and industry; whether they're for- or not-for-profit organizations; remote, hybrid, or in person; and how they implement the four-day week. Our findings hold across the various country cohorts and for all the time periods in the two and a half years we've been collecting data.

You may remember that in the previous chapter I mentioned rebounds—unwelcome blowback effects that we wanted to make sure we were capturing, if they were occurring. One was second-job holding. The historian Benjamin Hunnicutt found that after the Kellogg cereal company gave its workers a six-hour day in 1930, many of the men did eventually take on second jobs. We thought this might be especially true at our U.S. companies. We also wondered about whether overtime hours might go up. But no. There is zero evidence that people are more likely to have a second job. That number actually fell. And it fell even more in the United States and Canada than globally. Overtime hours declined as well. The other blowback issue we were interested in is work intensity. I take that up in the next chapter, but the short story is that it doesn't go up by much. People mostly get more productive, not sped up.

Table 2.7. Second jobholding and overtime hours

	Baseline	Endpoint	Change	% Decrease	% No change	% Increase
Second jobholding	10%	9%	-1%	4%	93%	3%
Overtime hours	2.1	1.9	-0.2	33%	49%	18%

Note. Percentage with a second job: (regular, irregular, freelance/gig). Overtime hours: frequency (1-4). Second jobholding change is significant at the $p<0.05$ level. Overtime baseline to endpoint change is significant at the $p<0.001$ level.

IS WHAT'S GOOD FOR THE GOOSE
ALSO GOOD FOR THE GANDER?

While all types of people were registering improvements in well-being and workplace outcomes, we were interested in whether the magnitude of those changes was the same for everyone. In sociology, differences across race, class, and gender (especially) are core research topics. We expected that some people would benefit more from this schedule than others. In particular, we thought that women, parents living with children under eighteen, and perhaps nonwhite employees would have larger well-being improvements. Women and parents, because we expected they were under more time stress. People of color, because they might be experiencing more microaggressions in the workplace, and likely have higher stress levels in general.

Researchers often begin to answer these kinds of questions by running simple t-tests to measure whether outcomes for the two groups differ. When we did this, we did find a few differences. The most important is by gender. Women experience more of a reduction in burnout than men. We also see gender differences for other outcomes—positive emotions, job satisfaction, mental health, sleep problems, life satisfaction, and work-family conflict. Overall, white men have less reduction in burnout than everyone else. On the other hand, we didn't see divergences by parental status, race (not accounting for gender), age, or education levels. That was surprising.

But simple t-tests aren't the end of the story. In our full statistical model, which I discuss below, these demographic variables are almost never consistently statistically significant. Once we take other correlated factors into account, we find that everyone has been benefiting roughly equally. This wasn't what we expected. Although many socioeconomic groups start out with differences in their well-being at baseline, our models are telling us that people benefit roughly equally from the four-day week. In other words, what is good for the goose is also good for the gander. The benefits of the four-day week help all types of people about the same amount.

One group that might stand out for having greater well-being improvements is employees with disabilities. In 2023, a CEO told us that she'd heard from an employee with an invisible disability who said the new schedule had allowed them to stay in the job. This is an important issue we hadn't been focusing on. When we added disability status to our survey, we found that at baseline those who told us they had a disability scored lower on almost all the well-being questions than those without. They are more burned out and report worse mental and physical health. They are more likely to have sleep problems, fatigue, and work-family conflict. At the conclusion of the trial, they were still worse off, but they experienced bigger increases in well-being than the nondisabled group. The differences aren't always statistically significant because the sample size is small, and we will be looking more closely at this issue as we get more data. From our early results it seems that the four-day week may be a powerful pro-disability reform.

DO THESE IMPROVEMENTS LAST?

The other big worry we had, and which doubters occasionally mentioned, was whether the improvements we were seeing might be short-lived. Maybe it was just the novelty of the schedule that people liked. Perhaps they'd get used to it and reset their expectations in ways that undermined their better mental states. We added a survey at twelve months. It's a short one, because we didn't think people would be motivated for another long slog through our questionnaire. So we don't know whether they fell off their exercise regime. But we do know that our main well-being results are robust. In some cases, there's a little backsliding. In others, continued improvements, although neither is always a significant change. The basic story is that the improvements are durable.

Table 2.8 Well-being improvements are long-lasting

	Baseline	Endpoint	12 months	Significance endpoint/12 mos.	Significance baseline/12 mos.
Work hours	38.6	34.3	34.3		***
Work intensity	3.5	3.6	3.4	***	*
Current work ability	7.0	7.8	7.5	***	***
Burnout	2.8	2.3	2.4		***
Job satisfaction	7.1	7.7	7.4	***	***
Work-life balance	2.9	3.8	3.8	***	***
Physical health	3.0	3.3	3.3	**	***
Fatigue	2.7	2.3	2.3		***
Sleep problems	2.3	2.0	2.0		***
Mental health	2.9	3.3	3.3	**	***
Life satisfaction	6.6	7.5	7.5		***
Trial rating	NA	8.9	8.9		NA

Note. Results at baseline, six months and twelve months later. Significance levels refer to change from endpoint to twelve months and baseline to twelve months.

We went back again at twenty-four months. The results remained similar. Working hours inched down a bit more. Most of the other well-being variables stayed constant or improved. People's rating of the trial rose. The one countertrend is job satisfaction, which fell. We suspect that as the four-day week normalized, negative aspects of the job returned to the fore. Overall, the results from the trials look durable, not just in the short run but even at two years after the new schedule is introduced.

There is one caveat about these longer-term results, especially the twenty-four-month ones. As time passes, the response rate to our surveys falls. One issue is that only people who have been there from the beginning are included in the survey because we are measuring how the same person fares over time. If people who are less enthusiastic about the four-day week are more likely to leave the company, that introduces what's called survivor bias into the results. Similarly, if less enthusiastic staff don't fill out the survey, that creates a similar slant. We're also seeing that companies are less willing to hang in there with us over time, as more decide not to participate in the surveys. That might also be correlated with their enthusiasm level. So the longer-term results likely suffer from a positive bias.

CONTROL COMPANIES

In the discussion of our research design in chapter 1, I explained that while a randomized controlled trial wasn't feasible, we did recruit a group of companies to compare with the U.S. and Canadian group that began in late 2023 and early 2024. We were able to persuade twelve companies to allow us to survey their staff on the same schedule as those going to a four-day week. They were mostly organizations that had attended 4 Day Week Global information sessions but weren't joining the upcoming trial. Ideally they would be perfectly matched to companies that were participating in the trial, but that perfect matching wasn't possible. The two groups are similar in most ways, but there are also a few differences. Gender, race, and the age structure were the same, but employees in the control organizations were 20 percent less likely to have a college education and were a bit more likely to have children living at home. We also found that while stress and work intensity didn't differ at baseline, a few of the other well-being variables did. Companies that were about to start their four-day-week schedules had higher levels of burnout and work-family conflict and more fatigue and sleep problems. They also scored a bit lower on current work ability. These lower well-being metrics at baseline suggest a rationale for going to a four-day week.

The purpose of adding the control group was to see if their well-being changes over the trial differed from the companies that shifted to a four-day week. We found that they did. Significantly so. In the treatment—that is, four-day-week—companies, everything got better, along the lines of what we'd been finding in all the prior trials. Work time fell by 5.4 hours a week. The productivity measures went up by 0.9. Work intensity nudged up slightly. But people were working smarter and less likely to be thinking about leaving. Stress and burnout fell. Physical and mental health rose, work-life balance got better. Satisfaction levels were boosted; fatigue and sleep problems declined.

In the control companies, we didn't see these improvements. They experienced no statistically significant change in work hours (as expected). As a result, the productivity measures didn't rise. Burnout didn't fall. Mental and physical health stayed the same, as did work-life balance, satisfaction with job, life, and time. Fatigue and sleep were constant. Where the measures show a small increase or decrease (for example, work ability, absenteeism, job and time satisfaction), these differences are not statistically significant, meaning we don't consider them real changes. There was true movement on two metrics. Exercise went up. We think that's seasonal. The trial began in the winter and ended in the summer. And stress fell a notch—by 0.1. That might be seasonal too. Summer is a more relaxed time.

The results from the control companies offer evidence that the well-being results we have found in the trials are attributable to the four-day week. That's the commonsense conclusion, and it's supported by what happened in similar companies that didn't change their schedules over the same period. Knowing that leads to an inevitable question: What *is* it about that third day off? Why does it improve well-being so much?

Table 2.9 Four-day week companies improve, control companies don't

Control companies

	Baseline	Endpoint	Change	Significance
Work time	39.4	39.6	0.2	
Productivity	7.5	7.5	0.0	
Work ability	7.3	7.1	-0.2	
Work intensity	3.4	3.3	-0.1	
Work smart	3.7	3.7	0.0	
Turnover intentions	2.3	2.3	0.0	
Work absenteeism	0.9	0.7	-0.2	
Work stress	3.4	3.3	-0.1	*
Burnout	2.9	2.9	0.0	
Mental health	2.9	3.0	0.1	
Physical health	3.1	3.1	0.0	
Job satisfaction	6.8	6.6	-0.2	
Life satisfaction	6.7	6.7	0.0	
Satisfaction with time	5.4	5.6	0.2	
Fatigue	2.7	2.8	0.1	
Sleep problems	2.4	2.4	0.0	
Exercise frequency	2.1	2.5	0.4	***
Work-life balance	2.8	2.9	0.1	

Four-day week
companies

	Baseline	Endpoint	Change	Significance
Work time	39.0	33.6	-5.4	***
Productivity	7.3	8.2	0.9	***
Work ability	7.0	7.9	0.9	***
Work intensity	3.4	3.5	0.1	*
Work smart	3.7	3.8	0.1	**
Turnover intentions	2.2	2.0	-0.2	**
Work absenteeism	1.1	0.8	-0.3	
Work stress	3.4	3.0	-0.4	***
Burnout	3.1	2.5	-0.6	***
Mental health	2.9	3.4	0.5	***
Physical health	2.9	3.2	0.3	***
Job satisfaction	6.8	7.7	0.9	***

Life satisfaction	6.6	7.7	1.1	***
Satisfaction with time	5.0	7.3	2.3	***
Fatigue	3.0	2.4	-0.6	***
Sleep problems	2.6	2.2	-0.4	***
Exercise frequency	1.9	2.4	0.5	***
Work-life balance	2.7	3.6	0.9	***

Note. There were 12 US control companies and 9 matched US and Canadian companies who instituted a four day week. We had 283 responses from control companies; 332 from four-day week companies. Baselines were from November 2024 to February 2024. Endpoints are six months later. All variables, including productivity and work ability are self-reported. More details in Fan et al (2024). Significance levels are based on paired-sample t tests to determine whether baseline and endpoint values are significantly different: +p<.1, *p<0.05, **<0.01, ***p<0.001.

EXPLAINING THE RISE IN WELL-BEING

What I've been discussing so far are top-line, descriptive results—the average change in our many well-being outcomes and work experience variables. Our next step was to drill down with a model that includes every individual's experience. We did this in a paper that asks the question, was the improvement due to the four-day week? To answer it, we needed to tie well-being outcomes to working hours. So the first question is, did the new schedule reduce weekly hours? And if so, by how much, and for whom?

In most organizations, not everyone works whatever the standard workweek happens to be. There is typically a big cluster around that value—often forty—but plenty of people work more and less. This was certainly true of our sample. Our first finding was that the schedule change worked as intended. At baseline, the mode—or the most common level of hours—was forty. At the end point of the trial, it had fallen to thirty-two. So far so good.

However, average hours did not fall by eight. For the full sample, the average decline was only 4.6 hours, or 12 percent. And although we found that 76 percent of people did reduce their working hours, 13.5 percent were working more at the end of the trial than the beginning, and for 11 percent there was no change. There are many reasons for this result. As I discuss later, some senior managers report being unable to take a day off. For some people, longer hours may be due to getting promoted to a more demanding job. It could also be that baseline and end point came at different times in terms of an annual work cycle. (Tax season for accountants, for example.) We have start-ups among our companies. Some were experiencing rapid growth, which means more work. Others had layoffs. So part of the explanation is these random changes, part is that not everyone wanted to reduce their hours, and part is that the four-day week can create more work for some people.

Table 2.10 Weekly working hour changes across the sample				
	Reductions			
	8 hours or more	5-7 hours	1-4 hours	No change	Hours increased
Fraction of sample	30.0%	24.2%	21.4%	10.9%	13.5%

Note. Changes of 8 hours or more, 5-7 hours and 1-4 hours are reductions.

Whatever the reason, we were able to use those changes in hours to explain well-being outcomes. We divided participants into four groups based on how their hours changed, and looked at five outcomes—burnout, mental health, physical health, positive emotions, and job satisfaction. We also included a large number of other variables (often referred to as controls) that might conceivably affect well-being. And we added company variables too, in case those mattered.

Our expectation was that the well-being effects were being driven by the changes in hours. And the model supports that interpretation. The greater the reduction in hours, the bigger the well-being improvement. It held for all five of our outcome variables. The size of the well-being effect is generally twice as large for people whose hours fell by eight or more than those who cut back by only one to four hours. Work less, feel better. Work even less, feel even better.

That finding was a start. But only a start. What is it about work-time reduction that improves well-being? To answer that question, we needed to do what's called a mediation analysis. That's the technical term for pathways of influence. The new schedule led to a lot of changes in people's lives—exercising and sleeping more, feeling less fatigued, being less anxious. It also led to them feeling more productive at work. Those are the two big areas we thought might be the pathways: things happening outside the job and changes in the work experience. Fewer hours at work leads to more sleep leads to better mental health. Personally, sleep was the horse I was betting on as we crunched the numbers.

We tested for pretty much everything. In the end, the intuition about inside- and outside-of-work turned out to be on the money. A big factor was that outsized jump in work ability. We knew people felt a lot better about how they were performing at work, and that translated into higher well-being. The outside-of-work variables also mattered, particularly fatigue, which was the largest mediator of all. Shorter hours reduce fatigue, and less fatigue yields more well-being. The second factor was sleep. Exercise also plays a role, particularly for physical health. The mediators explain how reduced hours affect well-being. Our model accords with the kinds of comments we got in the survey as well as in our in-depth interviewing. The four-day week has impacts inside and outside the workplace that make people better off.

NOT FIT FOR ALL

Of course, not *everybody* loves it. Among the thousands of open-ended comments we've received in our surveys we do find negative sentiments, although they are a small minority. People complain that the company didn't prepare properly. Or that it hasn't figured out the customer service piece. That their workload is too high. That co-workers aren't pulling their weight. That the pace of work is more stressful. That they didn't manage to reduce their hours. Quite a few of the unhappy comments came from employees in South Africa, where things didn't go as well as in our other trials. The salient fact about that trial was that hours fell a lot less than elsewhere. Our modeling predicts that those people would have less improvement in well-being, which is what we found.

One U.K. participant whom I quoted earlier in this chapter on how they're better able to manage their sleep threw cold water on the logic of the trial: "My job is also in no way compatible with the idea of a 4DWW; shrinking my intended working hours down by 20 percent makes negligible effect to how efficiently any of it can be done, and as such I work constantly in evenings and weekends." This is probably the most common complaint—that they aren't able to do everything in four days. But even that person ended their comment by saying, "Still better than 5DWW though." That sentiment makes them like more than 96 percent of all respondents, who want to continue with the new schedule.

By now you may be thinking, okay, it works for individuals. But I don't see how this is also a win for companies. Their staff are working fewer hours for the same pay. That sounds like a problem, not a solution. Explaining why and how it works for organizations is the subject of the next three chapters.

3

GETTING FIVE IN FOUR

Employees aren't the only ones who are thriving with the four-day-week model. Companies are also finding great success with it. We don't have nearly as many metrics for them as we do for employees, but the data we do have are very positive. One of the most powerful indicators is whether organizations stick with four days or go back to five. By that measure, less than 10 percent are reverting to five-day schedules after a full twelve months. Failure is mostly random, meaning our statistical modeling can't predict it with much accuracy. That in turn suggests that there aren't obvious categories of organizations that can't succeed with it. More on that later.

Here are some other results (also listed in table A.4 of the appendix).

- Revenue rose 20 percent at companies that had completed six months by mid-2024 and sent us data. If we weight by company size, that number is 10 percent.
- Employee retention improved. Pre-trial, the organizations

were averaging 1.8 resignations a month, or nearly two people per hundred employees. During the trial those quits fell to 1.4. We had expected hiring to rise during the trial since revenue growth was so robust. But it fell from 3.2 to 2.6, likely because fewer employees were leaving.

- Sick and personal days also declined, from 1.0 days per employee per month to 0.8.
- We asked companies to rate the trial on a scale of 1 to 10. The average rating was 8.2. Ratings for productivity and performance were both 7.3. At some point we added a question about ability to attract employees. That yielded the highest score of all—8.5. Companies (and their employees) were enthusiastic.

In this chapter, and the next two, I delve into how and why organizations are having such good experiences with the four-day week. While most companies use multiple strategies, this chapter is about those that mainly follow the 4 Day Week Global 100-80-100 model, which involves concerted attention to the ways time is used. Some of the improvement happens at the individual level. In our trials more than half of all employees report that they are working smarter on their new schedules. But it's far more than an individual adaptation. Companies are instituting productivity hacks. They're changing their cultures through the work reorganization process. Some go deeper into more profound questioning of what they're doing and why, in an effort to find mission clarity and a more strategic orientation. Both the hacks and the strategic repositioning are forms of getting more intentional. Intentionality plus more time off leads employees to value their jobs more, boosts their motivation, and yields company success. Those effects are the subject of the next chapter.

REPEALING PARKINSON'S LAW

We've all heard about Parkinson's law—the rule that "work expands to fill the available time." It's not a scientific fact. Many organizations are able to avoid it, and it's less a law than a curse. But it's real. Matt Juniper, partner at the advertising and public relations firm Praxis, figured out how to tame the Parkinson's beast, and in the process strengthened his company and improved his own life.

Matt is the son of Maureen Juniper. More than twenty years ago, Maureen founded Praxis, which is located in Toronto. The company has a strong orientation toward employee well-being. But they're also rigorously focused on growth and profitability. Matt originally planned for a communications career in politics but, after trying it out, was disillusioned by the difficulty of making meaningful change. While he was treading water and figuring out his next move, Maureen suggested he apply for an internship at her firm. He loved it and was soon hooked. Over the years he has had stints in various parts of the business, working his way up to director and eventually co-owner. While Matt cares passionately about the work, he also believes that it shouldn't be all-consuming (one difference from political campaigns). In the generation before him, he explains, it was a badge of honor to "pour everything you had into the job," whatever the cost to family and personal life. He has tried hard to instill a different philosophy at Praxis in which working until eleven every night isn't seen as the mark of a good employee. And while this reflected his personal values, he also realized that to be good at PR and marketing, you need to know what's going on in the culture. That won't happen if you're at the computer fifteen hours a day.

Matt started hearing about the four-day week through the media. While it aligned with his philosophy about needing balance in life, he thought it would never work for Praxis, because they're a client-serving business in an industry known for long hours and always being available. Matt felt they could only go to four once their clients had made the switch.

The pandemic changed his mind. At the beginning of the lockdown he was excited to reclaim two hours of daily commuting to the office, plus the forty-five minutes he'd normally spend driving to client meetings. However, that extra time lasted only a few weeks. Soon he found himself signing on earlier and "frantically working during every moment." Something was wrong. A friend suggested he talk to someone about the four-day week, and after learning more, he went from being a "complete skeptic" to pretty excited. Maureen was on board, because she's generally open-minded, but also because she had assumed remote work would never work for Praxis and that proved to be wrong. The four-day week might be the same kind of unexpected success. They were looking for something dramatic that would help the agency "stand out" and be a leader in the field. When they lost an unprecedented five employees in the midst of the Great Resignation, they decided it was time to act.

For Praxis, an essential element of success was a seamless experience for clients. So it opted for full-week operations, by dividing each team in half, and giving either Monday or Friday off. The aim was to have no reduction in quality, speed of response, and customer satisfaction. They achieved all that, and more. So how did they make up the missing hours? That's where Parkinson's law came in.

Perhaps because it specializes in digital marketing, Praxis has always been quick to adopt timesaving technology. But over the years, it had fallen into the trap of having work expand to fill the available time. According to Matt, "I joined the PR industry when people were faxing press releases, and now we have instant email communication. We had seen, going all the way back to email, Slack, all these technologies come in that in theory would save hours a day. But in fact, every employee was just as busy as they'd always been. And so the language about the work filling the time you create for it started to really seem true." Before the four-day week there hadn't been a clear incentive for individuals to harvest that saved time. Now there was.

Matt said the adjustments weren't particularly complicated. They scrutinized meetings, which had been ballooning during the lockdown. They got intentional about to-do lists and weekly planning. They did some of the usual things with calendars. They interrogated multitasking. But basically, people just tightened up, got more efficient, and were able to do their work in four days. One reason is that for Praxis the fifth day is not like the other four. Here's Matt again: "I was always my least productive on Fridays, and I could sense it with my clients—less emails, slowing down, more casual atmosphere, just a slower pace." Matt saw the staff avoiding that slowdown. "I have found in a four-day-week environment that that is not the case with my employees and my team. They are more productive and more energetic and they go right down to the wire, and then they are able to relax and enjoy the rest time that they are able to achieve as a result of that." Matt also credits what Praxis calls the rest day. "We saw some of these hours seem to condense and shrink just from people working smarter, faster, etc. And really, we attribute a lot of that to them being refreshed and working at their best when they do come back."

Praxis implemented its schedule change with meticulous attention to data. And the data have spoken. Praxis operates with ambitious growth goals; over the first year of the trial it was aiming for a 20 percent increase in its profitability metric. It slightly exceeded that target. Customers didn't bat an eye—the seamless experience Matt was hoping for happened—more on that below. Praxis also tracked things like employee well-being and resignations. The resignations stopped, and they saw strong improvements in satisfaction. When the company has had open positions, it has gotten more and better résumés. It is also looking at whether people are actually taking that fifth day off. Because its fee structure involves a significant component based on billable hours, they already tracked time use carefully. When Matt and I spoke, more than a year after the trial started, Praxis had hit 83 percent of the off time actually being taken. Matt aims to improve that number, and to make sure that when they do need extra people on a Friday or a Monday, the burden is shared equitably. From our surveying, we found that while hours of work didn't fall as much at Praxis as they did on average, they did see improvements in all the well-being measures that we tracked. Work intensity increased a bit, as would be expected from Matt's description of how things unfolded, but it was more than made up for if we take turnover intentions and the other positive impacts into account. Job satisfaction went up almost a full point—more than twice our sample average. Working a bit harder is a trade-off Praxis employees are clearly happy to make. They did institute a few changes, and continue to do so, which I'll discuss when we get to tweaks. But the bottom line is that it has been a tremendous success, and Matt is now an evangelist for the four-day week.

In large part that's because of how insidious Parkinson's law had become in his own life and his firm. When there are barriers to work-time reduction—whether they be economic or cultural—the work process is distorted. This came up in a number of my conversations with senior management. Sam Smith, whom we'll meet shortly, explained, "It's just such a simple concept, but something I've seen throughout my work life—just doing something today, if it can be done today and . . . how often that is not done in the normal course of things because of expanding the work to fill the time.

The five days a week is just the norm." It's a pervasive problem, he believes, that even affects employment trends. "I've also seen it in office environments and corporate environments, that the work expands to fill time and, even going as far as to say, work expanding to fill jobs."

Matt came up with an insightful modification of the Parkinson's adage: "Work expands to fill the space you give it." His version highlights the agency that people can have in controlling their time. Figuring out how to get that control requires recognizing the ways in which the five-day week has contributed to the problem. For Matt, it involved ongoing attention to containing work, or what he termed putting "guardrails in place" that prevent the creep back to five. For other companies, structural changes made the difference.

HACKING MEETINGS

The philosophy of the four-day-week trials has been that companies can figure out how to maintain 100 percent of their performance despite 20 percent less time at the workplace. With a little help, most of the companies figure out productivity hacks. The most common is to hack away at meetings.

Surveys, anecdotes, and hard data bear out the wisdom of this approach. The culture of meetings in many white-collar workplaces has careened out of control. In the early days of the first trials, I went to the annual TED conference and got a sense of the problem, even at some of America's most valuable and successful tech companies, and for people at the highest echelons. I'd been invited by Bill Gates to a private dinner he was hosting on the day of our session. I was sitting with the founder of a major software company, someone on Gates's staff, and a few other well-informed folks. Hearing about my research, they regaled me with tales about the meetings culture in the tech world. Their teams would spend months preparing for meetings with top decision makers, only to have their work blown off or rendered irrelevant in the space of a few minutes. There were more commonplace problems too, the kind that the smaller companies in our trials were facing: too many meetings that go on too long, involve too many people, and accomplish too little. I left the dinner surprised at the dysfunction they described. When I went to the literature, I found a whole research field called the science of meetings, with an army of people and products whose mission is to help companies make improvements in their meeting cultures.

It's hard to know exactly how much time workers spend in meetings, and of course it varies a lot across occupations and industries. The press is full of surveys on this topic, many funded by companies that are trying to sell products or consultancies that promise to cure the meeting blues. They report stats such as fifty-five million meetings held each week in the United States (pre-pandemic). Half of all meeting time is considered wasted. There are even surveys on particular types of meetings. A 2015 Harris poll found that employees average 4.6 hours a week preparing for "status"—that is, update—meetings and 4.5 hours a week attending them. Apparently these are so awful that 46 percent of respondents preferred unpleasant activities, such as watching paint dry or going to the Department of Motor Vehicles, to sitting through these meetings. Steven Rogelberg of the University of North Carolina is the dean of the science of meetings. His 2022 study with Otter.ai found that on average people have 17.7 meetings a week and professionals spend a third of their time in meetings. The fraction of meetings respondents feel are unnecessary is about 30 percent.

Meetings are clearly seen as a drag on performance. A 2023 global survey of 31,000 respondents by Microsoft found that the top "disruptor of productivity" is "inefficient meetings," with "too many meetings" as the third-most frequently chosen option. Management researchers at Harvard, Boston University, and Yale surveyed 182 senior managers about their views on meetings. They found that 71 percent said meetings are unproductive and inefficient and 64 percent agreed that they come at the expense of deep thinking.

Research on work interruptions suggests one pathway through which meetings might affect productivity: Interruptions lead to negative mood states. Meetings, particularly poorly run ones, have been shown to increase anxiety and depression and raise the likelihood of intention to quit a job. They also increase fatigue and subjective workload. Microsoft's Human Factors Labs put EEG (electroencephalogram) caps on a small number of people as they sat through online meetings. They discovered that brainwave markers associated with overwork and stress were higher than when the subjects were doing other kinds of online work. They also found that fatigue sets in once a meeting has gone thirty to forty minutes. On days filled with video calls, fatigue develops about two hours in. A real-world study of the quality of meetings at a variety of manufacturing companies found that poorly run meetings are associated with worse organizational outcomes a couple of years down the road.

Companies are catching on to the benefits of reducing meetings. Benjamin Laker and his colleagues at the University of Reading surveyed seventy-six companies across the world that had a thousand or more employees and had introduced at least one non-meeting day a week. They analyzed a wide variety of outcome measures: employee stress levels, productivity, collaboration, autonomy, engagement, satisfaction, and micromanagement. Almost half the companies (47 percent) had instituted two non-meeting days. Quite a few did more; 35 percent had three, 11 percent went for four, and 7 percent banned meetings altogether. The researchers found improvements in all of their measures before and after the meeting bans. The optimal number of meeting-free days turned out to be three, with some of the gains reversing if meetings were confined to one day or eliminated altogether.

It's therefore not surprising that for many four-day-week companies, ground zero for improving productivity is taming the meetings beast. Microsoft Japan is the poster child for this strategy. In 2019, it instituted a temporary four-day week, planned for five consecutive Fridays in August. To make it work, the company mandated that no meetings could go longer than thirty minutes. It also told managers to avoid unnecessary meetings and use face-to-face chats instead. Its widely reported results were striking. Productivity increased by 40 percent over the trial period. There were other positive findings as well. Employees were happier, time off fell by 25 percent, and there were environmental benefits: Electricity use in the office fell 23 percent, and employees printed 59 percent fewer pages.

THE LURE OF "DEEP WORK"

If the Praxis story underscores why the four-day week works (Parkinson's law), ArtLifting's experience shows how it can be done. ArtLifting is the ten-year-old brainchild of Liz Powers. During her college years at Harvard, Liz had volunteered with the homeless. After learning that many local shelters were stockpiling paintings done by residents, and had no use for them, she began organizing shows to sell the pieces. These successes launched the company, which is now a multimillion-dollar, twenty-five-person organization that sells art made by disabled and unhoused people, mostly to major corporations. The company provides income, community, and meaning for its artists and staff.

ArtLifting got into the business of reducing work time gradually. Like many other senior leaders, Liz was sparked by an article, in her case, from *The New York Times*. Leading her start-up was grueling, and Liz wanted more time for herself. She'd just come through a fiscal crisis that almost shut the company down. She was burned out and knew she needed to reset her work-life balance. With a standard workweek, finding that balance is very difficult for people in her position. She also knew that she couldn't institute shorter hours just for herself and recognized their value to her team. Many on the staff are people with disabilities who can't tolerate long hours and unlimited work demands. The need for balance was in their DNA. But Liz is a cautious person. Having just gone through that crisis and being mindful of how unusual it was to reduce work time in the start-up world, as well as what her board might think, she proceeded carefully, one baby step at a time.

Five years before transitioning to a full four-day week, ArtLifting began what turned into a stairstep test. In 2019, employees took every Friday off for three summer months. The next year they did it for five months. Then they went two years with every other Friday off year round. In 2023, the company launched a full-year, every-Friday-off, thirty-two-hour week. Liz and members of the team agree that it has been extremely successful, even "amazing." Since 2019, they've had average year-on-year revenue growth of 59 percent, and while many factors account for their growth, Liz feels the four-day week is a "huge" one. At a time when she sees her founder friends struggling to hire for their companies, within two weeks she had three hundred applicants for the company's latest job opening. "Whoa!" she exclaims. ArtLifting hasn't had anyone leave in two years. Liz now believes that the four-year ramp-up wasn't necessary and that six months is enough time to prepare. But when she started thinking about this so long ago, it felt "super radical."

When I asked Liz what was the most important thing they've done to maintain productivity, she didn't hesitate. It has been reducing meeting time, making meetings more efficient, and adding focus time. They changed their standing meeting from an hour a week to thirty minutes every two weeks. They get written updates in advance and have a real discussion instead of reports. Every calendar invite has to have a Google Doc agenda attached with differentiation between written updates and what needs to be discussed. And it needs to go out twenty-four hours before the meeting. But they haven't just improved and eliminated meetings. They've added new types of gatherings. They do "learning club" with homework in advance and thirty minutes of discussion. They increased the frequency of popular "meet the artist" sessions. And because they're all virtual, they added meetings that build team cohesion and sociability. These include "Huddle," a fifteen-minute weekend recap on Mondays at 1:00 p.m., and "Donut," a Slack add-on that randomizes people into small groups to re-create casual watercooler talk. They also created the "Culture Squad," a group of volunteers who organize a "shockingly fun," bimonthly staff get-together of games, dress-up, cooking, and other nonwork activities.

The flip side of cutting out meetings is providing time for people to focus. The Microsoft global survey found that 68 percent say they don't have enough uninterrupted focus time during the day. On Teams, the average user spends 57 percent of their time communicating with others—whether it's in meetings, on email, or in chat.

At ArtLifting, changes to meetings went hand in hand with expanding focus time. Liz reads a lot of management advice and really liked Cal Newport's popular book *Deep Work*, in which he advocates three hours or so of uninterrupted time as ideal for getting into a flow state. The company designated the period from 9:00 a.m. to 1:00 p.m. (eastern) as daily hours when people weren't expected to be checking Slack or email or holding meetings. (There were adjustments for people in different time zones.) This innovation was seen by employees as "life-changing" because it allowed them to actually "think." The sales team uses this time to strategize and then reach out to prospects they wouldn't have time for in the course of a constantly interrupted day. Liz uses the time for big-picture thinking.

For many companies, software plays an important role in how they save time, both by obviating meetings and by reducing communication time. ArtLifting installed software that automatically schedules meetings to maximize the amount of (unscheduled) focus time. When I met with a few of the ArtLifting staff, they were enthusiastic about Asana, their project management software product. (It was revealing that Liz, whom I'd already spoken to a few times, never mentioned Asana, an indication of how efficiency strategies vary by organizational level.) Other common practices include shared calendars and coordinating other kinds of information, such as tasks in progress. People also shifted out of more time-consuming ways of communicating, such as phone and in-person discussions, into email, Slack, Teams, and similar systems. That does entail a loss of informal social talk, but it helps get the work done.

And of course there are also low-tech ways of avoiding distractions and giving people more time to focus. One PR agency in the U.K. trial uses a stoplight system in its open plan office. A simple green light sign on an employee's computer means it's fine to interrupt; yellow means only interrupt for something important; and red is "Stay away, I'm busy." Our team members Phyllis Moen and Youngmin Chu also identified low-tech strategies in their in-depth study of BldWrk. The company had a culture of frequent distraction, which it needed to change when it went to thirty-two hours. Employees reported becoming more intentional and bundling their queries. According to one shop floor worker, "I don't get interrupted as much. We turn those interruptions into scheduled get-togethers. And then, I try to have all of my questions compiled, or all of my answers compiled, and I have noticed that everyone else is trying to do that so that we're taking more information away from the meetings that we do have. So while it may have resulted in maybe 10% more meetings, that's taken away 50% of the daily interruptions."

Creating a good culture of time use has another benefit that Liz identified. "If people feel like their time is wasted away on things that they're not using their brain on, then they'll be frustrated and leave. So the efficiency learnings aren't just about more revenue, or how to squeeze things into thirty-two hours. It's like, employee happiness and value."

ENHANCING CREATIVITY

To some extent, there's a mechanical aspect to how focus time works, which is that it eliminates interruptions and lets people get deeper into their tasks. But there's another aspect to the lack of interruption, which is its ability to enhance creativity and big-picture thinking. Alex Soojung-Kim Pang, our colleague at 4 Day Week Global, is an expert on creativity and has spent years studying and writing about companies that shift to shorter hours. In his book *Rest*, Alex delved into the scientific literature on creativity, which has made tremendous strides with the use of techniques like MRI. There's growing evidence that unconscious brain processes are key to aha moments, especially something called the default mode network. Mind wandering, low-demand tasks, background noise, absentmindedness—these are all states in which new ideas emerge (and one reason many people like to work in coffee shops). In *Shorter*, his sequel on companies that have reduced working hours, Alex details the ways in which working less makes people more innovative and creative.

Much of this can and does happen at the workplace, for example, during focus time. But Pang argues that uninterrupted time away from the office also matters. Liz Powers feels that her three-day weekends, during which she unplugs from email, calendar, and Slack, lead to those kinds of outcomes. "Having that space just frees up the brain to do the more strategic work.... While I'm driving an hour to see my grandmother, I'm not purposely trying to think of that strategic sales technique, but it might just be like, I have this aha moment. And then on Monday morning, first thing I can, send that ten-minute email." Much of the company's success is down to being proactive and developing long-term business strategies. At some point it figured out it could rent the art rather than sell it, which led to recurring revenue and helped the artists and the company. Liz credits the schedule. "Having the three days of unconscious problem solving makes people on the team more strategic." I noticed that while I was writing this book, the cooldown period at the end of my exercise classes led to new ideas.

As we heard more from participants about creativity and its role in the success of the four-day week, we got more interested in this dimension of reduced work time. In the fall of 2023, we included a creativity scale with items such as "I am a good source of creative ideas" and "I suggest new ways of performing work tasks." By the summer we had some findings from the U.S. and Canadian companies. We found a small increase in this self-reported measure (from 3.9 to 4.0 on a 5-point scale). Forty-six percent of the sample registered an increase in creativity, while 29 percent declined. One interpretation is that the former are able to take advantage of the schedule change to solve problems and do things differently, while the latter group feels more pressure at work and has less time to let their minds wander.

These ideas resonate with the phenomenon of slow productivity, explored by Cal Newport in his 2024 book of that name. Newport, a chronicler of knowledge workers, explains that the pressure to fill time and appear busy undermines quality and true results. He advocates doing fewer things, working at a natural pace, and obsessing over quality. Newport argues that this philosophy, which aligns with how some, although not all, of the organizations in our trials approach work, yields more creativity.

While I've described the measures that companies go through as productivity hacks, a lot of the experience doesn't fit the meaning of a hack, which in this case refers to a maneuver, shortcut, or innovation that increases productivity and efficiency. Those happen. But our survey results suggest something more profound, which is a sense of empowerment, efficacy, and command that people come to feel in the workplace. They feel on top of their workloads, are more able to focus, and can complete tasks expeditiously. They are less beset by anxiety and the Sunday scaries. They come to work refreshed, ready to dive in. They may use some maneuvers or short-cuts, but the bigger change is that work becomes less a problem and more a source of satisfaction and accomplishment. We think this is an important part of why companies are so positive about their overall productivity and performance as a result of the schedule change. As one trial participant told us, "I did not expect the 4 day week to impact so many areas of my life—especially my increased energy and creativity during the week. I felt keen to start on Monday, which has never happened in my career and [I] looked forward to it. I also felt closer to the company and more motivated to invest my own time even on the off day, to deliver better at work."

SERVING CLIENTS

All three of the companies I've profiled so far—Praxis, ArtLifting, and Tessa's ad agency—are client-service-oriented businesses, like many in the trials. You'll remember that Matt Juniper of Praxis originally felt he'd have to wait until his clients went to four days to make this schedule feasible for his agency. When Praxis decided to go ahead, it instituted regular client satisfaction surveys with questions such as "My agency's there when I need them, they are completing work, and meeting deadlines as necessary." Even with the reduced coverage on Mondays and Fridays, there has been a slight uptick in those metrics. In fact, Matt says that "clients have fully embraced the model." They have "noticed that our team is coming to client meetings energetic, more strategic, and more productive than they were before." Client satisfaction has shown up in the bottom line. By the end of the trial, revenue growth was coming mainly from existing clients expanding the volume of work they were contracting for, rather than from new business. "I attribute that to the team coming into the office more refreshed and they're able to sell in more business."

Some companies are up front with their clients before their trials begin. Tyler Grange, an environmental consultancy in the U.K., carried out a careful communications strategy before it started. It put together a write-up, complete with FAQs, that it sent to all three thousand plus clients. It did one-on-one phone calls or meetings with its top accounts. Its approach was ultimately successful, and some clients even asked for help on instituting the new schedule in their own organizations. The American Sociological Association, which shifted to a four-day week in January 2024, also let people know in advance. It posted the new policy on its website, along with its rationale (and some of our findings).

Other organizations figure they don't need to inform clients, because they won't be skimping on responsiveness. One architectural firm in our trials decided not to announce its plans in advance, leaving communications with clients up to the senior people on each project. A staff person explained that with some of the large clients "we're not going to call up and say, 'Hey, we're going on the four-day week.' First of all, they don't care. But also it's just inappropriate. With those smaller developers, I recommended after we had been doing it for four months that then they could let them know. And then if they had any concerns—it's been a while; we've actually been doing this for four months, and then it'd be like, 'Oh, okay, well. Right.' And there were two reasons for that. One of them was, of course, we didn't want to frighten any of our clients. But the other one was, in case it didn't work out. I didn't want to make this big grand announcement and then have to be like, we kind of failed."

Although our research team hasn't collected data on customer satisfaction, what we've learned indicates that customers aren't a barrier to success. Some participants, like Matt Juniper, feel that happier, healthier, more motivated employees can serve their clients better. Tessa Ohlendorf says that her clients are thrilled because she's giving them a superior product. Liz Powers is also confident that clients are not a barrier to closing on Fridays. Only a few of our companies gave us data from customers, but in those cases the metrics were either unchanged or better from trial beginning to end. In our communications with the small number of companies that have reverted to a five-day week, client or customer dissatisfaction hasn't come up.

Anecdotally, it seems that some clients are enthusiastic about a shift to four days because they'd like it for themselves. Liz Powers says that the responses from clients have been great: "Unbelievable. Like, this is the best, I love that you guys are doing this. I want to convince my company." Five years ago, when ArtLifting began its stepwise journey to four days, Liz was worried about client response. "But it's been nothing but support. I think a big factor was post-COVID [there's] much more awareness about mental health." ArtLifting crafted standard "Out of Office" (OOO) language that everyone uses on Friday. Liz says that client attitudes are revealed in their responses to those OOO messages. "Normally clients end emails with periods. I've had clients use all caps, and like five exclamation points in response. And it's been probably, like, thirty examples this year."

PROCESS ENGINEERING IN A MANUFACTURING SETTING

Because most of the companies in our trials are white-collar organizations, addressing meetings, distractions, and communication goes a long way toward making a four-day week feasible. In industries such as manufacturing and construction, time savings are more likely to be found by making the flow of work more efficient, through process engineering. Pressure Drop Brewing, a small London craft manufacturer, did just that to make its trial succeed. Our collaborators at Cambridge University conducted a series of interviews at Pressure Drop—pre-trial, midway through, and at end point. A year later, I contacted the founders to see how things had developed.

Until the 1990s, beer companies had a vertical monopoly in the U.K.; a few big brewers owned nearly all the pubs in London. As a result, when craft brewing took off in the United States, the U.K. didn't follow. However, the Tory government ordered a breakup of the industry in 1989, which set off a renaissance in artisanal brewing. Pressure Drop was founded about a decade ago by three men who were looking to reset their work lives. Ben and Graham had been volunteering at a small brewery, and Sam had business skills. The company currently brews about twenty-five hundred liters a week of high-quality, "luxury" beer. My imagination of their headquarters was of a rather cluttered, grimy space with belching vats and a nineteenth-century vibe. I was surprised to discover a spacious floor full of gleaming stainless steel. So much for the nine-teenth century.

Sam was the driver behind the four-day week. When they started, Graham had already left the company and Ben was skeptical. (Now he's a convert.) Sam's motives lay in his previous experience in the corporate world.

Sam had been an IT project manager at various companies, mainly in the City of London. He never loved the life; he would work for a while, save some money, and quit. He's an extremely thought-ful man, with big ideas about life and work that he shared freely, along with his personal journey. In his interviews he referenced anthropologist David Graeber's book *Bullshit Jobs* and the idea that conventional work patterns are kind of "insane." At one point he talked about how he'd rather be selling apples from a stall, in part because while it may not be intellectually challenging, there's a satisfying materiality and usefulness to it. That attitude informs everything that Pressure Drop does.

The impetus for starting the company came after he broke his leg playing football. While he was in the hospital recuperating, "mentally, something snapped" and it all felt so "meaningless and unimportant." He left the corporate world and founded the brew-ery. He wanted Pressure Drop not to be "some sort of awful piece of your life that you shut yourself off from at the end of the day. . . . We don't want to claim people body and soul. . . . You know, particularly high-paying companies tend to do that." Part of making Pressure Drop different was rejecting the typical growth trajectory of start-ups. Its vision is sustainability—being a mom-and-pop operation that's innovative and ambitious. We're not particularly "rapacious, in terms of wanting to take over the world or become a large corpo-rate or, or endlessly grow." What's important to Sam is giving em-ployees a great work life and staying afloat in a highly competitive and dynamic industry. It's pretty clear they're succeeding on the former, because job satisfaction levels register a full point above the other companies in our trials. The four-day week seemed like a natural for this larger philosophy. "There's a lot of bad stuff happening in the world that I think affects people in a negative way.... Part of the motivation for doing it in the first place was to sort of try to be part of a positive movement and create something positive for our employees."

Pressure Drop participated in the large U.K. trial that started in June 2022. It was a very difficult time in the U.K. economy, with high inflation and many of the company's competitors going bust. People were drinking less beer. But they've managed to make it work. Ben, who runs the brewing side of the business, explained that for the trial to succeed, employees would have to own it. That meant figuring out how to reorganize their activities. "Sam and I are not going to tell you how to do it; you're gonna work it out yourself. And that's exactly what happened." They had multiple sessions to plan the changes. "Everyone was on board with it, and everyone came up with ideas, but some guys really gave it a lot of thought and had whole lists of things we should be doing differently."

The regular schedule was that they brew on Tuesday through Thursday with packaging, cleaning, and other tasks on Monday and Friday. So an obvious plan was to divide the brewing staff into two groups and rotate Mondays and Fridays off. That was an easy decision. On the process side, they spent about two months, during which people timed all of their tasks to see how long each took. Ben encouraged people to be honest about break times; he wanted a real-world measurement. They found that some of the reigning assumptions were off by a lot. They'd assumed it takes three hours to clean one of the machines, but the exercise they went through showed it took only an hour and a half. They also incorporated new tools into some of their processes, to make them more efficient.

Brewing involves many different tasks; Ben's estimate was ten to fifteen. As one employee explained, they're often doing five of them at once. That offered multiple opportunities for sequencing things differently and slotting new tasks into unaccustomed places. For example, it takes hours to clean the canning line, but there are thirty-to-forty-five-minute periods when the operator is just waiting around. That means they can start setting up the next packaging run, lining up the kegs, and getting cans ready for the feed line. They also changed when they did cleaning and preparation. Pre-trial they'd had a Monday-morning meeting to list and allocate tasks. They moved that meeting to the previous week, which meant that if someone had a free moment on Thursday or Friday, they could set things up for the coming week. By cleaning the equipment, scanning (that is, labeling) the kegs, and lining them up in advance, they were able to save one to two hours on Tuesday. They got more organized with Mondays and Fridays as well, turning them into setup and clean-down days. And they added a quick check-in on Monday afternoons in case anyone had some free time to fit in an additional task.

The staff called it smart working. It's true that the overall pace of work went up. As Ben said, "That was the whole point of it." But he is confident that people enjoy that busier pace. Each day goes by faster. And the pace of work pre-trial was what Sam described as "mellow." I got a fascinating history lesson as he explained that this is intrinsic to brewing, which "lends itself to a mellow pace at times in the same way that agriculture does . . . where you'd have periods of intensive work and periods where people were basically idle. That's where the term 'furlough' comes from."

Management focused on meeting overall metrics, rather than individual performance. This likely helped create good team spirit and more "mucking in." Working for the common goal of getting finished in four days led employees to help out in new ways, doing things that aren't technically their job but that help meet production quotas and ensure quality. That's an outcome that is relevant beyond manufacturing.

More than eighteen months after the experiment began, it is clearly a success. Sam says they don't spend much time thinking about it because it is working "fairly smoothly." Pressure Drop has experienced one of the largest reductions in working hours among all our companies—a full 7.9. The new schedule has been normalized. Now the concern is inflation and the deteriorating market for high-priced beer. But the company doesn't have any debt and is holding on. It's also got the advantage of loyal and satisfied employees. Everyone's a stakeholder, Sam explains. They've gotten "people thinking like a manager would think in terms of how can we do this efficiently? What's the best way of doing this? That kind of thing. And, you know, we've got a good team."

While the role of process engineering was salient at Pressure Drop, we also saw evidence of it in white-collar workplaces. Wherever there's a workflow that can be studied, it makes sense to go through that exercise, whether it's the movement of documents or approvals from one office to another (as is common in finance and accounting), or the stages of product design (as in software), or the arrangements for preparing food in a restaurant. In the laid-back culture of Pressure Drop they hadn't done the efficiency studies that standard economics assumes all management goes through. When they did, they were able to realize a big benefit for both workers and owners.

The Pressure Drop experience also illustrates another point about the trials—the emphasis on employee involvement. Ben's view was that the employees were going to have to figure it out. This is something Andrew Barnes emphasizes, and that philosophy carried through into the onboarding sessions. In the later trials, we added a question on the employee survey about whether the respondent was part of the planning process or whether it was a top-down affair. We found that just over two-thirds of employees said they'd been involved in decision making for the new schedule.

SPEEDING UP OR WORKING SMART?

At this point you may be wondering whether the success of the four-day week is really about efficiency and working smarter. Parkinson's law suggests that people were operating at low intensity and the schedule change sped them up, as at Praxis. At Pressure Drop, there's little doubt the pace of work was mellow. If that's the story, it's a trade-off most prefer. But that's a far less compelling finding than the claim that the four-day week can catalyze innovations that actually save time. Workers have been subjected to management-driven speedup since the beginning of factory work. Was our team unwittingly part of another episode in that long process?

From the beginning, we'd been wondering—truthfully, I was worrying—about the speedup issue. As a result, we'd flagged it as one of those potential blowback phenomena we wanted to measure. In the early trials we used two questions about whether the job involved having to work to tight deadlines and at very high speeds. As the results rolled in, we were surprised to see that answers to these questions weren't changing at all between baseline and end point. By this measure, there was no increase in work intensity.

The result was encouraging. There didn't seem to be a lot of speedup happening. But we weren't convinced. Maybe we weren't asking about this the right way. So we decided to add direct questions on the pace of work and workload. At the time, we were approaching a trial end point, so we had to use retrospective questions. Those differ from the more accurate method of asking at baseline and end point. Looking back, people did think their pace of work and workload were rising a bit. Once we incorporated those questions into the baseline survey and measured again at end point, the increase disappeared. There was no change in pace of work or workload.

However, as the sample grew, we saw a subtle uptick in the two original intensity questions (tight deadlines and high speeds). It was less than a 0.1 rise on a 5-point scale. We had also started asking directly about the pace of work and intensity of the job, and those items showed a 1–2 percent rise. Surprisingly, for about 30 percent of the sample, pace, intensity, and workload fell. For about 30 percent, there was no change. And about 40 percent registered an increase. When I did the final update for the book, intensity had risen 0.1 and pace went up a full 0.3. So there seems to be some mild speedup.

However, the larger change is that people are working smarter, just as the 4 Day Week Global philosophy suggested. As I noted in the previous chapter, our original question about productivity asked people about their "current work ability compared to their

Table 3.1 Working harder or smarter?

	Baseline	Endpoint	Change	Significance	% Decrease	% No change	% Increase
Work intensity	3.5	3.6	0.1	***	30%	32%	38%
Pace of work	7.3	7.6	0.3	***	30%	29%	41%
Workload	7.4	7.5	0.1	*	33%	29%	38%
Productivity	7.3	8.1	0.8	***	15%	29%	56%
Current work ability	7.0	7.9	0.9	***	19%	26%	56%
Work smart	3.6	3.8	0.2	***	31%	18%	51%

Note. Work intensity: 2-item scale, working at high speeds, working to tight deadlines (1-5). Pace of work, workload and productivity: self-reported (0-10). Current work ability: compared to lifetime best (0-10). Work smart: 4-item scale (0-5). Significance levels are based on paired-sample t tests to determine whether baseline and endpoint values are significantly different: +p<.1, *p<0.05, **<0.01, ***p<0.001.

lifetime best." That measure rises in all the trials, generally by just under a full point (0.9), or 13 percent. For more than half the participants (56 percent), work ability rises. The results on productivity are similar. And "work smart"—a four-item scale—also rises, by 0.2 points.

I've already talked about the strategies that organizations are using to enhance efficiency and performance, such as changes to meeting practices and time use, and process engineering. They lead people to feel more productive and "smart" at work. A key point is that they involve the organization, or the team, as a whole. 4 Day Week Global and other groups advocate this whole-organization approach, rather than a focus on individuals and their performance. And companies in our trials mostly subscribe to that philosophy. But this doesn't mean that individual employees aren't also doing things differently to save time, especially those whose work is more self-directed. People develop personal strategies, even if they are often techniques that they're being taught in trainings and other organizational settings. To some extent it's a matter of becoming what one employee, from Healthwise, the first company in the U.S. trials, called "laser focused." She's more economical in communication, prioritizing, and getting the work done. At BldWrk, Moen and Chu found that reorganizing tasks was a big theme. By making to-do lists, and doing more up-front planning, people were able to move more quickly from task to task. Some shopworkers started coming in earlier, when the workspace is quieter. Others found they performed better by switching the order in which they do things. This was a very individual thing; there wasn't a common preferred way to order the day. At both Pressure Drop and Praxis, people were planning out their week in advance, becoming more intentional about what they needed to do and when it would happen.

And of course there's another issue that doesn't get talked about a lot but is surely at play for some people—pure time wasting. For many employees, there's enough slack in the day to sometimes be online, playing games, shopping, or browsing social media. Or that time might be spent chatting with co-workers, something that has come up in interviews. We don't know how much less any of that is happening, but we assume it's not a trivial savings. People are giving up what economists call "on the job leisure," in exchange for a full day off. A Healthwise interviewee was one of the few who raised this: "Let's be honest, I'm not goofing off or looking at Facebook—which I was."

A FORCING MECHANISM

For the three companies I've been discussing—Praxis, ArtLifting, and Pressure Drop—the focus was on efficiencies that allowed them to continue to be successful at what they were already doing. Ben from Pressure Drop recognized that the effort had a general positive impact: "If nothing else, this four-day-week trial was a great piece of exercise for any business, just to get people to think about their tasks critically and have a forum or an excuse to talk about those things." For Banks Benitez, the co-founder and CEO of an organization called Uncharted, the process of instituting a four-day week didn't result in more of the same but redirected the strategic positioning of the organization. The four-day week can be a "forcing mechanism." It's a term that's used a lot in climate science. In business, it's something that impels change.

Banks grew up in a family with two entrepreneur parents and has been interested in starting and leading companies since he was in elementary school. After college he co-founded a program called the Unreasonable Institute, which taught entrepreneurial skills to people around the world. Under his leadership the organization became active in more than forty countries. In 2017, he led a rebrand and co-founded Uncharted, a social impact accelerator. The organization was successful, partnering with major corporations and winning spots on "best places to work" lists. But Banks wasn't fully satisfied.

Banks had enough personal experience of burnout that the four-day week was attracting his attention. He was following the press reports on Microsoft Japan, Perpetual Guardian, and other companies that were going to four, which he found intriguing. This led to questioning his own work habits. He was a fifty- or sixty-hour-a-week person who said yes to just about everything, including plenty of low-value requests. He was coming to realize that he might be happier and more productive if he worked fewer hours. I originally met Banks at info sessions for 4 Day Week Global, where he recounted his organization's experience. When I asked him for an interview some months later, it wasn't lost on me that he scheduled a brief thirty-minute meeting.

Banks led the shift to a four-day week at Uncharted in June 2020. He had been influenced by a book called *Essentialism: The Disciplined Pursuit of Less*, which counsels that because time is such a scarce resource, people should figure out what's essential and focus on that. For Banks, that entailed a process that he called "reprioritization." With time at a premium, the organization started looking more closely at everything it was doing—how much effort it took, what the results were, and crucially, the relationship between effort and results. It discovered that there were widespread disproportionalities in its activities—things that took a lot of time but yielded little value. Some of the changes were fairly minor. They downsized their newsletter from biweekly to every six weeks. The newsletters got better and more effective, and not having to produce one every other week saved a lot of time. But the more important changes were big, strategic decisions. As it looked at the variety of programs it was running, the organization realized not all were sufficiently "mission aligned." When they decided to "de-prioritize" a corporate sponsorship program, it meant turning down a $1 million grant from a major tech company. By rejecting money people worried might lead away from their core goals, the organization was able to see a path forward that was truer to its original heritage. Banks felt that Uncharted had been "getting out over their skis."

I was skeptical about the relationship of that decision to the four-day week, because it didn't seem to be primarily about time use. I pushed Banks on whether Uncharted really needed the four-day week to accomplish strategic realignment. He agreed that prioritizing is something they were already doing to some extent and should be doing as a matter of course. But he feels "business as usual is such a powerful force." And the reality was that Uncharted hadn't been very good at it, compared with after the schedule change. In his view, four days got them there faster and, perhaps more important, forced them into ongoing practices of self-reflection, the recognition of trade-offs (temporal and other), and good leadership.

"Forced" is the operative word here. Time and again, as I talked to people in our trials, the idea of the four-day week as a forcing mechanism emerged. This was especially true when I pushed them on the question of why they hadn't instituted many of these changes before, especially the simpler, cheaper, or more obvious ones. One answer stands out. It was from Terry VanDuyn at Kickstarter, a company we'll meet in the next chapter. We were talking about organizations that regularly took the time to find the kinds of efficiencies that four-day-week organizations discover. Perhaps naïvely, I called them "functional companies." Why aren't there more of them? I asked. Terry didn't hesitate: "Have you ever worked at a functional company before? I promise you no one's doing that."

But why? "Because everybody is just tied up. . . . Everything is piled up, and everyone's just trying to keep their head above water." The four-day week forces people to take stock, reduce the piles, and get strategic.

ARE THERE REALLY $20 BILLS LYING ON THE GROUND?

At this point I need to ask, are you feeling skeptical? Thinking the story sounds too good to be true? Even if you aren't, I can guarantee my economist friends are. In fact, they have an old joke that likely sums up their attitude. Two guys are walking along the sidewalk. One looks down and says, "Hey, there's a $20 bill on the ground." The other quickly retorts, "Nonsense. If there were a $20 bill there, someone would have already picked it up."

That's the gist of the most common unconvinced attitude to the four-day-week movement—disbelief that it's possible to get a 25 percent increase in productivity via a schedule change. The idea of money on the ground, or any unexploited opportunity, runs counter to economists' view of the world. The standard model assumes that markets are efficient. If there's money to be made (or "found"), people will have already gotten going on making it. They capitalize on existing opportunities.

The corollary is that if there really are productivity gains to be had, why haven't companies already found them? Do they have to give their workers a day off to enact changes in meetings practices or processes? To make better strategic decisions? These things are in management's control. After my TED talk rehearsal, the head of TED, Chris Anderson, made just this point. Why aren't companies doing these things within the structure of a five-day week and getting even more performance from their employees? It's a great question.

One answer might be that productivity-improving change is expensive. But the four-day-week movement isn't telling companies they need to buy costly software or machines in order to raise hourly productivity. Only a handful in our trials have brought in consultants to figure out how to do this without reducing performance or production. In fact, they're making these changes with little to no cash outlay—by mobilizing people's time, energy, and creativity. This innovation is what people typically think of as a win-win. Economists generally don't believe in those. (Their terminology is "free lunches.") If there were changes that could make one party better off without making someone else worse off— what's called Pareto efficiency—management would have already enacted them. They would have picked up those $20 bills lying on the ground.

If that seems a bit unrealistic, or even extreme, remember that economists have an ace up their sleeve—competition. A big part of why they don't believe in unexploited opportunities is that companies that fail to capitalize on productivity-enhancing reforms will be outcompeted by those that see these opportunities. Competition ensures that there aren't free or low-cost ways to improve. Those "low-hanging" fruit get picked. Whatever is left is costly—machinery, expertise, software, or, on the labor side, higher wages or more training. If those strategies are available, companies will take them if the expected benefits exceed the costs. So the whole idea of today's four-day-week movement—that there's a way to give workers more that also benefits management and owners—is highly implausible in the world of conventional economics.

And yet it's happening. The companies really *are* finding $20 bills, using them to buy free lunches, and giving everyone a win. In the next chapter, I'll explain more about how and why I think it's working. But to do that, we need to take a look at another type of company experience. So far we've met organizations that are into time saving and efficiencies. For others, the well-being benefits for workers translate into better performance, fewer resignations, and reduced costs.

4

WHEN LESS IS MORE

The 4 Day Week Global model of 100-80-100 involves giving 100 percent of the pay in 80 percent of the time while asking employees to deliver 100 percent of their output. As we saw in the previous chapter, many succeed by changing the way they meet, focus, sequence tasks, and prioritize. In this chapter we look at those that follow a different strategy, having already squeezed out most low-value activity. Perhaps they're "too" efficient, because many of their employees are burning out. I call them 100-80-80 companies, because they don't ask employees to do five days of work in four. They just reduce work time. Their motives are to improve employee well-being, avoid burnout, stem the tide of resignations, and improve the quality of what they're producing. While many organizations combine aspects of both models, and I finish the chapter with a hybrid case, the examples I start with have had exemplary success just asking for less.

REDUCING BURNOUT IN A SERVICE SECTOR SETTING

M'tucci's is a casual restaurant chain that joined our second trial in April 2022. I'd read about fine dining establishments—famous for inhuman hours and stressful environments—that reduce working hours by closing for one or more days a week. Alex Pang profiled a number of them in his book *Shorter*. But most of those were owned by famous chefs, who had Michelin stars and were operating in the stratosphere in comparison with M'tucci's, which is selling pizza and pasta. Could this work in a setting where being open seven days was essential to the business model?

M'tucci's reasons for making the switch were familiar. John Haas, company president and a co-founder, read an article in *The New York Times* about the four-day week and thought it might work. It aligns with the organization's culture, which harks back to the 1950s model of a local business that cares for its people, has multiple generations of employees on the payroll, and supports families. At M'tucci's many of the senior managers are partners—that is, owners—in the business. The company believes in long-term investment in its workforce and has great benefits, including tutoring for the children of employees. That's the context in which it supports the four-day week. But believing in your people is one thing. Changing the notorious burnout culture of restaurants is another.

At the beginning, M'tucci's decided it would start the trial with only some of its staff—managers and salaried chefs. Their standard workweek was a punishing fifty-five hours. These employees would now have to work only four days. Amanda Cronin was one of them.

Amanda is a general manager who has been with the company since 2015. She began as a barback during her college days and rose quickly through the ranks to bartender, then hourly manager. She had been planning to get a master's degree in hospitality, but the owner told her not to waste her money. He'd train her instead. Now she not only is a general manager but was asked to open Roma, the company's new four-to-five-hundred-seat location, just as the four-day week was being rolled out. The tremendous success of that restaurant is one of the things that made M'tucci's experience even more impressive.

For Amanda, the big benefit of the schedule comes from the alleviation of what she calls "restaurant guilt"—the idea that if you're not at the restaurant, it's going to "crumble." Restaurant guilt is pervasive among managers and chefs, and Amanda suffered it from before the schedule change. No longer. She says the four-day week has helped her, and others, achieve work-life balance.

Our liaison at the company is Howie Kaibel, brand manager and "minister of culture." Howie oversaw the shift and is a big believer. He gave me the backstory of how they implemented the four-day week. Like many of the companies in our trials, M'tucci's is data oriented. It went to the National Restaurant Association for numbers on turnover and learned that the industry average in its segment was 80 percent a year, about twice the average for the private sector as a whole. (Fast food, he explained, is much higher, more like 120 percent.) During the pandemic, M'tucci's was well below its segment, at 40 percent, but burnout and turnover were still issues. That was part of the motivation.

Unlike most other organizations in the pilots, M'tucci's didn't follow the usual process of productivity hacks to conform to the 100-80-100 model. The general managers have a standing weekly meeting, but it is well run, held only once a week, and vital to keeping everyone on the same page. That didn't change.

Another difference from many other trial participants is that M'tucci's recognized that to make this work, it would need to add capacity. It wasn't going to ask its people to work harder or faster, especially post-pandemic, when staff had developed expectations of more humane schedules. It was already pretty efficient, without many costless ways to make up the time. So it hired new hourly paid managers for each of the restaurant locations. (Each restaurant has a general manager, a few salaried managers, and some additional hourly managers.) On the food prep side, it created a new position of team leader in each location and elevated someone from the cook team to it. That person was able to open and close the kitchen, and they were trained to work on final presentation of the food before it went to the customer. That eased the workload on the chefs, because the team leader was now doing some of their work. And it enabled the chefs' extra day off. It also added a promotion step for staff, and a ladder into the sous-chef position, which management considered a big plus. The strategy involved both new hires and changing the division of labor to give more skilled work to lower-paid employees.

When I asked about cost, the answer was that the additional managers and the slightly higher pay of the new team leader position were trivial enough that it didn't matter. The company didn't lose one manager during the trial period via resignation. Now it uses the four-day week in its recruiting messages. But Howie thinks the bigger benefit has been in the quality of its product. Its staff has so much energy when they show up at work, and it is reflected in the service and the food. Part of Howie's job is monitoring ratings, especially for the new locations: "The energy you get back plays out in the restaurant . . . the Yelp reviews have been 'wow' on the service."

Amanda also feels the shift has improved quality and service. One reason is that the teams are stronger. She says people are more willing to pitch in to do things that aren't in their job description, like go to other locations for special events. Morale has improved a lot. Existing staff has been "super excited" about the schedule, and for new hires it's a fantastic perk. In her view, part of why they needed to do this is that the pandemic changed prevailing attitudes among restaurant workers. They're no longer as willing to "commit to the restaurant 100 percent" as in the past, when they were expected to come early and stay late without complaint. Chefs expect more from owners now. At M'tucci's they're getting it, to the benefit of the company. "This has more longevity to it," Amanda explains.

The positive story I heard from Howie and Amanda is reflected in their survey results. M'tucci's has had bigger improvements in absenteeism, burnout, and mental health than the average company in the trials. M'tucci's employees also improved more on sleep problems (a particular problem in this industry, given the late nights). Satisfaction with personal relationships rose almost twice as much as the sample average. Job satisfaction is more than a point higher than at other companies.

The original plan was to expand the four-day schedule to all staff, which hadn't happened at the time I did these interviews in late 2023. There are complexities with the scheduling preferences of hourly staff that hadn't been worked out. Nor are managers' hours down to thirty-two a week. They're in the forty-five to forty-eight range. But they're on the road. And Howie and Amanda are both big believers—not only that a cool company with a throwback model and a minister of culture can do it, but that any casual dining restaurant can.

THE PARADOX OF WORK INTENSITY

The fact that 100-80-100 works for many companies suggests they are relatively low-intensity organizations. They've got inefficiency in their work culture and flow, or the pace of work is not too demanding. Many are suffering from Parkinson's law. However, there are also workplaces where there's no fat to wring out. I saw this firsthand in the 1990s, when I met with executives at Motorola to get them interested in a reduced work-time experiment. Competition with Japanese manufacturers had already led them to incorporate the management fads of the era—lean production, just-in-time systems, and a shift to teamwork. The organization had been sped up and processed out. I left the meeting convinced there was no scope for a costless hours reduction. Since then other industries have gone through similar experiences. In health care, consultants and economists have already cut to the bone. At successful restaurants, decades of fine-tuning have turned the kitchen into a fast-paced, well-oiled machine (no pun intended). Staff aren't playing games on their smartphones. And yet these high-intensity workplaces are also successfully implementing four-day weeks. They're the other end of the spectrum from organizations that have a clear path to 100-80-100. The paradox is that the four-day week makes sense for both types. The latter because they can. The former because they must.

In the high-intensity settings, employees are burning out in part due to the pace of work. These are industries that are demanding too much from their staff, who are responding by quitting in droves, getting sick from the stress, even leaving the field. It's a well-recognized problem among health-care professionals. Similarly, restaurants were extremely hard hit by the Great Resignation.

In these cases, burnout and turnover are so high that adding staff can actually be cost effective. In our trials, we see this situation in the service sector, in health care, and among nonprofits. Instead of productivity narrowly defined, what matters for success is the total economic picture. The company needs to pay attention not just to how much work people do every hour but to how well they do their jobs, how likely they are to quit, and what it costs to replace them. The operative word here isn't "efficiency" but "stability." These cases show that a four-day week can create team stability. And in some cases, that stability yields higher productivity and more business opportunities.

If Microsoft Japan is the poster child for raising productivity by cutting meetings, the town of Gothenburg in Sweden is the best-known example of cutting work time and adding capacity. It ran a two-year trial that reduced nurses' shifts in the Svartedalens retirement home to six hours a day and hired new staff to cover the extra hours. The nurses' well-being improved, and the town saved on unemployment benefits, sick leave, and health-care costs. Patient outcomes also got better. Ultimately, the direct staff savings didn't fully match the additional salary costs, although they came close. A new conservative city government ended the experiment. However, if it had done a full cost analysis, it might have made a different decision. In cases where the social costs of health-care professionals leaving the field and the benefits to patients are included, adding salary can pay for itself.

PRIORITIZING EMPLOYEE HEALTH

Grand Challenges Canada (GCC), which took part in a 2022 trial, is in this 100-80-80 category. The organization is financed by the Government of Canada and provides funding for innovative efforts to solve dire problems in middle- and low-income countries. It's a fast-growing entity and has tripled its staff in the last few years. At the time of the pilot it had ninety-seven employees. About a year after the switch to four days, I talked to Tracy Smith, senior director of people and culture, about why things had worked so well at GCC. Tracy felt the key was that "people are really respecting that time for each other. . . . It has really been almost a universal sense of crickets on Friday." That was important because the work is so psychologically draining. At the time Tracy and I met, conflict in the Middle East was the most difficult of the situations staff was dealing with. They're working on extreme poverty, ecological disaster, war, and the like on a daily basis. Tracy recognizes that this "emotional taxation takes a toll." COVID made things worse.

She also noted that this is a very diverse, aware staff for whom George Floyd's murder was a "key moment" that brought additional heaviness to the work. That awareness underlay the importance of making sure that the change in workload was absolutely equitable—that no one had to pick up someone else's unfinished tasks and that it was truly available to everyone in the organization. They were very careful to make sure that "there's not one role or any one group of folks that are being disadvantaged because of the seat that they sit in." At GCC, as in many organizations, the state of the world is an ever-present stressor.

The need to rachet down those stress levels meant that 100-80-100 couldn't be the plan. These people already put in many hours, in part to communicate globally. They are often dealing with high-stakes outcomes. Tracy repeatedly noted how productive and motivated they are. But the organization's survey results at baseline showed above-average levels of stress compared with our full sample. They were also doing worse on a few of the other well-being indicators, such as fatigue, anxiety, and work-to-family conflict, as well as some workload and pace variables—intensity of work, overtime hours, and second-job holding. When I asked specifically about the 100-80-100 model, Tracy was clear. The priority was to create well-being for the employees. And GCC achieved that. It had strong improvements on its well-being measures, mostly in line with our full sample, but a bit higher on stress and burnout. And that was its priority. If a little less got done, they would live with that. The organization had gone to thirty-two. Full stop.

Tracy explained that the technologies adopted during COVID were in fact making GCC more efficient; Slack, Zoom, shared documents, and other tools were helping "take away some of the bloat from the typical workday." Ultimately, Tracy felt GCC's success was less about technology or the number of days in the schedule than the organizational culture. "Culture is the soul of an organization . . . different people coming together with shared values and recognizing what matters most to them, and being really good humans to each other . . . being in a place that you feel morally, psychologically, culturally safe. That's a really, really, really rich culture where you can come and be yourself and do your best work every day."

KEEPING NURSES ON THE JOB

One of the questions that come up frequently in conversations about the four-day week is whether it can work in health care. When we were planning our first trial, in Ireland, we had the opportunity to meet with Leo Varadkar, who at the time was the *tánaiste* (deputy prime minister) and went on to become the taoiseach (prime minister). We were hoping for government support for the trial. After our presentation he pivoted, laser-like, to health care. How could this possibly work in that sector? Where's the wasted time? Varadkar was skeptical about the model. In time we'd have some answers for him.

In the first two trials, we didn't have health-care organizations enrolling. But by June 2022, a 5,500-person organization in the U.K. called Outcomes First Group joined. It offers mental health services in a variety of settings. In the first trial, it included 999 of its employees. The results were excellent—with significant improvements in all the usual measures. Our contact at the company reported, "It's going really well. So much so, we are now rolling it out for all colleagues in our schools by this September. Then we will roll out across all our residential homes." Since then there's been a slow trickle of health-care participants into our trials, in addition to other organizations we've learned about that are adopting the four-day week on their own.

As I was writing this section, I heard from someone at an organization I'd been talking to that provides nurses in the Pacific Northwest. She reported that the company had decided to go ahead with a trial that will enroll about two hundred nurses. Shortly before the book went to press I received their results, which were fantastic. Their stress, burnout, and productivity improvements were twice our trial averages. That's likely because health-care workers are experiencing especially high levels of burnout, stress, and attrition. These problems were already considered at epidemic level before the pandemic, especially for nurses, who are the largest group of health-care professionals in the United States. By one estimate, almost a third (31.5 percent) of nurses who left their jobs in 2018 did so because of burnout. When the pandemic hit, distress skyrocketed. In one study of East Coast nurses, 65 percent were experiencing high levels of "emotional exhaustion," and 70.5 percent had high overall burnout levels. The American Nurses Association's 2023 annual survey found 64 percent of respondents had been stressed in the last two weeks. Almost half reported turnover intentions of "Yes" (19 percent) or "Maybe" (27 percent) in the next six months, with 43 percent of those saying "Yes" or "Maybe" to leaving nursing altogether. This is the context in which health-care organizations are implementing four-day schedules.

Pre-pandemic, there were a few nursing homes and eldercare facilities we'd learned about that had started on the four-day week. In 2018, the Glebe in Virginia began offering its certified nurse assistants, with an annual turnover of 50 percent, a 30/40 program in which they got forty hours' pay for five six-hour days. It's had to start a waiting list for this position and, as of this writing, was expanding the program. Post-pandemic, others followed. Capri Communities in Wisconsin started a four-day-week program in early 2023. In 2022, Carrie Cadwell, the CEO of the mental health counseling provider 4C Health in Indiana, announced it was "excited to lead the charge in our industry's space. . . . We believe that giving a day back each week to staff for life outside of work without change to pay or benefits is the best investment any employer can make for employee wellness, while ensuring quality of care, and efficiency outcomes."

And now we're starting to see the four-day week adopted in hospital settings. At Temple University Hospital in Philadelphia the impetus was the loss of half its inpatient nurse leaders between January 2020 and November 2021. After an extensive planning process that included changing its reporting structures and adding some new leadership roles, it rolled out a four-day week for all its frontline nurse leaders. The new schedule was so successful that the executive team made it permanent thirty days after the trial. Voluntary turnover fell to zero, and multiple patient outcome measures improved.

One of the organizations in our trials had a similar experience. The company is a large (approximately thirty-five thousand) integrated health-care system in New Jersey. It came to 4 Day Week Global for consulting expertise on a trial that would include office workers and nurses. Our team covered the research for the office workers, but the nurses' group opted for continuing their data collection using the Mayo Clinic Well-Being Index. Heather Veltre, the chief nursing officer at one of their hospitals, filled me in on their experience not long after the trial ended.

Like Temple University Hospital, the company focused on nurse managers, identifying about forty-nine participants. (It ended up with thirty-eight, on account of leaves and other idiosyncratic reasons.) These positions are in charge of divisions such as oncology and surgery at the various hospitals, and everyone on that unit reports to them. One reason for limiting the pilot to managers is that frontline nurses are mainly on three twelve-hour shifts and are nonexempt, so going to a four-day week is more complicated to implement. Another is that the manager positions are grueling jobs, with a typical workweek of sixty hours and 24/7 responsibilities. As they did at Temple, Heather organized multiple planning sessions at which they agreed on goals and metrics and committed to progress reports and guidelines. Chief nursing officers would have the right to pull anyone out of the pilot at any time if they felt performance was slipping. As Heather said, "In health care, you can't wait. . . . Lives are at stake."

The model they used was to tap a nurse manager in an adjacent unit to cover for the off day. To ensure performance, coverage isn't just backup when problems arise. It's "true coverage." The substitute manager rounds with the team, is proactive, and pays attention to the workflow. And there is always an assistant nurse manager on the unit. Those positions do ten-hour shifts and weren't part of the pilot.

For participants, the program offered four days of work, although not necessarily a thirty-two-hour week. That was individual. If they could get their work done in eight hours, that would be fine. They're salaried and exempt, so the length of the day is really up to the workload they're facing. The point of the program was to give them a true day off each week—like a vacation day, without being on call or having the work pile up. Someone else would be doing it for them.

The program has been extremely successful. The nurse managers love it. Scores on the Mayo Clinic Well-Being Index were excellent, with the distress score coming in at a -0.82, a "wow" result, according to Heather. (It's a slightly complex scoring system that goes from -2 to 9 and includes a combination of yes/no questions and Likert scale agreement items.) A negative score, like the -0.82 of program participants, indicates thriving. They had a small nonparticipant group for comparison, which came in at 1.29. The national benchmark in 2022 was 2.11. The nurses in the four-day-week study were scoring almost off the chart.

There have been other indicators of success. Heather said they haven't lost any nurse managers since the pilot began. A few even rescinded resignation letters when they heard about the program. Metrics for patient outcomes, such as infections, improved, as did patient experience scores. When we talked, the status of the program hadn't yet been determined. Heather was due to report to the board soon. She did expect that board approval would mean the program would be rolled out throughout the system. She was unsure about how that would go and felt that if they canceled it, "we're going to have mutiny on our hands." But she also knew the rollout could be "dicey." There were a number of chief nursing officers whose personal experiences were of a 24/7 job. Would they be willing to go along with this? Heather feels it's necessary because "boomers aren't at the bedside anymore. . . . This generation of young leaders want flexibility, and they want to have a family. I think I'm the last of those who worked every day, all the time."

One of the notable things about both these hospital programs is that they did not involve additional up-front costs. At Temple, alterations in the staffing structure yielded savings that rendered the program cost neutral. In Heather's hospitals, the staffing changes involved using people who were already at work. They were able to make these changes because they thought through some basic questions and did careful planning. Not all organizations will be able to make these kinds of financially neutral adjustments at the beginning. But the economics of the four-day week in high-turnover settings aren't only, or even mainly, about the up-front investments. Calculations need to include the cost of losing people. In her report, Heather used a range of $132,000–$228,000 for every quit. This amount will vary quite a bit by region and time period, but the point is that if the four-day week stems resignations, it can pay for itself, at least in the early years. Over the long term other cost savings come into play, such as lower health-care and unemployment benefit costs. In a period of tight labor markets and rapidly rising salaries, keeping people in place can save the organization money. And that's just the labor side of things. We also have to factor in the monetary value of the better patient outcomes that come from a more rested, less stressed, more stable workforce.

The story gets more intriguing in other contexts.

TEAM STABILITY AS A BUSINESS STRATEGY

We met Tessa Ohlendorf in chapter 1. She's the media executive who transitioned her team to a four-day week during the pandemic.

As did so many of the companies in our trials, Tessa's team had great overall results, including an especially big jump in the all-important "current work ability" variable. You may remember from my earlier description that I was dubious that her success was due to productivity hacks. Her career achievements, as well as her obvious savvy and professionalism, made me doubt she'd run a shop with much wasted time. And when I asked if her team had already been "optimized," she largely concurred. "We were relatively efficient. We did use Google tools already, which, for example, if you're in a Google doc, and you have people across regions, or different time zones, or on different days off, you can still work on the same Google doc in real time. And we did all of that already." She allowed that they had too many meetings and that they could reduce time with clients. But for the most part, their success lay in the impact on turnover. Tessa's team of fifty-seven had lost only one person since the trial began. That not only yielded obvious cost savings but led to better work and additional business. As with the M'tucci's experience, guaranteeing team stability helped them make money.

Turnover is a chronic issue in marketing and advertising. Some teams in the industry experience 30 percent or even 40 percent turnover. Tessa's company, with its global reach, was no different. Tessa worked with the finance team to figure out how much that attrition was costing the organization. Using the standard figure of 30 percent of a salary for each resignation, they calculated that the company was spending $40 million a year on resignations. The teams that Tessa's people collaborated with were losing people at a rapid clip. One of the trouble spots was in Latin America, to which her Canadian team outsourced tasks. They had 40 percent turnover because people could easily jump ship and earn twice the pay. Tessa needed a way to keep them on board. So when she wrote thirty-two hours into a big new contract, she included the Latin American group on that schedule as well. The point was to stop the exodus and get some permanence on the team. That would ensure more consistent quality and delivery. As she'd seen with her own team, they would save an enormous amount of time in onboarding, mentoring, and training.

As Tessa recounted the situation, I recognized a phenomenon that economists call learning by doing. When people gain experience, they can get better at their jobs. Developments with one of Tessa's biggest accounts revealed how this works. She had three teams working with a fast food chain client. There was her ten-person media team, which had transitioned to the four-day week. There was the Latin American team, which was still on a five-day schedule. And the third group was the content team, also at five days. At the time we spoke, they'd had the business for twenty-nine months. The media team had zero turnover during that period. This "enabled the team to work on other opportunities with the client, bring in a lot of value. Know the business really well and do a great job. There's no onboarding and off boarding of new people. There's no new people making mistakes. There's no extra management in order to manage the team. So they get a better team." She contrasted her team to the content group, with 30 percent turnover, and the Latin American team, with 40 percent turnover. With media, "the client's getting an optimized team that understands their business, that does great work, that they can really trust. We brought opportunities to the client that we for sure wouldn't have been able to bring up because the team would have been so busy [dealing with people going and coming]."

The value of stability is showing up in Tessa's ability to secure business. "I presented to one major client, and when we were pitching them, I threw up the 1 percent turnover slide. And the client stopped us and the presentation. 'Go back to that for a second.' And then we sat there talking about it. And she's like, 'So you mean to tell me you have 1 percent turnover? That's what we can expect?' And I said yes. And it's just unheard of."

Tessa was clear that staff stability was key to the success of the relationship. "In our business, this is kind of groundbreaking, because in the agency world . . . everybody just assumes that there's going to be turnover. And so managers and the team are always working part of their day to help train somebody. . . . This is the first time in the history of my work—and I've been doing this for twenty-two years—where I have a team here, and a few of them now all they're doing is really focusing on their jobs, instead of training and onboarding, and supporting and getting to know this person and whatever." The client called the media team turnover result "truly incredible" and now they want that kind of result from the content team, which will likely require them to also go to four days.

When we spoke, Tessa was trying to monetize these results, above and beyond the ordinary savings that go with retention. She says that she's including clauses in her contracts that offer substantial bonuses if she is able to deliver a year's worth of a dedicated team, at a turnover rate of less than 5 percent. She muses about how if she has an initial price that is on the high side, she can come down 15 or 20 percent with the initial bid, because she knows she'll make it up with the bonus. That's because she trusts the four-day week, and her positive team culture, to keep people from leaving.

SUCCESS AT A LOCAL GOVERNMENT COUNCIL

We also have great evidence from a local U.K. government that saved quite a bit of money with a four-day week by improving retention and increasing applicants for its open positions. It began a three-month trial at the beginning of 2023 and then extended it for a year. Its experience is a counterpoint to the Svartedalens nursing home in Gothenburg, where the additional salary costs were slightly higher than the direct savings. In the case of South Cambridgeshire (or South Cambs, as it's called) the one-year savings were considerable—£371,500. This case has the most extensive data and analysis I've seen of a four-day-week trial, perhaps because it became very political. The local (Conservative) MP went all out to force the employees back to five days, and the Tory government threatened them with hefty fines. (He lost his seat, by the way, and the Tories lost the election.)

The council wasn't in our trial, but our British colleagues analyzed its performance data. The results are stellar. Recruitment and retention have improved markedly. Staff turnover has been reduced by 39 percent, and it's had a 53 percent rise in average applications for jobs, including increases in some of the positions it has traditionally found difficult to fill. It no longer has to pay signing bonuses (what it quaintly calls "golden hellos") to attract employees, or retention bonuses. Other recruitment costs also fell, as did its need to use agency staff for unfilled positions. It did have to spend to hire additional staff in cleaning and waste hauling. But overall, it came out ahead.

On well-being, changes were as expected. The council uses a commercial surveying firm with a simple scoring system. Before the trial began, it was registering in the "area of caution" (that is, poor outcomes) on a number of well-being metrics; now it's gone from negative to positive on mental and physical health, employee commitment, subjective well-being, and other measures. Many of its employee results have gone from red (bad) to green (good).

The story is similar with the key performance indicators (KPIs). Twenty-two of the twenty-four it is tracking have either improved or stayed the same. (One that declined is on-time rent payments, which are more a function of the cost-of-living crisis in the U.K. than council staff performance.) They are hitting or exceeding targets on answering calls, responding to emergencies, tenant satisfaction, the time it takes to process planning applications, and other indicators.

While this is a more documented experience than we have been able to carry out with our companies, it aligns with what we are hearing. Happier employees and equivalent or better performance. And in this case, there are also cash savings. The South Cambs experience is also important because it shows that the four-day week is not just viable for private sector organizations; it can be a lifesaver for struggling public sector entities too.

So far I've highlighted individual companies as examples of a particular strategy for success. Praxis got more efficient with time use. ArtLifting concentrated on meetings and focus. Pressure Drop restructured its workflow. Uncharted shifted its strategy. M'tucci's, South Cambs, Tessa's ad agency, and Heather's hospitals reduced burnout and kept people from leaving. But of course they all had more hybrid experiences, in the sense that most of them didn't just do one thing or have one outcome. The typical approach involves multiple changes that contribute to overall success.

PUTTING IT ALL TOGETHER

Nowhere was the power of multiple methods more apparent to me than at Kickstarter. Its experience runs the gamut of strategies and outcomes—productivity hacks, optimizing workflow, strategic realignment, hiring additional staff, plus well-being benefits, better talent attraction, and dramatically reduced turnover. This case also shows the need to tailor the approach to each level of an organization.

Kickstarter is a well-known crowdfunding platform for creative projects such as films, books, and games. It was founded in 2009 and has attracted media attention as a grassroots option for creative endeavors that might not be supported by existing funding agencies. It's a public benefit corporation, which means its mission is not just to make money for its owners but also to generate social and public good. In 2023, it was named one of *Time's* 100 most influential companies, in part because of its four-day week. As I talked with people at the company, it was clear that its mission attracted people from across the tech sector. It offered a home where people could feel good about the content of their work.

The familiar part of Kickstarter's shorter work-time origin story is that it began with someone in senior management. What's unique is that Jon Leland, the catalyst for the change, was already an experienced four-day-week activist. His interest in reduced hours was motivated by concern for the climate and how the growth mentality was helping to wreck the planet. After college, Jon went to law school. During that time he combined stints doing technology acquisitions for big companies such as Google with involvement in global and domestic climate policy. Not long after graduating, he joined Kickstarter as director of community engagement. After nearly a decade at the company, he became head of sustainability and chief strategy officer.

In August 2020, Jon co-founded the 4 Day Workweek Campaign. (It was subsequently renamed WorkFour.) At that point, it was slow going here in the States. But that changed with the trials, and Jon successfully persuaded the Kickstarter CEO and board to not only try a four-day week but be the lead company in our April 2022 pilot. At the time, Kickstarter was in negotiations with a new staff union—a relationship that resulted in its being the only tech company in the country with a wall-to-wall union. Jon was the lead negotiator for the company and brought the four-day week to the bargaining table. He described the union as "shocked" by the proposal, but in a good way. He believes it built trust between the parties.

My interviews at Kickstarter revealed the range of changes that occurred throughout the organization. When we talked, Jon focused on his group—the senior leadership team—and the steps they took. Leland describes the role of leadership as creating a culture of "high trust and high expectations," which means clarity on goals and metrics for "velocity, efficiency, and quality." This group's remit for the four-day week was to set targets and enact the necessary changes to make them realistic. They looked at bottlenecks— where projects were getting stuck and wasting time—and their own role in those slowdowns. They discovered that the guidance they were giving to the people below them wasn't clear enough. They needed a more developed understanding at the beginning of a project about what they wanted and why they wanted it. Once they could communicate that, they would be able to give more autonomy to the teams doing the work. Then, when a product team came to a fork in the road—a common experience in designing software—it would know which way to go because it knew leadership's goals. Leland explained that this shift involved "allowing them to navigate those decision points themselves with the context of what leadership's concerns and priorities are . . . as opposed to having to guess what's in the mind of some executives and making the wrong decision." It involved more up-front work on the part of senior management and more sharing early on. Leland felt that their adjustments definitely worked as a "clarifying and alignment" process that reduced wasted time. The leadership team also realized that the thirty-two-hour week would require adding capacity in some of the places that were understaffed. For example, they needed more investment in teams that required extra hands to complete the work, such as the group that responded to customer problems. They made those investments.

Wolf Owczarek, the company's director of operations, was given the task of overseeing the shift for the organization as a whole. For Wolf, the overriding philosophy was that the four-day workweek is a "grand bargain" in which "if you manage to find this extra time in your week, we will pay it forward to you." In addition to the logistics of that bargain, Wolf recognized the importance of the cultural aspects of the shift and how they affected morale. Monday mornings he started Slack threads about all the things people did on their three-day weekends, where people talked about trips, time with their kids, and the like. "To include [those threads] as part of our value proposition to employees, to me, became a very useful carrot. . . . We are proud we provide something better for our employees and the world by having this program." And, he added, "retention has been amazing."

But he was also clear that to make it work, they needed to "tighten up" a lot of their systems. "How were we going to measure this? How are we looking at general productivity, which is a black box in most tech companies?" For knowledge workers, what is it? "Lines of code? How often new updates break the site?" Step one was getting more serious about productivity metrics. Step two was letting the teams figure out how to improve them.

One of the people who spent a tremendous amount of time figuring out how to do that was Terry VanDuyn, director of product management. In product development the link between output and hours isn't always obvious, which left a lot of room to be creative. Terry led people through a premortem on productivity and the factors that were impairing performance, asking individuals and teams to fill out questionnaires and doing a lot of prep to alleviate anxiety about how this was going to work. They decided on Friday as a common day off. It was the obvious choice, but in addition having a common day meant that when people were off, their co-workers weren't busy creating tasks that had to be faced upon return to the office. That was important. The teams moved some tasks to be asynchronous, rather than doing them in meetings, and improved documentation so that anyone could pick up the assignment. (Improved documentation is something that came up in other companies as well.) They got more intentional about the meetings they did retain and made them more effective. Terry figures those changes bought them half a day. They interrogated the time-to-value ratio for nearly everything they were doing and tried to true that. They did a "process start, stop, continue" exercise. They looked at all the documents they ask people to fill out and the steps in that workflow. For hiring reports, they dispensed with the time-consuming post-interview form and distilled it down to the few essential things that HR needed to know. These changes weren't dramatic, but they helped. A more consequential change was in how they approached customer complaints. Rather than focus on every complaint, they prioritized those that affected larger numbers of people.

Kickstarter's success can be seen in a series of hard numbers, which the company has shared with us. In the past it typically hit 62 percent of its objectives and key quarterly results (OKRs); that number rose to 95 percent. Employee engagement rose from

51 percent to 73 percent. The fraction of employees who reported seeing themselves at Kickstarter two years down the road went from 39 percent to 62 percent. These results are especially impressive given the larger environment. Kickstarter was embarking on its four-day week during the depths of the pandemic and the Great Resignation. Tech companies were struggling with people leaving. Terry noted that "the market was paying suddenly, like, 20, 30, 40 percent more for the same jobs." That created both challenges and opportunities.

A similar story is found in our survey results. Employees at Kickstarter had a larger-than-average work-time reduction (six hours a week) without an increase in intensity and with a substantial rise in self-reported work ability. Stress, burnout, anxiety, negative emotions, fatigue, and sleep problems all fell. Physical and mental health and positive emotions improved. Satisfaction with job, life, and time increased and work-family conflict declined.

As of this writing, Kickstarter has had none of what the tech industry calls "regrettable departures," that is, people it wanted to keep who have left. As Leland explained, "We're in an industry where the average tenure at a tech company is, like, two years. I don't know what ours is right now. But it's definitely higher than that and barely anyone leaves."

The four-day schedule was a forcing mechanism of the type discussed in the previous chapter. For Terry, the big idea was looking at "hours that you weren't producing your core work product." By shaving those, she and her co-workers were able to find that second half of the day. For Jon, it was forcing leadership to reckon with the ways its decisions were playing out at the team level, and making sure they did their job better. For Wolf, it was creating a culture in which the grand bargain was operating. Ever the skeptic, he also wanted to downplay the schedule change. "Probably my headline here is just like everything that we did, it didn't really have much to do with a four-day week, it just created a co-incentive with employees to do it together."

Wolf's view is that the four-day week was one of many factors. "In the Jewish tradition of Passover, there's the song 'Dayenu'—it would have been enough." The song refers to the gifts that God has given, and that any one of them would have been enough. Wolf's point is that the company has many positive aspects and that I needed to understand the success of the four-day week in this larger context. "With Kickstarter, we're a public benefit corporation, and it would have been enough to focus on the mission instead of just profit. And it would have been enough to just be a tech start-up trying to exist out in the world as a business. It would have been enough to do that, while also having been the first tech company to unionize. It would have been enough to . . . Basically we keep adding more things on top. So the four-day workweek on top of everything else." Enough indeed.

Wolf was onto something important. Many of my interviewees attributed their success to the four-day week. But Wolf is right that it shouldn't be seen in isolation. It's not a Band-Aid you can slap on a dysfunctional or inhumane culture. It works when employees are truly valued, both as workers and as people. And in some cases, like Kickstarter, it's icing on a pretty tasty cake.

RETENTION, RETENTION, RETENTION

For employers, keeping people from quitting is like what location is to real estate agents. Almost everything. As I was writing this chapter, I got an email from a manager at a social service agency with an annual budget of more than $100 million. She said her people are "experiencing a very high burn out rate." The agency wants to pilot a four-day week, starting with one of its divisions, where the annual staff turnover is 50 percent (that is, half the people leave every year). While companies in high-turnover industries like advertising, restaurants, social services, and health care may be most advantaged by reducing turnover, Kickstarter's experience suggests it's also a factor in 100-80-100 companies, for which burnout may not be the main motivation for a four-day week. Across our whole sample, we find that from baseline to end point, 29 percent of respondents scored lower on the statement "I am seriously considering quitting or changing my current job." From the companies we also have evidence that resignations fall at four-day-week companies—going from almost two people a month on average at baseline to one every other month at trial end point.

Kickstarter achieved zero regrettable departures in an industry known for job-hopping as a way to raise salary. And while it's also the case that layoffs eventually hit the tech sector, Jon Leland credits the four-day week with his company's results. It is "by far the biggest asymmetric benefit you can offer people, and it's an amazing one, because it doesn't decrease productivity as an organization. So it's the most valuable thing you can offer employees and costs a company nothing. It's, it's remarkable. . . . [It] changes our position in the labor market." We hear this again and again from CEOs, executive directors, and other senior management. It keeps people from leaving. And it helps them attract the people they want. At Kickstarter, it has been key to its ability to hire very top talent—engineers who could go to Google or Microsoft but instead choose a comparatively tiny organization, one that lives its values and values its people. Of course, it almost goes without saying that the retention and talent attraction advantage is relative. If all companies go to a four-day week, it disappears. But we're currently a long way from that situation, and there's ample room for companies to improve their comparative position.

BACK TO THE $20 BILLS

Now that I've described the experiences of a variety of companies across multiple industries, we can return to the question I posed at the end of the last chapter: Is it really possible to make up a whole day of lost productivity? And if it is, why aren't employers finding those cost savings within the five-day structure? as Chris Anderson asked.

Let's start with the first question: making up that day. It's important to recognize that in many of the settings we're studying, not every one of the standard forty hours is spent working. One of the most common things we've heard is that people shift their "life admin" to the off day, rather than doing it during working hours. Doctors' appointments, teachers' meetings, and other obligations that can only be done Monday through Friday, from 9:00 to 5:00, are no longer scheduled during work time. We don't know how often people typically made up that work outside regular hours, but because they mention it so often, it seems to be an important part of what's changing. This isn't a true productivity increase, but a way to shift this cost back onto the employee. And it is mostly occurring for salaried workers who have the freedom to come and go and don't lose pay when they aren't at work.

A second thing to recognize is that not all days are created equal, and companies can take off the less busy—that is, less productive—days. That means they don't really have to make up a full day's work. Pressure Drop is an example of this point. It brews Tuesday through Thursday, so its off days are Monday and Friday. Matt Juniper tracked activity on Friday and saw that it was slower than any of the other days. It's the most popular off day in our sample. And that's likely because there's already an evolution away from Friday as a workday. Studies of stock market returns show that on Fridays earnings reports get fewer and more delayed responses, suggesting investors are paying less attention on that day. Responses to business surveys also reveal a Friday effect. Even before the four-day week, some salespeople in our trials had been required to report their weekly quotas at close of business on Thursday, in effect recognizing that Friday isn't a day people make sales. As a couple of book titles suggest—*Thursday Is the New Friday* (Joe Sanok) and *Friday Is the New Saturday* (Pedro Gomes)—we're already gradually moving away from a five-day week.

Another reason why companies are able to maintain productivity is that there's a long-standing relationship between working time and hourly productivity. Although there aren't many studies, especially outside manufacturing, the evidence suggests that there's a part of the curve where hours reductions yield higher hourly productivity. A classic paper on munitions workers in World War I found that after a certain threshold output per hour declined as hours increased. Recent data from a Dutch call center show that as hours rise, the amount of time it takes to complete a call also goes up. A Belgian study also finds that at the margin, additional hours reduce productivity. Alison Booth and Martin Ravallion cite empirical evidence showing that "hourly output declines dramatically towards the end of the working day as well as at the end of the working week," implying that cutting hours may raise productivity.

Historical evidence also suggests that shorter hours can sometimes be accomplished with no loss of output. In 1929, when the five-day week was in its infancy, the National Industrial Conference Board carried out a comprehensive study of manufacturing companies that had already instituted it. While more than half couldn't assess what had happened to output, the large majority of those that could reported either no change or an increase. At that time, about 75 percent of the companies reduced total hours when they went to five days, and among them 68 percent witnessed stable or rising output.

We also know that in the cross section—that is, at a point in time—countries with shorter hours of work tend to have higher hourly productivity. Of course the relationship goes both ways. High productivity tends to lead to hours reductions. But it's also the case that the cost of hours reduction is partly compensated for by higher output during the time people are on the job. This is one of the main reasons that work-time reduction has often yielded disappointing employment results; people get more productive, so the company doesn't need to add staff. When the French workweek went from forty to thirty-nine hours in 1982, work intensification replaced half the lost output. One review of the economic impacts of working time reduction concludes that productivity increases, which are generally predicted to compensate for about half the decline in work time, are typically underestimated before hours fall. The literature suggests that this is truer in white-collar service-sector settings than elsewhere. One reason may be that the mental energy required in the kinds of workplaces we're mostly studying begins to decline after a certain number of hours. The economists Gilbert Cette and Dominique Taddei take the view that "the bill"—that is, the cost of work-time reduction—"is always paid for by productivity gains."

Literature aside, this is what we're hearing from companies, especially those that are able to follow the 100-80-100 model. And we're hearing it from employees too. They're working smarter, more efficiently, and with higher work ability. They report their productivity is going up. Those measures are all rising from baseline to end point.

Finally, and perhaps most important, productivity is only one of the factors that determine whether companies can succeed with a four-day week. As this chapter shows, there may be gains in retention and talent attraction that offset any productivity losses. Tessa's story, and to a certain extent that of Praxis, suggests that team stability can create new business opportunities. What the organization cares about is *all* the impacts—the full costs and benefits of the change. Sometimes the conversation about the four-day week has been too narrow—focusing just on hourly productivity, rather than on the total package.

Our results—from productivity hacks to strategic realignment to employee retention—show that there is a win-win possible with a schedule change. Achieving it is not as easy as picking up a $20 bill from the ground. It takes planning, hard work, and the right kind of culture to begin with. But for many of the companies that are trying it out, the results have been superb.

THE GIFT OF TIME

This leaves us with the question that TED's Chris Anderson asked. For the 100-80-100 companies, why not make these timesaving changes in the context of the five-day week? Is it necessary to go to four? Of course, organizations do attempt to save time and get more efficient. They get new technology, change their policies, and make improvements on an ongoing basis. But in many of our companies there was still plenty of scope for improving productivity.

As I put this question to participants in our trials, I heard a few different explanations. I've already told you about Terry VanDuyn's response to my quip about "functional" companies. For her, there wasn't time and space to optimize. They're too busy surviving. Banks Benitez's experience suggests that people just aren't strategic and intentional enough on an ongoing basis. They forget what's "essential." That all makes sense. Continuous optimization is exhausting.

I had given Chris a different answer. None of our trials had ended yet, so it was just a hunch. I said that management had to offer something back to employees to get them to work smarter or more intensively. There needed to be reciprocity. (Back then, I didn't know that work intensity wouldn't actually rise much in most of our organizations and just assumed that it would be going up.) Jon Leland gave a similar answer when I asked him the question, putting it down to human nature. "Companies are made of human beings and human beings are inefficient. We aren't machines." This is what the economists don't realize, he explained. "And there is that feeling that we're all privileged to be able to do this. This is not the norm. And so there is a kind of gift there."

The idea of the four-day week being a bestowal came up throughout our research. It was reflected in the terminology that some companies used to describe the program. One calls it "unlocking" the off day. An ad agency executive wrote into a 4 Day Week Global message board, "Our six-month pilot has concluded with positive outcomes. Hours spent down by 800+, revenue up considerably, team motivated and proclaiming 4DW to be a 'gift.'" From our open-ended comments, one employee, after telling us how much they appreciated the time off, reported, "I felt so much better about doing my job because it felt like a reward that I could have a day off and it wasn't coming from my annual leave. I felt appreciated because I was being gifted weekly." Another explained, "One thing that I just wanted to mention specifically is that I do feel good to be a part of an organisation that give value to their employees personal life. And because of that I sometime feel that I have to put in more effort to pay back the favour (I considers it a favour as I signed the contract to work for 5 days a week)."

In many companies, an important dimension of this gift is that it's for the group and is not just between employer and employee. As Leland explained, the four-day week "makes everyone super motivated to implement these changes, which aren't easy. It makes everyone more honest. It makes the stakes really high, because you're not only gaining these efficiency gains just for yourself, but you're doing it for everyone else around you." This accountability to co-workers is an important part of why people are willing to make the extra effort to find efficiencies, forgo goofing off, and do the hard work. They develop more team spirit. Leland felt that at Kickstarter it wasn't mainly "an issue between management and labor. At least in our sort of business, those things are blended." His colleague Wolf agrees about the importance of the "co-incentive with employees to do it together. Whereas otherwise, it would be unnecessarily hard." Leland again: "And we know how valuable it is to people. It's a win-win, because they get the work done. They're getting it done not just for themselves, but for their co-workers or other members of their team. So they can all be with their families on Friday."

The alternative is a more fear-based culture. Leland feels that "if the only motivation you're offering people to maintain their productivity and efficiency is the threat of being fired, that doesn't breed, honestly, very good work cultures. That's not a place that people want to continue working at. So you lose employees, which dramatically impacts organizational productivity." Matt Juniper had a similar analysis, referencing the idea that if he would try to make people work harder without giving them a gift in return, they'd be resentful. "You're going to see a decrease in motivation, you're going to see some burnout, you're going to see employees that are less invested in giving back to the company. And so that's been my personal experience—you give it back."

It's not surprising that so many experience the four-day week as a gift. At this point, it is happening as a result of management initiative, rather than through collective bargaining. It doesn't require a cut in pay. It's a benefit few people have. However, not everyone in our trials liked this interpretation. When I asked Sam Smith from Pressure Drop what he thought of the idea of the four-day week as a gift, he agreed that people at the company "see it that way." But he resisted the formulation because of the implied need for gratitude. "You [the management] should do this because you think it is the right thing to do, not because you want people to pat you on the back for it. . . . If you want thanks for it, you're not going to get it. And you shouldn't be doing it for that reason." To Sam, everyone deserves the right to a job that makes it possible to have a balanced, fulfilling life.

THE VALUE OF A FOUR-DAY-A-WEEK JOB

While both companies and workers use the language of gifting, which comes from the anthropological tradition, there's also strong economic reasoning to explain why productivity can rise with this model. The four-day week raises the value of the job to the employee because it gives them something better than what is generally available on the market. My PhD research, from the early 1980s, was about the value employees place on jobs and how it affects things like wages and labor effort. My thesis was part of an emerging body of literature called efficiency wage theory, which offered a novel explanation for why market economies typically suffer from unemployment. That's a fact of economic life that had been puzzling neoclassical economists for decades. Their model says that markets achieve equilibrium, in which supply equals demand. So if there is unemployment—that is, excess supply—they expect wages to fall. That in turn leads companies to hire more workers. And it leads some people to drop out of the labor market, because they want better pay. The result is that supply and demand will again come into balance; that is, unemployment will disappear. Efficiency wage theory explained why, in the real world, labor markets don't equate supply and demand. If there's zero unemployment, and people can easily find other equally valuable jobs, employers have a hard time keeping workers. The Great Resignation was a good, indeed dramatic example of this unstable condition. Achieving equilibrium requires that workers have something to lose when they quit or are fired.

Employers have a variety of ways to make jobs valuable, but the most generic is to raise wages above the market-clearing rate. As they do that, it raises the value of the job and creates a positive "cost of job loss" to the worker. When many firms do this, it leads to unemployment. It's a commonsense idea. If losing one's job means earning a lower wage, or suffering a spell of unemployment, the job becomes more valuable. My adviser Samuel Bowles and I created an actual economy-wide measure of the cost of job loss. By today's standards, it's very crude. However, even crude, it had a lot of explanatory power. We showed that it affects all sorts of things. Sam and I used it to predict how often U.S. workers went on strike. I showed its connection to wage growth. My colleague Jerry Epstein and I even used it, successfully, to predict the Fed's interest rate decisions.

The research I did that's most relevant to the four-day week was about the intensity of work. Using a rare dataset from the U.K. that literally measured how hard factory workers were working, I showed that work intensity varies with the cost of job loss. That's part of the economic reasoning behind the productivity impacts of a four-day week. People are more productive in jobs they value more. This analysis also explains the retention effects I've described in this chapter. *By raising the value of the job by so much, the four-day week brings quits to a standstill.*

We can see how much employees value their four-day-week jobs via one of the questions in our survey. We asked about what economists call willingness to pay. First, we ask for their schedule preference (four versus five days). As I noted earlier, almost everyone prefers the four-day week. For those who do, we then asked them to consider the following hypothetical: "Imagine that you are looking at alternatives to your current job. How much of a pay adjustment (as a percentage of your current pay) would you require to take a new job with a five-day schedule?" We find that most people require a fair amount to revert to five days. The biggest group (45.5 percent) requires between 10 and 25 percent. Twenty-seven and a half percent want quite a bit more—a 26 to 50 percent raise. Nine percent require a really large increase—at least 50 percent. And 13 percent say that "no amount of money" would induce them to go back to a five-day-week schedule.

Table 4.1 How much more pay do employees require to take a five-day-a-week job?	
Pay increase required	Fraction of respondents
Less than 10% pay raise	4.7%
10-25% pay raise	45.5%
26-50% pay raise	27.5%
50%+ raise	9.0%
No amount of money would entice me to work five days	13.2%

We also heard similar sentiments in some of the comments. For one person, their valuation went beyond the hypothetical. "I have already been approached by head hunters offering a 30% pay increase and have declined. Once you get settled into the four days week there is no going back. I have never felt more balanced in my personal/professional life." Another expressed what we heard from the 13 percent: "This is so valuable to me that I don't think I'd go back to a five-day workweek for any amount of money." The value of the job—and by extension, the cost of job loss—is very high for four-day-week employees. It's what explains the big argument of this chapter—why retention improves so much in these companies.

Now we can give a full answer to Chris Anderson. He was proposing that people produce more in five days—that is, give more to the company with no accompanying reward. That might not only produce resentment à la Matt Juniper but also lower the cost of job loss and destabilize the current bargain. In contrast, the four-day week represents a whopping increase in the value of the job. There's the hourly wage increase it results in. We know from our surveys how valuable people find this schedule. We know that many describe it as "life-changing." It's not a fear-based phenomenon. In this case, people experience it in a positive way—because it's usually given in the spirit of the gift. And in that spirit, people are willing to put in more effort, apply themselves more diligently, and pitch in for the good of the team. There's both an economic and a cultural dimension to why it works.

5

CHALLENGES, FALSE STARTS, PAUSES, AND FAILURES

So far I've been talking about the ways organizations are successful with the four-day-week schedule. For many, like Praxis and Pressure Drop, the transition is fairly easy. Others, like M'tucci's or Grand Challenges Canada, also made it look relatively seamless. At Kickstarter, which has had one of the most successful transitions, people emphasized that it was hard, but they figured it out.

In this chapter I look at some of the ways in which companies need to tweak the four-day-week model in order to succeed, why some need to pause, and why a few revert permanently to the five-day week. One lesson is that it's important to be flexible. If something isn't working, change it. For some, ongoing iteration is a bedrock principle for how they approach the four-day week. Pay attention and adjust.

A LITTLE EXTRA TIME

A common tweak was creating at least some employee availability on the off day. That's how The Architects Group* (TAG) went from thinking the experiment wasn't working to having a smoothly functioning program. TAG is a design firm that does high-visibility urban projects, such as schools and cultural centers, as well as multi-unit residential buildings, many of which offer affordable housing. It works across North America and Europe, winning awards and creating impressive buildings. It's a very successful place, which was founded by a solo practitioner decades ago and is still fully owned by him. Emma Smith is the studio manager at the practice, and she was responsible for overseeing the pilot. As part of our ongoing surveying of organizations, Emma reported that they weren't continuing with the four-day week. I was curious about why, and she was willing to explain. As it turned out, they hadn't really ended their program. They had tweaked it to create some on-call availability during the off day.

The idea for the pilot came from the founder, who felt that going to four days made sense, given what other companies were finding and due to long-standing issues of overwork in the profession. When he came to her and suggested it, Emma admitted she thought, "Well, this is crazy, because, you know, we can't possibly even service the projects that we have right now with the staff we have. But we were listening to all the, I don't want to call it rhetoric, but all the information that was out there about how working smarter and better would produce better work and more engaged employees." A key concern was attracting and retaining people among their staff of about seventy-five. One factor was the

---

* The Architects Group and Emma Smith are pseudonyms. This company chose not to be identified.

long-hours culture in architecture and its growing mismatch with younger professionals. Emma described the way things used to be. "In the past they'd have charettes [intensive workshops] all weekend long, and working sixty hours was quite regular. Now people understand that in order to attract good, especially younger talent, we cannot maintain those kind of working hours."

They started with a common model: Everyone would have Fridays off. While most employees loved the new schedule, project managers were having trouble with it. Architecture is a highly collaborative field, and multiple people work on a single project. To accommodate the change, they'd set Thursday at 6:00 pm for the deadline when the week's changes would be due. But that left project managers—who then pick up the work—unable to communicate with their colleagues until Monday morning, three full days later. So the project managers found themselves making corrections and changes they would have normally given to others on the team. They were now working more, because their obligations bled over into Saturdays and Sundays. Some of the upper management also complained about being unable to reach people when they needed them.

The firm couldn't find extra time via adjustments to meetings. Unlike in many organizations where meetings are inefficient or unproductive, in architecture meetings are the medium through which the work process is organized. People come together, pore over drawings, and push the designs forward. It's a tried-and-tested methodology that they needed to maintain. Emma explained, "There is just no time saving. There is no reducing those hours. . . . Because of the size of most of these meetings, shrinking them from what are sometimes two hours to even an hour and a half, there is not enough time for everyone to say their piece and to go through the drawings. So although we were looking for efficiencies and time management, in the end there physically are this many hours that need to be consumed by a project." That meant they couldn't push back the deadline for weekly work to Wednesday. Instead, they needed to create some availability over the long stretch from Thursday at 6:00 to Monday at 9:00. One option would be to extend the workday on Monday through Thursday, but they felt people were already so worn out by the intellectual and creative demands of the work that they would just be crashing on Friday.

Instead, they solved the problem by asking for on-call availability on the Friday. Emma described the policy: "We will try and allow people to have their Fridays. First of all, they don't have to come in to the office. So that's definitely a work-from-home day, whether it's a workday or not a workday. But we would try, to the best of our abilities and to the project's deliverables and deadlines, to minimize work on Fridays. However, the expectation is that you will have your phone with you. And you also have to be available in case we need you to work." Rather than treating it like a fairly inviolable weekend, it functioned similarly to those occasional weekend days people would be called into the office. They also encouraged people to do continuing education on this day, given its importance in the field. While there was some pushback from staff, the change has worked for the company, and for the employees. Mostly people get their Fridays off. And project managers get their answers, if they need them.

After nine months with the original model, they shifted to the on-call option. Emma explained, "We're going to keep looking at this every few months and determine whether or not we have to change course, add new policy, revise policy, whatever it is." That stance of ongoing evaluation and iteration is one that many of our companies adopt. It aligns with the basic philosophy of being intentional and strategic and paying close attention to work time and performance.

As it happened, the four-day week helped address other issues in the company. One was excessive "chitchat" and time wasting. There were some senior members who spent a fair amount of time "going from one desk to the other, wasting everyone's time." There's far less of that now. They were worried about maintaining the social atmosphere of the office and impacts on morale. So once a month on Fridays they have beer and chips. And there's a lot of outside-of-work socializing. They also encourage people to have lunch together off-site or to take short breaks for walks. They did find some efficiencies in their processes; they've been able to reduce the number of iterations that designs go through. "The work is never perfect and never, never complete. So, instead of doing twelve iterations, let's do eight." And they've improved some of their workflows and technology. Emma thinks it's working and will continue to "as long as everyone understands that Thursday at six is not a mic drop."

The tweak made by The Architects Group is one of the common ones we've learned about—creating some availability on that out-of-office day. Companies are finding different ways to implement that change. Praxis adjusted its program to solve some of the same issues the architects were having. Matt Juniper explained they've created a kind of "standby" status. It's not for working a full day, more like "usually zero" but "sometimes you're called in to work a very small amount." However, the company was also mindful of wanting to protect some of those days so people could make commitments and keep them—things like doctors' appointments or vacation plans. So it gave eight days a year, if staff prebook them, when they can completely switch off. Grand Challenges, the Canadian nonprofit, shifted to a slightly more available model after hearing about lack of response from the organizations it serves. Even so, people get called only once or twice a quarter, what Tracy Smith described as "very minimal amounts." However, a guiding principle for Grand Challenges has been equity, so it was unwilling to ask for that Friday availability for just a few staff. It renamed the program Flex Friday. Tracy explained, "The words are changing, but the philosophy is very much the same. This is a time for you to unplug or recharge. But flex means that you should be reachable. Because if something happened, and it was an urgent request, we still need to be able to facilitate that request."

OTHER CHALLENGES

Another common tweak involves weeks with holidays. During the trial, some organizations discover that those three-day weeks don't work for them. So if there's a holiday, employees don't get another off day. It's too difficult to complete all the work in just three days. We've also gotten reports from some companies that they are no longer offering unlimited PTO (paid time off) after shifting to four days. And one company reported that if people haven't finished their work by the end of their fourth day, they're expected to complete it on the fifth.

Small changes to the basic program are common across our trials, including for organizations or divisions with uneven work-flows. Accounting is a field with peaks and valleys in workload. In addition to monthly closes, there are the annual crunch times for taxes and audits. One way this is being addressed is by annualiz-ing time off. People get more days off in the quiet times, including clusters of days, on the expectation that they have to work five days during the busy seasons.

Another issue is that for companies following the 100-80-100 model, it's not clear what 100 percent should be for new hires. Even for existing staff, calibrating can be difficult. One tech company I heard about put its support team back to a five-day schedule tem-porarily in order to create a baseline for what they should be doing in four. To address this issue, some organizations ask new hires to start on a five-day schedule, in part to figure out what their baseline workload is and to make sure they can handle the higher expectations of the four-day week. Starting at five days can also mitigate the "adverse selection" problem of people who want to take the job because of the four-day week and haven't got the kind of work ethic the organization is expecting. That's an issue that is complicated and needs to be handled well when hiring new people. Some of our respondents mention being wary of applicants who focus too much on the four-day week in their interviews.

Organizations also have to make sure the four-day week doesn't spoil the good things about their culture, in particular the benefits of sociability and cohesion. While in some cases, like at The Architects Group, there can be too much of some kinds of socializing, the pressures of getting everything done in four days can also take a workplace too far in the other direction. Most aren't as intentional as ArtLifting with its "Culture Squad"; however, many are scheduling lunchtime get-togethers, retreats, outings, and other dedicated social times. But were those efforts working?

One respondent offered a very negative picture in their survey comments: "Company culture really takes a hit due to the 4-day work week. I've felt very isolated from my coworkers because we're all so nose-down in a shortened work week. And while they haven't admitted it in our staff 4-day week surveys, in one-on-one conversations with coworkers I've learned that they're as stressed as I am! Overworked, exhausted by the pace, and with little time to build or care about company culture. Morale is low, disillusionment high." In this case, the isolation and nose-down culture were compounded by overload. "I don't know anyone who isn't exceeding the 32 hours allotted. In fact, the company feels more busy and strapped for time than ever, with many team members seeming to be working long nights, Fridays, and/or weekends." If that was the end of it, it would be a damning picture. But this person went on: "That all said, everyone I've spoken to—including me—doesn't want the 4-day week to go away. Because on the weeks when we CAN, in fact take the extra time to ourselves on Fridays, it's really great to have." While this organization clearly needs to figure out why its workload is unmanageable even in forty hours, it also should be more intentional about social interaction.

There has been a lot of concern about whether working from home will undermine social connectedness in the workplace. We wondered if taking away a day of work would have an impact. From the beginning, we had been asking about how connected people felt to others in their workplaces and hadn't seen any change. At some point we added a four-item scale that was explicitly focused on social interactions. We also found no change in that measure from baseline to end point. It doesn't seem the four-day week erodes valuable aspects of workplace sociability.

Another issue we'd heard about is tension when only some groups are shifted to a four-day week or the offer isn't made to everyone. Tessa Ohlendorf faced opposition from some at the company because her group was in a privileged position. The leadership team wanted to keep things on the down-low, but of course word leaked out and it created friction. One employee from the South African trial reported, "This can only work if everyone in the company participates. Creates disharmony between those who could participate and those who couldn't. If you can't participate you should be compensated for it."

Keeping customers happy is always difficult, and in organizations that couldn't split into teams, coverage was sometimes elusive. But perhaps the biggest problem we see is when there's not enough preparation and support for the shift. If people are expected to find efficiencies, they can't only be left to their own devices. Some people complained about not getting the help they need. And circumstances other than the schedule change can make things hard.

If the company has a downturn and lays people off, that can affect success. So can rapid growth and failure to add new staff quickly enough. Personnel issues in small organizations can sometimes be paramount. One very small organization paused its trial because it had half its staff on long-term leave. It didn't feel the four-day week would work with contracted employees and newly hired staff. It plans to revisit it when its team stabilizes. Pausing can be a useful way to ensure eventual success with a four-day week.

PAUSING BETWEEN PILOT AND
FULL IMPLEMENTATION

Who Gives a Crap, an organization that produces high-quality, affordable, recycled, and earth-friendly paper products, found that it needed to step back after its first trial ended. The company is a values-oriented organization that was founded in 2012. According to the National Resources Defense Council, Americans, with 4 percent of the world's population, consume a fifth of all toilet paper. Much of that comes from the magnificent Canadian boreal forest. The company's toilet papers reduce the use of virgin forest through recycled materials and sustainable alternatives such as bamboo and sugarcane. Who Gives a Crap also donates half its profits to organizations pursuing the goal of ensuring everyone on the planet has access to clean water and a toilet by 2050.

Remember the TP panic in the early days of the pandemic? It resulted in soaring demand at Who Gives a Crap. Sales ballooned to thirty to forty times greater than usual, with long waiting lists for its products. That in turn led to a considerable amount of investment funding and rapid growth. In August 2022, it became a late sign-on to our Australasian pilot. A year later it officially ended the experiment, after concluding that a successful company-wide four-day-week pilot wasn't feasible at that time. Catalina Lopera, well-being and workplace director, shared that "the 4DWW remains a significant focus for us, especially for me as director of wellbeing." Long-term, the company is committed to revisiting the initiative.

Originally, Catalina got approval from the executive team for a small trial—just twenty-three people, or 10 percent of the total workforce. The executive team was supportive while also expressing some caution about the potential impact on business performance. So they decided to be very systematic in terms of who could participate and how they would evaluate it. They positioned it as a conditional benefit—a gift that would be available if people had finished all their work—and used the terminology of "unlocking" the fifth day. That highlighted its conditionality. They also set some guardrails to guide participants. It couldn't be combined with vacation days (or other PTO). It had to yield three consecutive days off. It couldn't be taken during a week with a public holiday. I wondered if insistence on the 100 percent productivity and strict rules about the off day undermined the program, in part by eroding trust. While I got the sense that Catalina, and likely most others at the company, cared about well-being for its own sake, the language and tone of the trial was performance-centric. Perhaps that mattered.

Nevertheless, at the midpoint, employee outcomes were heading in a good direction. Work time was down by 5.7 hours a week—an excellent result. Stress, burnout, and turnover intentions improved. All the satisfaction measures were better. But three months later, at end point, the trends were reversing. Working hours rose, as did overtime and work intensity. Current work ability, which typically goes up a lot, didn't improve. Compared with the baseline, the well-being indicators were worse. Not by a lot, and not significantly so in statistical terms, given the small number of people involved. It was also notable that they got only a 65 percent response rate at the end point.

In their comments, nearly everyone was positive about the schedule, with some reporting it as life-changing. However, a number of people did say that they were having trouble completing their work in four days and either extended their hours or worked on the fifth day. Compared with the kinds of results we were seeing in almost all the other companies, this trial wasn't succeeding particularly well.

What happened? Probably the biggest issue was capacity. The company was growing at 20 percent a year, and even before the trial began, it was having capacity challenges. As Catalina explained, "We're just growing a lot, which made it challenging to really embed [the four-day week] while concurrently addressing essential groundwork on enablement and performance metrics." The company was adding staff during this time, but it was cautious, in order to avoid layoffs in the future. Catalina also noted that "capacity is about more than head count. It's also about team structure, ways of working, and upskilling. . . . There was an uptick in the amount of work that we had in the last few months of the trial. For sure for the majority of people. You could see that and so therefore people were not unlocking the fifth day as often and they didn't have the uplift in well-being." As we've learned from other fast-growing companies, it's important for hiring to keep up with a growing workload.

Catalina is determined to move forward and sees the first trial as a stepping stone to a full company switch. That raises another reason results might not have been stellar. Including only some people made it harder to succeed. "A piece of feedback that we got is, 'Hey, unless the whole company is doing this, let's not do it.' We understood that as a risk, but we felt it was better to take action, knowing full company approval wasn't feasible at this stage." It's one thing to pilot with a subset of employees in a thousand-person company; it's another in a company of two hundred. Our positive results have almost all been from organization-wide trials.

Another issue was that while senior management wanted hard data, they didn't have the kinds of metrics they needed to assess how things were going. As a high-performing organization in the early stages of scaling up, Catalina acknowledged the lack of "measurement maturity" and how it "affected the clarity they were striving to achieve. . . . So we were telling [people], 'Hey, make sure that you finish your work. And if you finish it, then you can take the fifth day off as a gift.' [But] there was no way for people to know when they had finished their work . . . if they were on track towards their goals." As they plan for an eventual second try, they're figuring out what to measure and considering getting outside help. That may be a good idea, given their measurement concerns. As the field of four-day-week experts has expanded, there's a lot more known today than when the trials began. Some consultants conduct readiness evaluations, to see if companies are good candidates, and to pinpoint where they need work before a trial.

The data issues at Who Gives a Crap raise the issue of conditionality—a situation in which the four-day week is not guaranteed but depends on performance. In its case it was the ongoing conditionality of being able to "unlock" the fifth day. This kind of uncertainty came up in other companies and can be tricky. In some sense, all the pilots had a conditional aspect: Companies are trying out the new schedule to see if they can reap its benefits while also maintaining performance objectives. But there's a difference between conditionality for the organization as a whole and for individuals or teams. In interviews for the U.K. trial, our Cambridge colleagues found that at one of the companies the policy was repeatedly described as "a privilege, not a right." If a person, or a team, hadn't completed all of their work, they weren't permitted to take the fifth day off. This created some resentment. The interviews suggested that the company had adopted a "light touch" approach, that is, not much up-front support for the policy.

Joe O'Connor of Work Time Reduction feels this kind of targeted conditionality—whether toward individuals or teams—is counterproductive. If individuals or teams are struggling, the organization needs to take responsibility for helping them to be successful with the new schedule. Other teams need to step up and share what they've learned. That seems right to me. The four-day week is an organizational innovation, and problems need to be addressed at that level. This issue came up repeatedly in the onboarding sessions. The advice from 4 Day Week Global was that companies should focus on organizational or team metrics more than individual ones. That creates the team spirit I discussed in the context of the gift. O'Connor believes that rather than exercising the threat of withdrawing the four-day week, organizations will succeed with what he and his colleagues term "trust cultures." In a trust culture, "employees are granted greater autonomy and flexibility in exchange for elevated performance accountability."

CAN SENIOR MANAGEMENT GET TO FOUR?

So far I've been emphasizing the successes of the four-day week at the companies in our trials. That's because success is the overwhelming experience. But there's a group for whom taking a full day off turns out to be difficult: founders, owners, and senior executives and managers. The sentiment is "the buck stops with me." We heard this from small company owners. One, when we contacted them after twelve months, explained that when their one-person customer service person was out, "I, as the Founder, have to handle it." Another small business owner reported that they couldn't take the day off, but their team did and they were a lot happier. It's also an issue in the bigger companies. Tessa Ohlendorf confided to me about one of her senior managers, a "wonderful guy." But "wonderful guy just is of the mindset that 'the higher up I go, the more I work.' And he wants to just take over the work so that people can have the benefit. That's cascading down to his two major managers that haven't been able to take the benefit because they see their boss working all the time."

I've raised this subject in many of the interviews I've done. Liz Powers reports that senior managers at ArtLifting often work a few hours on Friday. Matt Juniper says that he usually works on Friday mornings. When we talked, Emma Smith said that she'd worked every single Friday since they'd started, although she allowed it was from home. While many of the senior managers may not fully benefit from the innovation they've worked hard to implement, that doesn't mean that the four-day week isn't also a benefit for them. Some report that the off day serves as a buffer or catch-up day. They don't have meetings, or interactions with the people they supervise, so they get a chance to breathe, work through their to-do lists, and get on top of their (often) heavy workloads. That frees up other times during the week, so while they may not get to four days, at least they're no longer doing six or seven.

Work on the off day is also less taxing. Tracy Smith says she's typically working on Friday, but it's not like the other days. "I have to tell you, there's a psychological factor. Even though we're working at home, if I were to do a load of laundry on a Monday to Thursday, I'd feel guilty about that. . . . On the Friday, I don't feel guilty. So there is a bit of a safety or a freedom factor to it, where I'm still okay to work, but I also feel good that I'm running around the house more or I'm also getting some personal things done at the same time. . . . Or if I clock out to pick up my daughter from school early, I feel very free to do so. . . . I like to clean out as much of my week as possible before coming into the next week." While she works on Fridays, it's less like regular work.

My favorite conversation about this was with Wolf Owczarek at Kickstarter. He explained that being in senior management means "you can't just clock out at the end. If you're bad at setting estimates, you just screw yourself up and your team. I'm able to take some Fridays off, but it is inconsistent." He often worked on the train, on weekends, and at night. "I like to say my prime hour in the day is the witching hour—3:00 to 4:00 a.m. . . . the most precious time . . . When I'm able to give the company 3:00 to 4:00 a.m., you will get the best output from me that you will get at any time, anywhere. So there's some days that I provide that." Seeing my reaction, he admitted, "Yes, I think cringing is the right response."

THE HARD NOS

As I explained earlier, we do have companies that decide not to continue implementing the four-day-a-week approach. So far, there are twenty that have reverted after a year. And even that number is a bit overstated. Out of 203 companies that have passed one year, we lack information from six. Seven dropped out very early or never really got going. (Those organizations didn't even participate

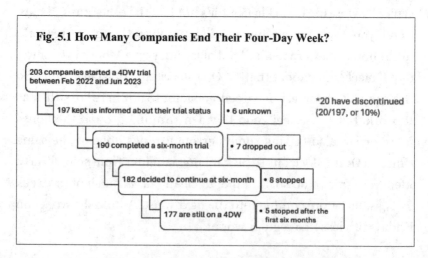

Fig. 5.1 How Many Companies End Their Four-Day Week?

203 companies started a 4DW trial between Feb 2022 and Jun 2023

197 kept us informed about their trial status • 6 unknown

*20 have discontinued (20/197, or 10%)

190 completed a six-month trial • 7 dropped out

182 decided to continue at six-month • 8 stopped

177 are still on a 4DW • 5 stopped after the first six months

in the research. Four were in the South African trial and were very small—together employing only eighteen people.) Among those that completed at least six months, only thirteen (or just under 7 percent) went back to five days.

We ask companies why they are not continuing, and while there are so few that it's hard to draw firm conclusions, we have gotten explanations. One is new management. One of the largest companies in the first trial, a global software firm, had a great experience with the schedule change. Then it was bought by a private equity firm that canceled the program as it instituted a series of sweeping changes. We experienced a similar situation with one of the largest organizations in the U.K. trial, even before it started. A new CEO arrived and withdrew from the trial. New management also resulted in the cancellation of a successful scheduling intervention studied by our team member Phyllis Moen at a large U.S. IT firm, as described in *Overload*, co-authored with Erin Kelly. BldWrk, the fabrication company that Moen and Youngmin Chu studied, ended its four-day-week experiment when it found itself unable to meet deadlines for completing projects.

A second issue is small size. One small office said it just didn't see enough change, although the measures it instituted were beneficial. Another reason is hard economic times. An Australian firm referenced a downturn in sales and missing Friday social time. One company said it was facing "organizational" problems that were affecting business performance, but that it was interested in trying again, although with more preparation than the first time. The U.K. trial took place during a terrible time for the economy. There were large layoffs in tech during one of the trials. One organization had the opposite problem: New business opportunities were opening up for which it needed more staff time.

Our team hasn't done an in-depth investigation of cases where companies reverted to five days. But Julie Yen did, as part of her dissertation research at Harvard Business School. She was invited in to a start-up that sells a restaurant and hospitality software product. Its software is "purpose driven," and the company is highly attuned to employee well-being. The co-founder CEO wanted to shift to a four-day week to align with their employee-friendly work culture. His co-founder, the CSO, was also in favor. The three other members of the leadership team (CCO, CFO, and CTO) were either skeptical or opposed, but the group agreed to try it out. The policy was sold as a win-win, which would improve both employee well-being and productivity. After three months, strong resistance on the leadership team developed, and they rescinded the policy. It wasn't because they had failed. Well-being went up, and employees were very positive about the new schedule. Productivity trends were ambiguous; there were some improvements, some regressions, and some unclarity. The bottom line was that productivity hadn't clearly increased, as supporters predicted it would. This gave the three "resisters," as Yen dubbed them, an argument for reversion. Their opposition was also colored by their personal experiences: They hadn't reduced their own hours. One worked every day and felt resentful about others taking the time off. "I'm working on [projects] on Fridays and Saturdays and Sundays. . . . I can't personally keep working eighteen hours a day to make up for everybody else's 4DWW. . . . I'm just telling you, that's impacted me. I mean this has personally been a disaster from the standpoint of my ability to function." One reported that he was "a lot less productive." Only one agreed he could accomplish everything he needed to in four days, compared with 79 percent of workers. Yen argues that the shift challenged the resisters' sense of identity as "hard workers" or even "workaholics" and "destabilized their self-understandings." One offered that "I'm old school, I used to work fifty to sixty hours a week, and hire people that I coached to expect that, so I'm still coming to grips with it personally." There was a belief in "sacrifice" and concern that high-performance people won't join the company due to the four-day week. I'd also heard this sentiment in one of our interviews, from a senior executive who also didn't reduce hours. In the end the CEO acquiesced to the naysayers, in order to keep their trust.

PREDICTING FAILURE

Two years into the trials, we went back to companies to find out if the explanations we'd heard, plus a few others we thought of, would predict failure. We began by thinking about structural factors, because those are hard to change. If it turns out that manufacturing companies fail, or large companies can't do this, or in-person work leads to reversion, those are pieces of information that tell us a lot about the viability of this innovation going forward. We also asked about another type of factor, which is more contextual. Was there a leadership change or a merger? (Some of the case studies suggested this could end a trial.) We asked whether the company had experienced layoffs, legal or regulatory shocks, or other disruptions, such as an economic downturn.

Using these variables, we constructed a model to predict whether or not companies continue with the four-day week after a full year. We included the factors I mentioned above plus others such as industry, company size, the age of the company, whether they were a for-profit or a nonprofit, and when the trial took place. We looked at whether they were remote or not. We tested whether having employee involvement in the planning of the trials affected the outcome. We added revenue growth to the model, as well as the resignation rate. We included leadership changes, mergers, layoffs, shocks, and so on.

Our findings? No, no, no, no, and no. The model wasn't yielding much in the way of prediction. That is, there weren't identifiable variables that were linked to whether a company continued with the four-day week. We wondered if it was a statistical problem due to having so few failure cases. We were using what's called a rare events model, and doing what we could statistically to address rarity.

One variable that did matter was the rate of new hiring. As the Who Gives a Crap story suggests, growing very fast may be an impediment to a four-day week, especially if new hiring doesn't keep up with growth. That should be a temporary problem, however. (On the other hand, we'd heard elsewhere that in a rapid-growth environment the four-day week makes expansion possible by preventing burnout among staff. That seems like a smart take.)

A few characteristics did seem to matter but weren't statistically significant because of the small numbers. Four of the twenty discontinuing companies were in retail. They were small. One was a teensy bike shop with just a few employees that decided to stay open five days and didn't have the staff. There was a higher failure rate in Australia. We don't know if that's because the Australian pilot wasn't as robust as the earlier ones, or because the economy wasn't in great shape. Two architecture firms reverted; maybe that is due to the long-hours culture in that field being too hard to crack.

We also tested a variety of other theories, and here we had a bit more success. One explanation had to do with worker experiences. Maybe the discontinue group had worse employee well-being results. Or maybe they had changes in efficiency that caused some blowback effects. These theories did get some support. Companies with less improvement in worker stress were more likely to revert to five-day schedules. Although strangely, other well-being changes, such as burnout, didn't matter. Companies whose employees scored higher on the "work smart" scale also reverted more often. This one is puzzling. Based on the verbal explanations from the companies, we don't think it's that they got the efficiencies and then decided to take advantage by adding that fifth day back in. But we don't have another explanation.

We also looked at the demographics of the workforce. Maybe the age distribution mattered, with older workforces less enthusiastic about the schedule. That wasn't the case. Then we hit on one demographic explanation that *is* statistically significant: the fraction of white men at the company. It's a consistent finding. Perhaps white men are more inclined to adopt the ideal worker norm and resist cultural change that decenters work. But we also tested attitudes to the trial at baseline, and those aren't predictive. Average well-being outcomes for white men are not as good as for everyone else. If they're in charge, that might help explain things.

After all this modeling, we didn't discover many structural factors that predict failure, because there really aren't many, or at least many that are measurable with the kinds of information we have. While that was disappointing to us as researchers, it's actually a good result from the point of view of the feasibility of the four-day week. It means that all those things we tested don't prevent companies from succeeding with this schedule. Being remote versus in person, country, size, industry, and profit status don't determine whether the four-day week will work. Reducing employee stress is important; that can help avoid reversion. And diversifying the workforce away from white men should also boost the likelihood of success. But beyond that, failure is basically random. So it should work for organizations across all these categories. Our "non-findings" tell an optimistic story.

DOES THE FOUR-DAY WEEK EQUAL LESS PAY?

One of the critiques I've heard about the four-day-week trend is that it will lower wage growth going forward. To a large extent one's point of view about this prediction depends on what model of the labor market one subscribes to, as well as how shorter hours affect productivity. It's worth spending a bit of time untangling the arguments.

The neoclassical economics view is that pay is determined by individual worker productivity. The alternative view is that there's a certain amount of value created in production and that it's shared between workers and the owners of businesses (that is, between labor and capital). In the second model, the balance of power between the two groups determines how much each side gets.

If productivity falls at these companies, then in the neoclassical model pay will also fall. But if the four-day week doesn't involve a reduction in productivity, which is what we're hearing from many companies, it shouldn't have any impact on pay. It's just a shift in when tasks are done, but the outcomes are the same. Okay, that's a bit too simple. Maybe the shift has other impacts. If it improves well-being, it might even enhance productivity, which should lead to higher wages. In the first model, it's all about productivity.

What if the second model is right? Things get trickier. I argued in the previous chapter that the four-day week raises the value of the job to the worker. (That's one reason hourly productivity rises.) On those grounds, the employer could conceivably reduce wages, knowing employees are unlikely to quit. That's because the employer's four-day-week gambit has given them more leverage over workers, who now value their jobs so much they'll stay on even at lower wages. Our willingness-to-pay findings suggest that possibility. Participants in the trials are saying that to go back to five-day schedules, they'd require a lot of additional salary. Maybe, over time, they'd be willing to stay in a four-day-a-week job for less money.

One possibility is that we get a bifurcated market. Some companies stay at five and pay more. Others go to four and attract those employees who are willing to trade income for time. If you believe that five-day workers are more productive than those on four-day schedules, which is also something skeptical neoclassical economists are more likely to assume, then this might be the predicted outcome. One reason is that in their view, for any given technology, worker preferences ultimately determine labor market outcomes such as hours of work and days per week. However, there's also evidence to the contrary. As I argued in *The Overworked American*, and others have shown, there's not a well-functioning "market in hours," as the standard model assumes. Mismatches between desired and actual hours are chronic. The bottom line here is that it's hard to predict what will happen.

Then there's the issue of how things evolve over time. The economists who think shorter hours imply lower wage growth assume no productivity benefits. However, as I've argued, if the forcing mechanism of shorter hours leads to less time wasting and more productivity, it should result in a higher wage path at these companies. That forcing mechanism may also lead to four-day firms being more profitable, as Banks Benitez thinks happened with Uncharted. If that's the case, both models would likely suggest that wages get higher over time. That's what Liz Powers thinks is happening at ArtLifting. She's convinced her company's growth is occurring in significant part *because* of reduced working time. She pushed back against the idea of a lower salary path. ArtLifting has been able to maintain its competitive goals with respect to salaries. "But I think if someone's just looking at it, overly black and white, yes, I can see how they interpret . . . of course, people are less efficient. But from actually experiencing it for five years, I think people might even be more efficient and accomplish more in the thirty-two hours than they did in the forty."

When I put this question to a few CEOs and managers, they disputed the lower-wage scenario, often vigorously. Matt Juniper is adamant that it's always salary first and then benefits come into play. No one will sacrifice salary for shorter hours, he argues. That might be true in his industry—PR and advertising. Tracy Smith took a similar view: Salary and benefits are thought of separately. Because she's in the nonprofit world, where salaries are lower in any case, she saw the four-day week as key to talent attraction. But in no way does it "cause" lower pay. That's already a given.

This is a question that's going to take some years to answer. We need many more four-day-week companies to see how it plays out. There are reasons to think that over the long run there will be a trade-off between hours and income. However, there's an X factor that makes the future hard to predict. That's artificial intelligence, the issue we turn to now.

6

WILL AI GIVE US A
FOUR-DAY WEEK?

We had just started our fifth trial, in November 2022, when OpenAI released the first version of ChatGPT. While discussions about the Future of Work had long included predictions about robots and digitization, this bot is different. It writes text and code and can even brainstorm. Within two months, it had a hundred million users.

Suddenly the Future of Work, and by extension the four-day week, were big question marks. Will there even *be* a Future of Work—other than for the people building new versions of Chat? Whole occupations might become unnecessary, or at least radically downsized. Many tasks within companies will be done by AI. How will employers respond? Will millions of workers lose their jobs to this new technology? Who will benefit from these enormous time savings?

Within months, the Writers Guild of America organized a strike, in part to forestall its members' replacement by AI-written scripts. After one of the longest work stoppages in Hollywood history, the guild was successful in securing an agreement that prevented AI-generated scripts and source material, such as a novel or play for adaptation. The idea was to provide guardrails, rather than out-lawing this "intelligence" altogether, and to commit to a future in which it complements, rather than substitutes for, human labor.

The Writers Guild of America had the ability to wage a long strike and the power to rule out scenarios that would leave many of its members without jobs. Not many workers will be able to do that. But for both groups—those with and without protection—there's also the question of how AI will impact working hours. Will its introduction occur within the five-day-week structure? If that's the case, as AI enhances productivity, we can expect job losses—either small or large, depending on how widespread AI becomes. Alternatively, the higher productivity it enables could be the occasion for going to a four-day week. AI tools are widely expected to make it easier to do more in fewer hours. Don't workers deserve to benefit with time off? There's also the question of wages. When productivity rises, shouldn't employers and employees share that added value? It's important to get this right, because if we don't, our economic system could become even more precariously unbalanced, with excessive concentration in both income and access to work.

Our surveys were designed before ChatGPT debuted, and we hadn't included questions about general AI. Surprisingly, it almost never came up in employee interviews, even those conducted in late 2023 and early 2024. (We added questions about it in mid-2024.) In my conversations with senior managers, only one person talked about it in any detail. To try to figure out how AI will likely affect work time, we'll have to depart from our team's findings to look at a much wider range of research.

The first place to start is past experience, that is, history. We've been through this before, at least once on a scale that seems comparable to AI, and that's during the Industrial Revolution. The surprising thing about that episode is that it first led to big increases in hours of work. In fact, working hours peaked in the mid-nineteenth century. Work-time reduction kicked in late. Taking this longer view, we get a complex story about how technology affects hours of work.

WORKING HOURS AND THE
INDUSTRIAL REVOLUTION

It's a common belief that the spinning mule, the steam engine, and the conveyor belt freed humans from overlong days and weeks of toil. It's also a profoundly myopic one, tenable only from the vantage point of the late nineteenth century—the usual start date for the conventional narrative. By that time, England had already experienced a substantial increase in hours, from the early Industrial Revolution in the mid-eighteenth century to the first quarter of the nineteenth. To get a handle on how AI will likely affect hours, we need to dispel the myth that capitalism, or industrial society, has led to major declines in work time.

We know this from work by the historian Hans-Joachim Voth. For decades, historians had thought that the emergence of industrialization and capitalism led to a decline in days off and, once factories arrived, a rise in daily hours. But direct evidence was sparse, and eventually this view came under scrutiny. Voth had the ingenious idea of using witness testimonies at London's Old Bailey court to create an hour-by-hour account of how people spent their time. He reckoned that by combining thousands of witness testimonies that pinpointed when crimes happened and what people were doing at those times, he'd be able to create an account of when Londoners slept, ate, relaxed—and worked. In addition to this precision, the court records have the advantage of including all kinds of people, unlike the fragmentary occupational data that economic historians had been relying on. The results are striking.

Voth discovered that between 1750 and 1800, men's working hours rose by about a thousand a year, or an average of about twenty per week. The pattern of change is important. Daily hours didn't go up much, but men were working more days per year; holy days, which include both political and religious holidays, declined. Even more relevant for our purposes is how the workweek changed. In 1750, Voth found, Saturday, Sunday, and Monday stood out as different from the other days of the week. People worked much less on these three days. The idea that Monday was a rest day may be surprising in the modern context. But E. P. Thompson, one of the great postwar British historians, had famously written about this widespread practice years earlier. St. Monday, as it was called, was a quiet day in which men didn't do much work, as Voth's data show. They eased back into the workweek slowly, suffering a bit from their weekend drinking, then building steam as the week progressed. Apparently, Yorkshire miners flipped coins on Mondays to decide whether they should go into the pits. That said, it's important to note that St. Monday was always a men's holiday; women and children had to be at work.

It is no surprise that St. Monday wasn't approved of by everyone. Thompson cites one "indignant" observer, from 1681:

> When the framework knitters or makers of silk stockings had a great price for their work, they have been observed seldom to work on Mondays and Tuesdays but to spend most of their time at the ale-house or nine-pins. . . . The weavers, 'tis common with them to be drunk on Monday, have their head-ache on Tuesday, and their tools out of order on Wednesday. As for the shoemakers, they'll rather be hanged than not remember St. Crispin on Monday . . . and it commonly holds as long as they have a penny of money or pennyworth of credit.

It wasn't just British workers who practiced St. Monday. Evidence for it has been found in many places, including Mexico, France, Belgium, Prussia, and Stockholm. It's rarely mentioned in the context of the four-day-week movement, but it's worth considering why it was so popular and what we might learn from it. But for now, back to Voth's findings.

Fifty years later, after the Industrial Revolution and related changes had occurred, Monday looked very different. In fact, it was no longer distinguishable from other weekdays. St. Monday had virtually disappeared. Voth estimates that by 1800, men's hours were nearly thirty-five hundred a year, or an average of sixty-seven a week. Voth's findings can't be tied directly to new machines in factories, because those developed outside London, where his data are from. But he is studying the period when capitalist production and the factory system took off.

Of course, hours eventually begin to fall. The brutal schedules of the factory system, where women and children were kept at their machines for ten, twelve, or even more hours per day, generated resistance across society. Government regulations, union pressure, and employer farsightedness led to reduced hours. The nineteenth century ushered in a sustained period of work-time reduction across all the early industrializing countries.

What can we conclude from this history? The first point is that technology does not determine hours of work. In the case of the Industrial Revolution, new technologies first led to a substantial increase in hours. Decades later that trend reversed. Labor-saving technological change may or may not save labor. This fundamental point is often lost in the debate about the Future of Work, robotization, and AI. When factory owners bought expensive machinery, they wanted to use it as intensively as possible, and as a result the early textile factories had terribly long hours. It's also why, today, capital-intensive industries such as steel, auto, and mining have much longer hours than industries with less physical capital, such as retailing, where there are many more part-timers. You might ask why the factory owners didn't just have multiple shifts instead of keeping people at their machines so long. I think the answer is that expanding the labor force can lead to lower-quality hires or more expensive ones.

There will typically be pressures in both directions after the installation of new tech. Employers want to keep the machines running, and push for longer hours. At the same time, it is clearly possible to achieve more production in less time. There are also other important questions, such as what happens to the number of jobs and how wage and income inequality evolve. These are the issues that have occupied economists.

ECONOMISTS' VIEWS OF AI

So what do economists have to say about how AI will affect working hours? The simple answer to this question may be "not much." One reason is that in the post–World War II period, work time became something of a stepchild in the profession. At the end of the first seminar I gave on working hours back in the 1980s, at MIT, a senior economist suggested I give up the topic; he was puzzled that I was interested in hours, because all that really matters is income. Needless to say, I didn't take his advice. But his view wasn't atypical. Employment, wages, incomes, the income distribution—those are better things to study. The profession wasn't always like this. Historically, many influential economists wrote about hours of work and how technology would affect them. Marx chronicled long hours in the "Satanic Mills" of the Industrial Revolution. Keynes predicted increasing leisure over the twentieth century. That said, there *is* a robust literature on technology, and increasingly on AI.

A lot of the research is about jobs. Will the labor-displacing dimensions of AI lead to what's called technological unemployment? Are we headed for a dystopian labor market in which an elite group of highly skilled technologists have work, and the rest of us are left idling? Will we need a basic income to adapt to this inevitability, as some in Silicon Valley have suggested?

There was a time when most economists had stock answers to these questions. No, no, and no. For decades, there was a widespread belief in the profession that technological change does not result in long-term unemployment. One reason was past experience. We'd already gone through something similar with the Industrial Revolution, and it turned out well. While there will certainly be an initial displacement effect with people losing jobs, they can be reemployed elsewhere. Economists point to the new occupations that didn't exist a century ago and expect that a similar process will again occur. Many new types of work will be invented, even if we can't imagine them today, just as our ancestors couldn't predict the rise of computer programmers or content moderators on social media.

The second reason for economists' optimism is grounded in their model of how the economy functions. By definition, technological innovation raises the productivity of inputs into a production process. Let's call those capital and labor. When both become more productive, the result is more output. Let's call that growth. The idea is that the incentive to grow leads to a higher demand for labor—even enough additional demand to absorb those who have lost their jobs. Therefore, the initial displacement effect is overridden by the positive productivity impacts of technological progress. Prosperity gets shared by capital and labor, in the form of profits, higher wages, and ample jobs. Over the years, I have been on a number of panels on this topic, and this is the story my fellow panelists usually tell. A recent one summed up this view in one of his slides: "Takeaway: we should not be afraid of technologies that increase productivity!"

That's not to say that economists haven't been worried about other impacts of digital technology. As wage inequality intensified in the last half century or so, attention turned to how technology can change the content of jobs in ways that advantage or disadvantage certain types of workers. One effect is called skill-biased technical change. The bias at present has been in favor of the more highly educated (that is, higher skilled). There has been a lot of ink spilled on the declining fortunes of people without college educations. That research led to a focus on the actual tasks that workers perform and, by extension, a reconsideration of the usual rosy views about robots and AI.

This revisionist approach, which has been championed by Nobel laureate Daron Acemoglu and his collaborators, argues that the impacts of AI on workers will depend on the balance among three effects. The first two are what the traditional thinking emphasizes: the (negative) labor displacement effect and the (positive) productivity/growth effect. Acemoglu and Pascual Restrepo add a third (positive) factor they call the "reinstatement" effect, which includes new occupations in which labor has a distinct comparative advantage. Analyzing data since 1947, they find that over four decades the displacement and reinstatement effects were roughly equal. But after 1987, things changed. There has been a lot of displacement, with very little reinstatement. As a result, labor demand has stagnated.

David Autor reflected the shift in economists' thinking in a subtitle to a paper: "From Unbridled Enthusiasm to Qualified Optimism to Vast Uncertainty." He noted that "traditional economic optimism about the beneficent effects of technology for productivity and welfare has eroded as understanding has advanced." A 2017 poll of leading U.S. economists found that 35–40 percent believe robots and AI will raise long-term unemployment rates. Another study by Acemoglu and Restrepo provides evidence for that view. Tracking the installation of robots in automobile manufacturing locations around the country, they show a subsequent rise in unemployment in surrounding areas. Exactly how exposed workers are to AI remains a point of contention. The most extreme estimate was an early (and widely criticized) one that claimed that 47 percent of U.S. employment was at risk from "computerization." A McKinsey report estimated that 30 percent of activities in 60 percent of occupations were able to be automated.

While there's still a tremendous amount we don't know about how AI will affect the labor market, I'm with the revisionists, and suspect the rosy market-driven scenario is unlikely. There will be labor displacement, perhaps a great deal of it. And that doesn't begin to address the many other negative effects that AI may bring in its wake. We've already seen that algorithms are often pernicious agents of racial and gender discrimination and bias. They're contributing to the rise of hate groups and extremism via social media. Deepfakes threaten to destabilize democracy. AI can be used by governments to control populations. A not insignificant number of AI pioneers have been warning about its potential to cause human extinction. And then there are its current energy requirements. An AI-powered search uses ten times the electricity of standard googling. We desperately need to get serious about what we're doing on this front.

However, the revisionists remind us that the future is in our control; the impacts of AI and robotization are not inevitable, or even natural. They depend on what we decide to do today. The four-day week is a vital part of a sane response. And while it doesn't address the political or existential dangers of AI, it could be key to reducing painful labor market impacts. In fact, all those pessimistic findings that economists are producing have a silver lining. Displacement means we will need less human labor to do things. Instead of reacting by eliminating people's jobs, maybe we could all work less?

This is where economists' disinterest in working hours has been a bit of a liability. Instead of just thinking in terms of numbers of jobs destroyed and created, let's focus on reducing hours per job. It's an obvious point. But it has been a blind spot in the debate about why technology didn't lead to mass unemployment in the late nineteenth and through the twentieth century. It wasn't just growth and new occupations that kept people employed. It was also declining work time. Between 1870 and 1970, average annual hours of work fell across nearly all the high-income countries. For many years, the consensus figure for annual hours in 1870 was about three thousand a year (or sixty hours a week). A century later, we were at roughly two thousand (forty hours). That was critical to providing jobs. But since then things have stalled out in ways we need to address to make sure AI delivers benefits to everyone, and not just its owners.

WHY DO AMERICANS WORK SO MUCH?

In chapter 1, I talked about the time squeeze and the common feeling that "two days is not enough." There I mostly focused on the rise of women's hours of paid work and the high demands of household labor. The other half of today's time squeeze is what I call the "long-hours economy." It's long in two ways: in comparison to other comparably wealthy countries and in comparison to our own history. I reported that the average U.S. worker is on the job hundreds of hours more than European counterparts, and even more than the Japanese.

Why *do* Americans work so much? The conventional answer is

that it's cultural. We're a nation of workaholics. This perspective points to the Protestant work ethic or the power of the American dream as a root cause. The argument also gets circular. Sometimes, evidence of long working hours and the status value of being at the office all the time are offered to support the cultural explanation. But it doesn't hold water.

The main reason is that for many decades, the United States was a place where people worked less. Before 1900, American hours were lower than in a number of European countries, such as Belgium, France, Germany, the Netherlands, and Italy. The United States was first to go to the five-day week. In 1950, Germany, France, the U.K., Italy, and Spain all had longer hours. Even through the 1960s, work schedules in Europe exceeded those in the United States. Then the two regions took different paths. U.S. hours stagnated and rose. Europeans continued a century-long trajectory of reducing work time.

It is hard to credit "culture" when the thing to be explained departs from the nation's history and is of recent vintage. As one influential paper on the differences between European and U.S. working patterns asks, "Why did 'culture' start diverging in the early seventies across the Atlantic so dramatically?" Why indeed? The authors find that unionization and regulation of mandated holidays account for the differences. In fact, the influence of unions raises a fundamental question about how labor markets operate.

The standard model says that workers have preferences between work and leisure and that employers offer jobs that match those preferences. The key assumption here is that employers are perfectly happy to let workers choose their hours. The other way to express this is that there's a "market in hours." Workers can "buy" more or less leisure according to their preferences.

But that's not how labor markets work. Employers actually care a lot about hours and have their own reasons for preferring particular schedules. In the United States, if you want a job with low hours, you have traditionally had to sacrifice benefits and a career ladder to get it. Companies offer what economists have called "tied wage-hours" offers. The wage and the hours go together, and traditionally, to change hours, workers have had to change jobs. This is why unions matter. They can be powerful enough to overcome what employers want.

And what do employers want? In *The Overworked American*, I argued that they want long hours. I identified three reasons why. Reason number one is that in the United States, employers offer health care, which is paid by the person, rather than prorated by hours worked. It functions like a tax on employment, giving employers an incentive to hire fewer people for more hours. This was an accidental and unfortunate pairing; during World War II, employers began offering health insurance to attract workers because wages were controlled by the government to keep wartime inflation at bay. Little did anyone expect this would distort the labor market eighty years later. There are also some employer taxes, such as worker compensation and unemployment insurance, that have a similar incentive structure, because they are capped at a certain level. Hours above that level become cheaper for the company. To continue the contrast, this makes the U.S. system different from the setup in most European countries, where health insurance is financed independently of employment, thereby avoiding this disincentive. Employer-provided health care also helps explain why benefits aren't paid for part-time work.

The second reason employers prefer long hours goes back to the cost of job loss, which I talked about in chapter 4. Longer hours (with more pay) raise the cost of job loss. That makes the worker more manageable, cooperative, or productive—pick whichever of those words you like. The easiest way to see this is to think about the difference between having two twenty-hour-a-week jobs and one at forty. Challenging the boss is more costly in the forty-hour job, because getting fired from it entails twice as much income loss as from one of the twenty-hour positions. My research found that work effort and the propensity to strike move up and down with the cost of job loss.

The final reason is the practice of paying by salary, rather than by the hour. In 2022, 44 percent of U.S. employees were paid on salaries, a fraction that has grown over time. Because additional hours are "free" to the company, these workers end up with elastic hours. (Have your hours crept up over time in a salaried job?) Years ago, I estimated that merely switching from being an hourly to a salaried worker would increase annual hours by a hundred a year or more. Together, these three factors serve as structural disincentives for work-time reduction in the U.S. economy.

Other researchers have found an additional structural feature that has been driving up hours in the United States—the growth of inequality. As income flowed to the top of the distribution, that created competitive pressures for people to work more to keep their incomes up as well as to avoid falling further behind. Given that U.S. inequality was already high and has increased more than in Europe, this also helps explain the U.S./European divergence.

So where does this leave us in terms of what to expect from digital technology and AI? The main takeaway is that there have been powerful structural factors operating to keep hours high. We saw this in the Industrial Revolution. Those technological breakthroughs led to longer, not shorter, hours of work. In recent decades, digitization has transformed work in many occupations and industries, but in the United States hours haven't fallen. I've argued that's due to biases in the economy that have operated against hours reductions. Europe has some of these biases, but stronger unions and welfare states and a more equal income distribution have reduced those pressures, so European countries have continued to translate productivity growth into free time. Since 1973, I've calculated that the United States has taken less than 8 percent of its increased productivity to reduce hours, while western European countries have taken much more—generally three to four times that amount.

This history suggests that we can't just sit back and let the market determine the impact of AI on our societies. Yes, there are structural pressures going in the direction of unequal benefits, unemployment, and maintaining long hours of work. But those outcomes are far from inevitable. As Daron Acemoglu and Simon Johnson argue in *Power and Progress*, whether new technologies bring widespread prosperity "is an economic, social, and political choice."

Our U.K. collaborators at the Autonomy Institute have generated estimates of how many U.S. workers could be enjoying a four-day week within a decade as a result of AI. They estimate that the productivity gains of this technology could enable 28 percent of the U.S. workforce, or 35 million workers, to transition to thirty-two hours by 2033. A less stringent, 10 percent work-time reduction is feasible for 128 million, representing 71 percent of the workforce. We shouldn't lose this opportunity.

Among my conversations with senior managers, only Matt Juniper of Praxis raised the specter of AI. As we saw in chapter 3, he was a big believer in Parkinson's law. "What I was saying around work always expanding, I think we've always seen this experiment play out in the other direction. For a hundred years technologies allowed employees to work faster and more efficiently. . . . Never at any point has that been given back to employees. . . . The productivity enhancements have just been baked into employers' bottom line." Matt sees AI as a chance to escape that trap. "And so I guess the hypothesis is, what if you do that the other way? So as we see AI come into the mix, there's all these rightfully concerned individuals that say, what if this replaces humans and takes jobs away?

But I would argue, why can't we look at it the opposite way? Why can't these technologies, if they're able to do 20 percent of what a human does—or did—why can't that 20 percent be given back to the employee? Maybe that's a philosophical debate. But I feel it's an important one. Maybe we could take some of these efficiencies and give them back to the employee, so that [you have] people who are happier, healthier, etc., working for you."

The impact of AI on work is ultimately a question about control—at many levels. Control over how the technology is used. Control over who reaps its rewards. Control over who has access to jobs and hours of work. And control over who is controlled—and surveilled—by it. To understand the big choices we are now facing, it's worth returning to St. Monday, because its demise was not just about changes in hours of work but a symptom of the disappearance of an entire way of life.

A NEW CULTURE OF TIME

The trends in daily time use that Voth identified were part of the evolution from a society dominated by agricultural and artisanal production to an industrial economy with factories and modern workplaces. Thompson's classic account is about this broader cultural and economic shift and how it affected attitudes to time and work. For Thompson, St. Monday exemplified the task-based orientation to time that prevailed in preindustrial societies. Agrarian duties (sowing, reaping, pasturing, milking) structured what needed to be done. There was little sense of time scarcity, or even time itself, apart from its connection to the daily and seasonal rhythms of agriculture. Industrialization, he argued, created a novel, economical attitude toward time, which he describes as the shift from *passing* to *spending* time. In this sense, industrial capitalism created its own time consciousness. One precondition for modern time culture was the development of a common sense of time, something we now take for granted. This required the diffusion of clocks and watches, and then their standardization. Railroads were key to synchronizing widespread local variations in time. Setting foot on a train and arriving at a destination "before" one's departure time, which did happen, was impractical. At the mid-nineteenth century, railroads went onto Greenwich mean time and society followed.

These developments had profound consequences for workers' experiences, because they ushered in temporal cultures dominated by a mentality of time scarcity, the importance of not "wasting" time, and a general antipathy toward idleness. What Thompson has called "time-discipline" transformed the workplace. Payment systems for labor switched from piece rate (which was task based) to wages (which were paid by time units such as the week and day, and of course eventually the hour). Time-based practices meant employers pressured people to show up early, stay late, and work diligently. Josiah Wedgwood, whose innovative potteries helped create modern industry, instituted the first reported system of "clocking in." Much that we take for granted about how time is spent, especially at work, is still rooted in a time-discipline system that began in the eighteenth century. Fixed hours. Centralized workplaces. The idea that the employer owns the worker's time. The paramount role of productivity and the belief that it is well measured by how many hours a person logs at the office.

While there's no doubt this culture enabled phenomenal increases in production, the emergence of digital technology and AI—twenty-first-century technologies—suggests it might have outlived its usefulness. There's a growing understanding that turning humans into machines is far from optimal in a world where so much of what we're producing is knowledge, human care and connection, and the next generation. We encountered its limits in Alex Pang's discussion of how shorter working hours foster creativity and Cal Newport's plea for "slow productivity." Busyness, face time, "productivity theater," clocking in, and the ideal worker norm are all part of an outmoded way to work. As machines become able to do so many jobs, we would do well to free ourselves from the rigid temporal mindset of the modern era.

So back to St. Monday. It taps into a deep human need for a more extended break from work than the two-day weekend affords, at least if we're still in the world of the contemporary workplace. The passion with which participants in our trials describe how the four-day week has transformed their lives suggests its power. Before the advent of factories, when adult male workers were able to control their time, five days of concerted effort was too much. It seems that is again the case for many.

POWERING DOWN FOR
PEOPLE AND PLANET

E. P. Thompson published his paper on the changing culture of time in 1967. Since then the trends in workplace discipline he wrote about have intensified. I'm thinking about developments like the algorithmic management of Uber drivers and DoorDashers, and dystopian sci-fi-like computer monitoring, in which workers' every keystroke is recorded. But perhaps the change that is most notable, because it affects nearly everyone, is the acceleration of daily life. If, as Thompson showed, the first stage was the consolidation of a common consciousness of time, the second has been the pressure to do more, better, faster. Even Thompson, who was keenly attuned to this process, would likely be amazed at how intense the culture of acceleration has become. We've got pervasive multitasking, an increase in speeding on the roads, two-hour Amazon delivery, TL;DR, and the mini-crossword. Showing up a minute late for a Zoom meeting prompts an apology. While many blame smartphones, and they have undoubtedly contributed, this trend long predates digital technology. It's a predictable consequence of a world in which time equals money. And it's at the heart of why so many people are overloaded, burned out, and pressed for time.

The fast life doesn't just affect people. It's also destroying our planet. The two major ecological crises we face—climate destabilization and the sixth mass extinction—can both be traced to the speed of human activities in relation to nature's time scales. In many ways, nature is resilient. Atmospheric pollutants disperse over time. Plants and animals migrate as the climate shifts. Ecosystems are adaptable. But after 1950, when humans began what scholars have termed "the Great Acceleration," the speed of change has far exceeded what nature can manage. That's the crux of the ecological breakdown: Humans are altering planetary ecology on a scale that far outpaces nature's adaptability. A landmark effort by scientists around the world has identified nine planetary boundaries that are dangerous to exceed; we have already crossed six.

The role of speed in ecological outcomes can be seen most clearly in the link between transportation and carbon emissions. To get somewhere quickly requires using more energy. The highest footprint option is generally a plane, which is fastest (except for short trips). Internal combustion engine cars come next, and they're generally speedier than buses, trains, and ferries. Walking and cycling are very low carbon. There are complexities of course. These include the size of a car and the number of people in it, accounting for calories expended when walking, and of course in cities traffic can make cycling or walking faster than driving. (High-speed trains are an exception; they're energy efficient and fast.) But exceptions aside, the speed of travel generally equates to energy use.

There's also a more general lesson here. The fast-paced, long-hours lifestyles that are undermining human well-being are also implicated in environmental decline.

The impact of working hours on ecological outcomes is one of the topics we covered in our research. We don't yet have a full accounting; however, our data reveal some promising signs. But before reporting on our findings, I'll start with a bit of context on the climate crisis to see the contribution that work-time reduction can make. I focus on climate, rather than some of the other planetary boundaries, because it is the most urgent and most clearly connected to working hours.

THE CHALLENGE OF CLIMATE

Climate destabilization is increasingly wreaking havoc on people and planet. Temperature rise causes heat waves, droughts, extreme weather events, rising sea levels, biodiversity loss, crop failures, and insect-borne diseases. Loss of livelihood leads to migration. Climate impacts destroy infrastructure and property. Indigenous ways of life are under severe threat. While we don't have definitive evidence yet, I suspect these changes are already contributing to the widespread political instability we're experiencing today.

The main global organization addressing climate, the UN's Intergovernmental Panel on Climate Change (IPCC), figures out where we are and analyzes possible futures. In 2018, it published a special report on requirements for keeping temperature rise to 1.5 degrees Celsius, the threshold that will avoid many of the worst climate impacts. Its answer was that we must achieve 40 percent emissions reductions by 2030 and get to net zero by 2050. As of 2024, we're not on track. After a brief decline during the pandemic, global greenhouse gas emissions began rising again. In June 2024, the level of carbon dioxide measured at NASA's Mauna Loa Observatory was a whopping 427 parts per million, 50 percent more than two hundred years ago.

While we're seeing some progress, as countries shift to renewables and phase out coal, current global rates of decarbonization are far below what's necessary. We need about seven times what we're managing at the moment—17.2 percent annual reductions versus the current 2.5 percent. This means that hopes for a 1.5-degree rise are nearly extinguished. But holding to a 2-degree increase is still important and requires a demanding 6.5 percent annual rate of decarbonization. Another way to think about what's necessary is in terms of greenhouse gas emissions per person. Globally the current average is 6.8 tons. (The United States is far above that level—at 17.7.) We need to get to 5 tons in the next decade and then to 2.5 tons by 2040. It's a tall order.

The good news is that working less can help.

THE ROUTE TO DECARBONIZATION

To understand exactly how working hours affect the climate, we need to start with the rate of decarbonization—the pace at which emissions are falling. Whenever we produce things, we use carbon. That means there's a close link between output (economists' word for GDP) and carbon emissions. Rates of decarbonization are driven by those two factors: how much carbon is used for every unit (let's say dollar) of GDP, and how much GDP we are producing. When carbon is delinked from GDP, we call that decoupling. What's termed relative decoupling occurs when each dollar of GDP uses less carbon. That happens as a result of improvements in energy efficiency, a shift to renewables, or changes in what is produced, such as fewer carbon-intensive activities like mining and manufacturing and more low-carbon services such as teaching. Relative decoupling isn't a solution; an economy can be experiencing a lot of relative decoupling, but if energy demand and GDP are expanding rapidly, emissions can still be rising. That has been the experience of wealthy countries for most of the time they have been negotiating about climate change. We need the second kind of decoupling—absolute. That's when GDP growth is occurring, but emissions are actually falling.

Until very recently, virtually all the attention has been focused on reducing carbon emissions per dollar of GDP. Governments have been investing in energy efficiency, shifting away from the dirtiest fossil fuels (like coal), or in some cases getting off fossil fuels altogether. While we've made progress, emissions are still going up, because GDP is also rising. For decades, rates of decarbonization were fairly close to rates of GDP growth, which means we've been running in place. That 2.5 percent rate of decarbonization I mentioned above? GDP growth has been hovering at just about 3 percent lately. As Al Gore famously noted, climate change is an "inconvenient truth." And there's no more inconvenient part of its truth than the connection between growth and emissions.

The emphasis on carbon intensity keeps the conversation centered on technological solutions, avoiding difficult choices about how much energy is being demanded, which in turn raises questions about growth and the structure of the economy. But even the global community is now realizing that technology alone won't be sufficient, because we can't keep undoing the progress we're making. We're going to have to learn to live differently. In 2022, the IPCC's Sixth Assessment Report introduced a new possible future—a "Shared Socioeconomic Pathway"—in which "consumption is oriented toward low material growth and lower resource and energy intensity." Finally! The report relied on research showing that high quality of life can be achieved with small carbon and eco-footprints. As part of this discussion, for what I believe is the first time, the IPCC raised the issue of work-time reduction and the role it can play in controlling emissions.

WORKING HOURS AND THE CLIMATE

I published my first paper on work time and the environment back in 1991. At the time I was thinking about the big divide between rich and poor countries in terms of their use of ecological resources. For climate, wealthy countries are the "legacy" polluters. They got rich on fossil fuels and are most responsible for building up the stock of carbon dioxide and other gases in the atmosphere. Poor countries want cheap energy so they can grow and lift their populations out of poverty. Therefore, the equitable path is to ask the rich to cut back on their pollution to give more ecological space to the Global South. But inhabitants of wealthy countries will be unlikely to accept a way forward that doesn't also benefit them. That's the beauty of work-time reduction. It provides tangible, durable improvements in people's lives. And if it's not accompanied by reductions in the income people already have, it is very popular.

In the early 2000s, I began modeling the connection between hours and carbon emissions. I studied two main pathways of influence. The first I've already discussed—the linkage between GDP and emissions. The best way to think about this relationship is through the simple arithmetic of productivity. When productivity increases, an economy can either keep its working hours unchanged and produce more or keep production steady and work less. (And of course it can do a bit of both.) Countries that reduce their working hours are in effect taking some of their productivity growth as free time, rather than producing to their maximum levels. So there's a trade-off between GDP and hours of work. I called this the "scale effect," because it refers to the size or scale of the economy over time. Countries that reduce their hours of work are "scaling up" less rapidly.

The second pathway has to do with households' energy use. We know that income affects how much carbon each household uses. Actually, it's the biggest factor. In 2019, the richest 10 percent of the global population was responsible for nearly half (48 percent) of global emissions, in contrast to the bottom half, who emitted only 12 percent. Researchers estimate that inequalities across households are more important than across countries.

But time matters too. Doing things more sustainably, by using less energy, is usually more time intensive. Conversely, time stress activates that speed/emissions connection I discussed above. So my hypothesis was that households with less free time have higher energy use, after accounting for their incomes. I called this the "composition" effect because the mix, or composition, of household activities varies with working hours.

You're probably already thinking of counterexamples. If people get a three-day weekend, won't they use it for a trip to the Bahamas or Disneyland? And even if the extra carbon use isn't as high as with an airplane trip, aren't other leisure activities carbon intensive? People drive locally and go to theme parks, hotels, and other attractions. Those all use a lot of energy. Researchers call these rebounds. They are the second-order effects that reduce some of the savings from an innovation. Rebounds are rampant in the energy space because nearly everything we do involves energy. Efficiency improvements lower the cost of operating a vehicle or a household appliance, which in turn can lead to driving more or buying a second fridge. Installing solar panels can induce a household to use more air-conditioning. And so on. We need to take these into account if we want to know how the four-day week affects carbon footprints. And with work-time reduction, there's another possible rebound. If people take on extra jobs during the off day, they'll earn more money, which they will spend. That's a scale effect that could increase emissions.

HAS THE FOUR-DAY WEEK
REDUCED EMISSIONS?

When we developed our strategy for measuring climate impacts, we were in largely uncharted territory. Most of the research on work time and emissions has looked at weekly or annual hours. The four-day week has unique features, most of which haven't been well studied. The design and timing of the trials also created complications. As a result we've got indications but not solid conclusions. One other point is worth mentioning: Because these trials didn't involve any reductions in pay, they would just be tapping into composition, rather than scale effects. Therefore we didn't expect large impacts. The most likely place for savings would be in commuting. That was top of mind for us.

Environmentalists have long advocated for the four-day week on account of its potential to reduce the number of times people travel to and from work. Research on compressed (four-day) workweeks had shown savings. A California study of a 1990 Los Angeles program found that employees' daily trips fell by 9.1 percent and total distance traveled was reduced by 17.1 percent, which amounted to just over a U.S. ton of carbon dioxide per person. It turned out that having Fridays off changed a number of travel patterns, such as when people did errands and took weekend excursions. Those longer trips were shifted to Saturdays, which left Sunday as a stay-at-home R&R day. A widely publicized experiment in Utah was estimated to have reduced emissions by 14 percent, although those measurements were partial. These studies suggested not to expect a full 20 percent reduction in driving, because there would be some rebound, but that the savings were considerable.

We certainly expected our participants would be commuting

less. But we were also mindful that remote and hybrid work had already reduced commutes by a lot. To complicate matters, our trials were occurring during a transition period when people were coming back into their workplaces.

We also wanted to look at how energy use in buildings was changing. With a day off, offices would have fewer people in them, and homes would have more. So we expected less commercial and more residential energy use. But how much less and how much more? Were companies shutting down for the day, which meant a significant energy savings? Or were they still open and staff were taking different days off? That wouldn't make much of a dent in heating, cooling, and lighting. Similarly, were houses going from being empty (with low energy use) to having someone there turning on lights, heat, and air-conditioning? Or were they already occupied so that an extra person didn't add much?

The literature contains some clues about how these scenarios might play out, but most of it is geared to different questions. Energy research often focuses on peak use, rather than total. It does have one potentially relevant way to think about these questions: differences between weekday and weekend use. Adding an off day is like expanding the weekend. Historically there has been about 10 percent less energy use on Saturday and Sunday. Could we assume that holds here? Apparently not, because over the last decade that difference has narrowed. Weekends are still less energy intensive, but the gap is closer to 5–7 percent. We might find some modest savings. Another piece of evidence comes from research on the impact of the pandemic and the shift to remote work. A comprehensive study found that household electricity use went up about 8 percent during the lockdown period. (In our case the increase is probably lower, because during lockdown computer use for work was high and people were also in the house nearly all the time.)

This study also found a 6.9 percent decline in commercial and an 8 percent reduction in industrial energy demand. So changes in building energy use were close to a wash.

In the end the questions about building energy use were too complex for us to answer. One reason is that we had so many companies doing different things. Only some were closing their offices on the off day. We asked for energy data from the companies, but we didn't get much. Many of the small companies didn't have data on their usage, because it was included in their rents. We'd also asked employees for their spending on utilities, thinking it would be easier to get dollar amounts than kilowatt hours or gas consumption. But then energy prices shot up, and at different rates around the world. The final complication is that energy use is very seasonal. Some trials started in the dead of winter and ended in summer. Others did the reverse. (As the sample grew and included companies starting at all times of the year, seasonality became less of a factor.) After toying around with various models that attempted to account for all these factors, we put that exercise aside because the data were too messy.

But we have other indicators. We have questions about commuting. We track out-of-town trips, to see if there is a travel rebound. And we included a three-item "pro-environmental" behavior scale to see whether sustainability practices changed during the trial. Once we discovered that the household energy questions weren't panning out, we asked people to estimate their personal carbon footprint, at baseline and six months later. Our findings are shown in table 7.1.

Overall, the results are suggestive that there may be some decline in energy use. Looking across all the trials, we find that average hours spent commuting fell by about half an hour a week (3.6 to 3.1 hours). Forty-eight percent of participants reduced the time

Table 7.1 Carbon use and environmental outcomes

	Baseline	Endpoint	Change	Significance	% Decrease	% No change	% Increase
Personal carbon footprint (self-rated)	5.0	4.9	-0.1	**	39%	30%	31%
Walk or cycle instead of drive	2.8	3.0	0.2	***	23%	47%	30%
Encouraged others to protect the environment	2.9	2.9	0.0		28%	47%	25%
Volunteered to protect the environment	1.6	1.7	0.1	*	19%	61%	21%
Hours of commute time per week	3.6	3.1	-0.5	***	48%	19%	33%
Percentage commuting to work by car	57%	56%	-1.0	**	5%	91%	4%
Domestic trips in past four weeks	2.7	2.2	-0.5	***	40%	32%	27%
Round-trip international flights in past four weeks	0.2	0.2	0.0	**	10%	78%	12%

Note. Personal carbon footprint: self-rated compared to others in one's country (0-10). Environmental behaviors: never to always (1-5). Commute time per week: in hours. Domestic travel: trips taken in the past four weeks. International travel: round-trip international flights in the past four weeks. Significance levels are based on paired-sample t tests to determine whether baseline and endpoint values are significantly different: +p<.1, *p<0.05, **<0.01, ***p<0.001.

they spent commuting, in comparison to 33 percent for whom it rose. For the 33 percent with more commute time, it's likely due to the fact that they were going back into the office a bit more; remote workdays fell from 2.8 a week to 2.6, with 37 percent reducing the number of days they work from home. There's also a very small (1 percent) decline in the fraction of people who report getting to work by car.

Our pro-environmental behavior scale included a question that's relevant to driving. We asked people to think back over the last four weeks and to indicate their level of agreement with this statement: "I chose to walk or cycle instead of using my car when I could." The average response was between "sometimes" and "often," and increased by two-tenths of a point (from 2.8 to 3.0). Thirty percent of the sample increased their frequency of avoiding using cars. With the remaining items on the pro-environmental behavior scale, the results don't indicate much change. There's a slight uptick in volunteering (a one-tenth increase in the average level), although nearly as many are doing less than are doing more.

But there's other good climate news in our data. We don't find much of a travel rebound. The number of domestic trips taken over the previous four weeks fell on average from 2.7 to 2.2 from baseline to end point. International flights held steady, at 0.2. The other rebound we wanted to look at was second-job holding. As I reported in chapter 2, in the full sample, the rate of second-job holding fell by one percentage point. In the U.S. and Canadian sample, second-job holding declined by 2 percent.

Another finding is that about two-fifths of people register a decline in their self-reported personal carbon footprint. The question we asked was, "Thinking about your personal carbon footprint, which includes your household energy use, transportation, diet, and purchasing behavior, how would you rank your footprint compared to others in your country?" On a 0–10 scale the average level at baseline was 5.0, and at the end of the trial it had fallen to 4.9. Thirty-nine percent of the sample reported a decline. Findings for the United States and Canada are quite similar to the global sample, although there's an additional one-tenth of a point decline in car commuting.

We had one more way to look at how the four-day week might be affecting emissions, which is information on how people spend their off day. There's not much existing research on this question, but there are a few studies of how variations in working hours affect household emissions. This literature doesn't analyze interventions like ours but uses large-scale surveys of time use. One of the best studies, from Sweden, finds that for a 1 percent reduction in working hours, emissions fall about 0.8 percent. But like most of the research, this study assumes a 1 percent reduction in income too, which drives most of the emissions decline. When people have less money, they spend less, and therefore emit less. We expect less reduction, because pay stays the same. However, like other researchers, what we mostly see is a lot of low-carbon, close-to-home activity.

We ask people to fill out a time diary about their most recent day off, in which they record their activities in 30-minute time slots. Here we're not following our before-and-after design, because there is no off day in the "before." Mainly we're worried about rebounds. So we look to see whether people are using the time off to do carbon-intensive activities. For the most part, our findings suggest not. The most popular activities are low carbon. People spend most time on hobbies and leisure activities (TV and radio, sport and exercise, hobbies and reading). Together these take up just under 235 minutes, or just about four hours. Second is household work and caring labor (cleaning, food preparation, household maintenance, all types of child, elder, and pet care), which totals 195 minutes, or more than three hours. People also sleep a bit (46 minutes) and on average work at their main job for about an hour and a half. Time spent in travel to and from activities averages just 36 minutes. Mostly people stay close to home and do things that aren't too carbon intensive.

So where does this leave us in terms of the question we set out to answer—how does the shift to a four-day week affect carbon emissions? We found small commuting benefits, no significant travel rebound, and fairly low carbon use on the off day. We have no findings on how building energy use changed. Overall, indications are that emissions might have fallen, but not by much. To get more robust findings, we need new approaches to data collection. We're starting on that soon and hope to have a first set of results in 2025.

Do these modest results mean that people like me, who have advocated for work-time reduction for climate reasons, have been wrong, or have oversold the case? I don't think so. But to see why, we need to zoom back out to the macroeconomic and long-term pictures.

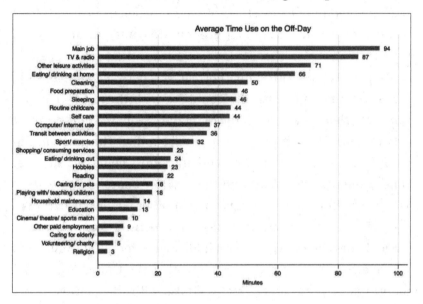

Average Time Use on the Off-Day

Activity	Minutes
Main job	94
TV & radio	87
Other leisure activities	71
Eating/ drinking at home	66
Cleaning	50
Food preparation	46
Sleeping	46
Routine childcare	44
Self care	44
Computer/ internet use	37
Transit between activities	36
Sport/ exercise	32
Shopping/ consuming services	25
Eating/ drinking out	24
Hobbies	23
Reading	22
Caring for pets	18
Playing with/ teaching children	18
Household maintenance	14
Education	13
Cinema/ theatre/ sports match	10
Other paid employment	9
Caring for elderly	5
Volunteering/ charity	5
Religion	3

TRADING INCOME FOR TIME

To understand the working hours/emissions relationship over the long run, recall my discussion of scale and composition effects. At the household level, the four-day-week trials are an example of a pure composition effect. Only the time budgets of households are changing; income is held constant because pay doesn't change during the trials. From the existing literature on households, we would expect that the response will be fairly modest.

But what if work-time reduction isn't a onetime thing, from five to four days, but an ongoing process in which productivity growth is used to gradually give people more free time? That's mostly what happened after 1870 in the first group of countries to industrialize.

Some, like the United States, have stalled out. But with the advent of AI, using productivity growth to reduce hours is one of the most important things we can do to maintain employment, share the benefits of this technology, and protect the climate. That's the future that the IPCC pointed to in its most recent report. Reducing working hours in line with productivity growth keeps us from undoing the progress we're making on decarbonization via the transition to clean energy.

We can see this with simple correlations between annual working hours and emissions. The countries with the lowest hours—Germany, Denmark, France, the Netherlands—have made the most progress toward achieving absolute decoupling. This relationship holds in the statistical models. Looking across countries and over time, a number of studies find that shorter hours are associated with lower emissions, holding constant other factors such as population, urbanization, and industrial structure. And conversely, longer hours are associated with higher emissions. Colleagues and I have also looked at this question within the United States and found that it holds across states. Those with the shortest hours have the lowest emissions and vice versa.

This literature is correlational and doesn't illustrate all the moving parts in the economy. For that we need structural models. A recent European one has looked carefully at the impact of work-time reduction on emissions within one country. It assumes that all productivity growth is translated into shorter hours and games out various scenarios. The size of the emissions reduction depends on whether employment and exports increase (those both add to emissions), and whether trading partners are also on a path of work-time reduction, which reduces emissions. The bottom line is that shorter working hours have the ability to deliver major declines in emissions, and yield between 0.6 and 3.5 times more cuts than technology-only approaches.

If we think long-term, it's also important to recognize that other factors also affect how potent work-time reduction can be. An important one is inequality. Not only do increases in inequality lead to longer hours, as I noted in the previous chapter, but higher levels of income concentration at the top strengthen the link between hours and emissions. That means that for the United States, with its relatively high levels of inequality, hours reductions could yield even larger climate benefits. And of course reducing income and wealth concentration is a benefit in itself.

A future in which productivity growth is exchanged for more free time, rather than more income, does raise the question of whether we need to keep growing to give people quality of life. In many rich countries, there are plenty of reasons to think the answer is no. One reason is that wealth is highly concentrated in the hands of a few, and growth isn't "trickling down." In 2017, the three richest men in the United States—Bill Gates, Warren Buffett, and Jeff Bezos—had as much wealth as the bottom half of the population. A more recent analysis found that the top 1 percent of Americans, 3 million people, are worth more than the bottom 90 percent, a combined 291 million. Nearly three-quarters (72 percent) of all wealth is held by the top 10 percent of families. If the distribution of income and wealth were fairer, more of the population would have a decent standard of living.

People also desperately need more time, suggesting that income growth isn't required for improvements in quality of life. Our trials show that well-being improves dramatically with no change in pay.

The third and most compelling reason for getting off the growth train is that it's destroying the environment on which we rely not just for quality of life but for life itself. Until we can figure out how to expand the scale of production without crossing dangerous planetary boundaries, we need to power down and protect our ecosystems. This is especially true for wealthy countries that already produce enough for everyone but fail to distribute it equitably.

The Shared Socioeconomic Pathway that the IPCC laid out in the Sixth Assessment Report recognizes an important fact about quality of life. It doesn't need to depend on high levels of energy. There is a group of countries with high well-being outcomes but low energy use. This finding was originally discovered by José Goldemberg, a Brazilian physicist who served as his country's minister of the environment. The subsequent work of Julia Steinberger and her colleagues has dived into the nitty-gritty of the relationship between resource use and well-being. This line of research tells us what we know from everyday experience. Once our basic needs are met, a life that is rich in people, time, and meaning is the best way to ensure happiness and well-being.

A four-day week with no reduction in pay is not a climate panacea. That's especially true if it ends up being a onetime change that leads to another era in which work time fails to decline. But there's another possibility, which is that the four-day week breaks the logjam and leads to a longer period of gradual declines in hours. I hope that's where we're headed. The next chapter is about why we might be.

8

ACHIEVING FOUR FOR EVERYONE

In March 2024, I had the privilege of testifying at a hearing of the Senate Committee on Health, Education, Labor, and Pensions (HELP). Bernie Sanders, the chair, had just introduced a bill to reduce the standard workweek from forty to thirty-two hours, and this was the first Senate hearing on the topic since 1955. It lacked the theatrics of some earlier meetings of this committee— Oklahoma senator Markwayne Mullin and Teamsters president, Sean O'Brien, nearly came to blows a few months earlier—but it had plenty of passion. Sanders opened the proceedings with a rousing speech reminding his colleagues that for decades productivity gains have gone to people at the top as wages have stagnated and hours have risen. The United Auto Workers president, Shawn Fain, whose union included a thirty-two-hour week in its recent bargaining demands, took umbrage at accusations that working people are lazy and suggested that if anyone fits that description, it's the "Wall Street freeloaders." There were absurd moments as well. A GOP witness claimed our research doesn't accord with "statistical statistics" as she made a number of laughably false claims.

Near the end of the hearing, Chairman Sanders noted that he didn't expect the bill to become law anytime soon. But he was planting a flag. The buzz in subsequent weeks suggested his strategy was working as the media took notice. Stories included an interview with the hedge fund billionaire Steven Cohen predicting "a four-day week is coming," a *Forbes* piece titled "6 Jaw Dropping Clues That the 4-Day Workweek Is Already Underway," accounts of individual company successes (including organizations from our trials), and articles about the bill—pro and con.

Politicians' interest in the four-day week makes sense given its enormous popularity. Poll after poll finds that most people prefer a four-day week. The conversation has also started to shift from assessing desirability to feasibility, an indication of momentum. Three-quarters or more tell pollsters they can complete all their work with a four-day schedule. In one survey, the average answer to "how many hours a week are you productive?" was thirty-one hours, and 21 percent reported "at most 20." Other polls have similar findings. It seems that employers are buying the argument. A 2024 KPMG survey of American CEOs found that 30 percent were "exploring organization-wide work schedule shifts such as the 4-day and 4.5-day week."

I was thrilled in late 2023 when Francis Ford Coppola contacted me to talk about his upcoming movie, *Megalopolis*. In addition to being a movie director, Coppola is a humane, family-oriented employer. He mentioned that his Inglenook winery was offering a four-day week and arranged for me to speak with the staff there. It's a popular schedule.

Popularity and feasibility don't necessarily translate into action, however. There are many popular reforms that are stymied for years, or forever. And while companies in our trials have had great success, there are likely only hundreds, not hundreds of thousands, of organizations in the United States on four-day, thirty-two-hour schedules. Yet I am optimistic that we're going to get there. AI, climate, and a

tight labor market are some of the macro forces that should acceler-
ate the transition. There are also signs that we're organically evolving away from Friday as a workday. But to me, the most compelling
argument is that things are playing out very much as they did a hundred years ago, when the United States shifted to a five-day week.

HOW THE UNITED STATES GOT TO FIVE

At the dawn of the twentieth century, the normal workweek was six
days, and 70 percent of industrial wage earners worked fifty-four
hours or more. So how did the five-day week come about? One view
is that labor made it happen—perhaps because they take credit for
it, including on a popular bumper sticker: "Unions: The Folks That
Brought You the Weekend." A second explanation credits Henry
Ford going to five, in 1926. So far there's nothing comparable for
the four-day week. No mega-employer has switched, and unions
haven't gone all in yet. But if we look at the 1920s, the picture looks
similar to what we're seeing today.

In 1929, the National Industrial Conference Board, a think tank
for manufacturers, published a long report on the working week. It
began by noting that "in the short space of a few years, the five-day
week has passed from the status of a vague future possibility to
that of an accomplished fact in several hundred establishments,
and has become a live question in many others." That feels like
where we are now.

The first recorded company to institute a five-day week, in 1908,
was Malden Mills, a New England textile concern owned by Henry
Feuerstein. (Decades later, the company would invent Polartec
fleece.) Feuerstein was the first of a group of Jewish business-
men, almost all in the garment trades, who closed on Saturdays.
A Jewish Sabbatarian movement had begun a few years earlier,

when Orthodox rabbis tried to discourage a Reform Judaism trend toward Sunday services. They would continue their activism throughout the second and third decades of the twentieth century. Like many companies offering compressed workweeks today, Malden Mills didn't reduce total hours. The first to do that was the Curtis Publishing Company, a year later, when it went from fifty-four to forty-eight, over five days. By 1914, a number of New York department stores were closing on Saturdays through the summer.

In that first decade, only a handful of companies converted to five days. Momentum built in the 1920s, with hundreds of manufacturing enterprises joining the movement. The garment industry, which was heavily Jewish, dominated the trend, and by the end of the decade a majority of firms in men's clothing (53 percent) had ended Saturday work. Companies in printing, automobiles, and many other products also shifted.

The most obvious similarity with today's movement is that in the first stage business owners were at the forefront. In addition to Sabbatarian concerns, they were motivated by the same issues employers are articulating today—the most common being the desire to give workers more free time.

Another point of convergence with the present is that many of the first-wave companies felt they could make the switch without loss of output, and that they could achieve business efficiencies. Saturday was already a half day, and for many enterprises it was inefficient to set up for only a few hours. Absenteeism was high and morale low. In manufacturing establishments, Saturday could now be used for maintenance, which reduced machine failures during the week. Productivity findings from the National Industrial Conference Board survey align with what we're hearing from companies in our trials. Many didn't know what was happening to output, but among those that did, 49 percent said it hadn't changed and 19 percent said it rose. (Almost a third reported a decline, a difference with our results.)

Other similarities include the fact that the majority of early adopters were small companies. Two-thirds had fewer than a hundred employees, and 91 percent had fewer than five hundred. There was also a great deal of variation in how the schedules were implemented, in order to meet individual situations. Another commonality is that many companies had already begun to reduce summer hours.

There was also a strong emphasis on productivity among many of the early adopters. Richard Feiss, the general manager of the Joseph and Feiss Company, a Cleveland garment manufacturer that eliminated Saturday work in 1917, sounds strikingly like Andrew Barnes almost exactly a century later when he cautions, "Days off are not given—they are earned." The company allowed people to skip Saturday work, but only if they had met their production quota by Friday evening. It was a piece-rate shop, and the opportunity was eagerly taken by the workers. The company saved money on electricity, experienced less absenteeism, attracted new sources of labor (especially women), and was better able to meet its quotas. A century later, Barnes required his employees to sign an opt-in contract which specified productivity metrics that the signer had to meet. He had similarly positive results.

As the 1920s wore on, the movement changed in ways that haven't yet developed, but that we're seeing early signs of. Unions came to play a bigger role. The Amalgamated Clothing Workers of America, which represented men, began to push hard in the second half of the decade. The building trades also made significant inroads. By 1928, twenty construction unions with 514 locals had gotten a five-day, forty-hour week. In 1930, the General Sprinkler Fitters' Organization signed the first national agreement with no reduction in pay. The American Federation of Labor (AFL) also signed on, after some initial reluctance. (One worry was that pay would fall.) Unions are less powerful today, but they still matter on issues of work time. The UAW's 2023 demand for a thirty-two-hour week was a stunner.

While they didn't win it, the union has vowed to keep fighting for shorter hours. The AFL-CIO, the Service Employees International Union, the United Food and Commercial Workers, and others have also endorsed Senator Sanders's bill. It's likely we'll see more union activity in the next few years.

The other difference is that by mid-2024, no major employer had yet announced a shift to a four-day week. Edsel Ford originally signaled his company's intentions in 1922 and began small steps before the wholesale switch in 1926. As a leading employer, Ford had a big impact. I'm hopeful we'll get some large companies moving soon, and I've been contacted by a few. The fact that countries such as Belgium, Spain, and the U.A.E. have already started to legislate means that multinationals will have to reckon with the four-day week.

After 1929 the landscape was dramatically altered. The financial crash and the long depression that followed turned work-time reduction into a strategy for boosting employment, rather than improving laborers' lives or achieving business efficiencies. Debates about work time were prominent throughout the 1930s. In the first years of the Depression, sharing the work became the dominant policy idea for addressing unemployment, even from employers, many of whom voluntarily reduced hours and pay to avoid additional layoffs. Labor also cemented its stance in favor of shorter hours. In the 1932 election, both parties supported shorter hours, and legislative efforts for a reduced workweek got serious in April 1933, when the Senate passed a thirty-hour bill. A week later, Roosevelt's secretary of labor, Frances Perkins, announced the administration's support for thirty hours. It seemed inevitable that the House would follow. Indeed, the historian Benjamin Hunnicutt reports that it was widely believed that "the 30-hour week was within a month of becoming federal law." Alarmed at these developments, business sprang into action to oppose the bill. Roosevelt, who was never a wholehearted supporter of work-time reduction, hastily put together an alternative plan that would become the National Industrial Recovery Act (NIRA). It focused on increasing government spending rather than work sharing. The NIRA did contain some hours provisions, and these fights would go on for a few years, but the thirty-hour work-week was dead. After his reelection in 1936, Roosevelt attempted to pacify the unions with the Fair Labor Standards Act, which set a minimum wage and maximum hours. The FLSA passed in 1938, with a forty-four-hour week, which was reduced to forty in 1940. (Of course, it wasn't really a maximum; it only made hours over forty more expensive for the employer.) The battle for shorter hours had effectively ended. It would take eighty-five years, and Sanders's bill, for the Senate to take up this question again.

A TIGHT LABOR MARKET
CREATES MOMENTUM

In the 1930s, the impetus to reduce hours of work came from the mass unemployment that was gripping the country. Paradoxically, in the 2020s, a tight labor market is having a similar effect. When employers have trouble attracting and retaining staff, they offer not just higher pay but other benefits that people want. Many workers want a four-day week.

In chapter 1, I reported on the reasons that employers are offering shorter schedules; the Great Resignation and abnormally high numbers of quits were among them. There are other indicators of a tight labor market. Since April 2020, the U.S. economy has added a net twenty-eight million jobs. But population and labor force haven't kept up. One reason is aging. The fraction of the population fifteen to sixty-four years old peaked in 2007 and has declined by 2.5 percent since then. Fertility, which is also on the decline, fell to a historic low in 2023. Another factor is the impact of long COVID, which is now considered a "mass disabling event" that has debilitated 3.8 million Americans. As a result of these trends, the nation's labor force participation rate has been on a sharp downward trajectory, peaking around 2000 and falling by 4.6 points as of March 2024. The Bureau of Labor Statistics projects that the labor force growth rate will continue to fall in coming years as aging continues.

It's not just demographics that make me think we're in for tight labor markets going forward. The political winds have shifted such that both political parties want to keep jobs plentiful. The 2016 presidential campaign of Bernie Sanders led the Democratic Party to be more responsive to demands for better wages and working conditions. So far, the GOP seems disinclined to push back on worker gains. Another reason is the pandemic. Historically, after major disruptions such as war and depression, which exact significant sacrifices on working people, governments are loath to inflict more pain. Even the Federal Reserve has been reluctant to undermine labor scarcity. In the 1970s, when inflation was high, there was elite consensus on the need for a punishing recession, which the central bank engineered over the period 1980–82. This time it has moved gingerly and hasn't done enough to reverse current labor market trends. Remember my cost of job loss measure, from chapter 4? Decades ago, Jerry Epstein and I used it to predict interest rates and found that the Fed raises rates when the cost of job loss gets low, as is the case today. Back then, our model was spot on. Today, the Fed is acting differently.

I think employers also expect a tight labor market going forward. If so, that'll create more momentum for change.

WHY FOUR TENS ISN'T THE ANSWER

In mid-2023, a *Washington Post* reporter contacted me in advance of releasing a major survey on the four-day week. I was excited because most of the polling I'd found had been conducted online and is not as accurate as the thousand-plus-person, nationally representative survey I assumed the paper would be fielding. But when I got the results, I was disappointed. They didn't even include the option our trials offered. Apparently, the *Post* thought the only choice is between five eight-hour days and four ten-hour days. Or full pay at five versus taking a pay cut to get four. The results were predictable: Three-quarters preferred four tens, and about the same fraction also opted for staying at five with no reduction in income. (There's long-standing evidence that people are averse to giving up income they already have. After a bout of high inflation one expects even more unwillingness.) Four days (with no stipulations about hours or pay) was by far the most popular schedule: 52 percent chose it, in comparison to just 25 percent who preferred five.

The Washington Post isn't an outlier among pollsters. A curious fact about many of the surveys on the four-day week is that they either don't specify the number of hours or assume that switching to four requires longer days. Even so, four days elicit overwhelming support. A Gallup–Bentley University report from 2024 finds that 77 percent of respondents predict that even four tens will have either an "extremely" or a "somewhat" positive effect on their well-being. Other findings are similar, in that large majorities prefer a shorter workweek, even if daily hours rise.

You won't be surprised to learn that I'm not a fan of the ten-hour day. Labor fought long and hard to get to "eight hours for work, eight hours for rest, and eight hours for what you will." Ten hours on one's feet, in front of a screen, or driving is not healthy. It's true that many people prefer a compressed workweek because they may have long commutes, childcare responsibilities, or maybe just want another day to themselves. However, it doesn't yield the significant well-being benefits we see in our trials. A review of research on nonstandard schedules found that with a compressed workweek, stress is higher on working days, although there's some countervailing reduction on the off days. While there are positives about this schedule, it's unlikely to be better for workers than four eights. Americans already suffer a sleep deficit during weekdays, and experts caution that weekend "recovery" sleep doesn't reverse the negative health outcomes of not sleeping enough during the week. As we've seen in our modeling, better sleep and lower levels of fatigue are the main contributors to improved well-being. The fact that people are willing to do those long days in exchange for an extra day off is an indicator of how valuable a three-day weekend has become.

However, there *is* one intriguing aspect of the compressed workweek: It may be a transitional schedule on the road to thirty-two hours. We've had organizations approach our team with that idea in mind—taking a first step that opens the door to later reductions. The Belgian government might have been thinking similarly when it passed a law in 2022 allowing employees to choose four nine-and-a-half-hour days rather than five eights. On the cusp of AI, going to four with the expectation of cuts in the near future isn't a bad bet. And while we don't yet know whether a four-day week will ultimately prevail in the eight-, nine-, or ten-hour variety, there are indications that it is on the way.

EVOLVING TOWARD FOUR

There are very few studies of how working hours are spread out over the week, because most look at weekly or annual hours. As interest in the four-day week grew, two economists researched trends in days worked. They found that four-day schedules are becoming more common, and at a fairly brisk pace. Depending on how they defined full-time work—a prerequisite to identifying these trends—they discovered that between 1973 and 2018, the number of people in the United States on a four-day schedule either tripled or quintupled. Trends in the Netherlands, Germany, and South Korea are similar. The authors concluded that the desire for "bunched leisure" (that is, a three-day weekend) has been the driving force behind the trend. That accords with scattered pieces of evidence that suggest the United States, and perhaps other countries, are evolving toward a four-day week by gradually changing how people spend their Fridays.

In chapter 4, I cited evidence for lower market activity on Friday, in finance and other industries. Those data came from the business side. There's also anecdotal evidence about consumers. A piece about Fridays from *The New York Times*' style section particularly caught my eye. "Doesn't anybody work on Fridays anymore?" it quoted someone asking as they walked crowded streets in lower Manhattan one Friday. The answer: aside from essential workers, "Not really." The article went on to discuss how people are holding birthday parties on Friday afternoons and drinking hard on Thursday evenings because they can recover the next day. It ended with one woman declaring, "I know that a two-day weekend isn't enough. I think it should be illegal to work on Fridays."

There's other anecdotal evidence that Friday is evolving for white-collar workers, and not just in trendy city neighborhoods. My exercise of choice is barre, a combination of ballet, Pilates, and yoga that's popular with women. When my instructor learned about our research, she told me that Friday morning classes in her suburban Boston studio were very popular, with attendees letting her know they were able to come because they were "working" (in air quotes) from home. ClassPass, an app through which people schedule fitness and salon appointments, reports that the most popular salon day is Friday.

Another indicator is summer Fridays. In 2019, one study found that 55 percent of U.S. employers offered either early closing or a full day off in the summer, an increase of more than 40 percent from just seven years earlier. That number has fallen with the shift to work from home, however. Alternate Fridays off is another schedule that seems to be in use, but I haven't found data on its prevalence.

The intersection of Work from Home and No Meeting Fridays is also affecting Friday work. The most common work-from-home day is Friday, by a large margin. Pair that with a No Meeting policy, and the possibility of going to barre class while "working" emerges. Of course, many people make up the time on another day, or are already working more than a standard workweek. The Stanford economist Nicholas Bloom and colleagues' research finds that work from home does not reduce productivity. My point isn't that people necessarily achieve less but that they have more opportunity to avoid working on Fridays. A study of computer performance found lower output on Fridays, especially in the afternoon, as well as more mistakes. There are other indications that the standard Monday–Friday, 9:00–5:00 week is disappearing. Microsoft Teams data find a decline in people being online after 3:00 p.m. Research using satellite images and vehicle tracking data found a large increase in Wednesday golfing, with the peak time being 4:00 p.m. Four to six is described as a new "dead zone." And so on. Most of these studies involve computer use, and therefore pertain to white-collar employees who are eligible for remote work. But that's a growing number of people in our economy. This group is also reporting that they are having difficulties staying productive during the standard workweek.

LEGISLATIVE PROGRESS

Senator Sanders was of course right that his thirty-two-hour-week bill wasn't about to be passed into law. However, he is not the only legislator advocating for work-time reduction. Representative Mark Takano had already introduced a similar amendment in the House a couple of times. The Congressional Progressive Caucus, which has almost a hundred members, has endorsed these bills. No country has yet passed a four-day reduced workweek, but some are beginning to experiment. The Spanish were the first to act, in 2021, when they announced a three-year four-day-week pilot with government subsidies for the fifth day's wages. If history is a guide, the companies could count on a 10 percent productivity boost at the beginning, and additional productivity growth through technological innovation over the three-year period, as the subsidies declined. The regional government of Valencia also did its own pilot, which got going earlier than the national one. Not to be outdone by its Spanish neighbors, the Portuguese government sponsored a pilot in 2023, in collaboration with 4 Day Week Global. That one ran like the private sector trials—voluntary participation, no financial incentive—and has had similarly positive results. In 2023, the Scottish government organized a pilot with public sector workers, which we are researching, in collaboration with the Autonomy Institute. The Belgians, after passing their four-day-compressed-workweek law, began a pilot program for companies wanting to reduce hours. And beyond these trials, the Spanish government announced its intention to reduce the standard workweek in 2025 from forty to thirty-seven and a half hours. Perhaps this is a first step on its way to thirty-two. There is also movement in eastern Europe. The current Polish government included work-time reduction as an election promise and is deciding between a four-day week and shorter daily hours, with plans to implement the change by 2027. The Slovakian prime minister announced support for a four-day week in January 2024. He referred to a compressed workweek, but Slovak unions are pushing for work-time reduction as well, with the president of the main confederation stating it's a question no longer of whether but of how.

There's also activity at state and local levels. In the United States, by mid-2024, more than one hundred legislators across twenty states had taken some kind of action to enable a four-day week. In four states, bills have been introduced to run pilot programs like the ones we've been involved with. In a number of states bills have been introduced to reduce the standard workweek, like Senator Sanders's and Representative Takano's federal legislation. None have passed yet, but lawmakers aren't giving up. At the local level, the most common actions have been to move public sector workers to a four-day week. More than 650 school districts in twenty-four states are operating four-day school schedules. Many public sector employees are also on four days with thirty-six or forty hours.

And localities are starting to institute thirty-two-hour schedules. The city of Golden, Colorado, worked with 4 Day Week Global to implement a thirty-two-hour workweek for its police force. It found that response rates to calls increased, overtime costs fell, and it had a 50 percent decline in resignations and retirement. Satisfaction rates with the program have been consistently over 90 percent. Overall, the results have been so positive that the city is now planning to expand it to other departments. I've been getting queries from local governments in Massachusetts that are interested in the four-day week.

CAN ALL COMPANIES DO IT?

As legislative activity increases, a common question is whether this is a feasible schedule for every employer. Some opponents of government interventions in the labor market have no issue with voluntary actions by companies but draw the line at rules for everyone. One of the GOP themes at the HELP Committee hearing was that this schedule isn't viable for "people who work with their hands." The ranking member of the committee, Bill Cassidy of Louisiana, sent me various questions afterward about manual workers, including whether any "assembly line workers" participated in the trials. (Since I calculated that only 0.09 percent of U.S. workers are on assembly lines, that one didn't feel too relevant.) But there are many industries and occupations for which costlessly going to four days feels difficult.

The issue of manual workers is a bit of a red herring. The manufacturing sector may currently have less wasted time than white-collar, or knowledge, workplaces, but there's nothing more inherently time wasting about one type of workplace than another. The pace of work, levels of efficiency, and how time is spent are matters of culture, power, and history. Those vary over time within industries and occupations. Labor scholars are well aware that a factory can be riddled with self-defeating practices or hum along at full speed. They know that some industries are much more efficient than others. And manufacturing is the sector that has experienced by far the most productivity growth, which means it should have scope to reduce hours of work without squeezing profits. That's the beauty of productivity growth. While we don't have any large manufacturing concerns in our trials, we do have smaller ones, and as I've argued earlier, they have had success with this model.

That said, I don't believe that the model of squeezing five days' work into four can work everywhere right now. It seems to be easier in white-collar settings at the moment, if only because that's where it is being implemented and those businesses face less global competition. But over time, industries that aren't facing existential threats, and where productivity is rising, can afford to reduce work time. That means most can.

It also doesn't make sense to conclude that the kinds of companies that have enrolled in trials are the *only* ones for which this model will work. Consider the issue of size, and the fact that we have a strong skew toward small companies. That may be because the model will work better for them. It's also partly due to the setup, as I mentioned in the first chapter. Big companies don't need an NGO to partner with in order to change their schedules. But it's also likely that a change as "out of the box" as giving workers a day off without reducing pay is more daunting for entities that operate like large ocean liners. They need time to shift direction.

And then there's the issue of selection bias, which in this case is about whether the companies in the trials are different from those that haven't taken the leap. They surely are, at least in some ways. We didn't collect data on why organizations were opting to try the four-day schedule. We heard about various reasons—burnout, resignations, the possibility of efficiencies. In most cases, there are probably multiple motivations, which is one reason we didn't try to track them. But one through line I've noticed is that many of these companies have humane work cultures and are led by people who care a lot about their employees. Not all companies fit that bill. However, many do. That makes me think that there are many more organizations that could also successfully adopt this model now, because they're *enough* like the early adopters that they could replicate many aspects of their experience. The companies we work with don't seem exceptional in lots of ways that matter.

But for the sake of argument, let's say it's true that only some companies can successfully go to four right now. That's the wrong way to think about whether all companies can. The right questions are, "How many can get there over some reasonable period of time?" and "Will legislation that forces the transition help or hurt?" I think the answers are most can, and legislation will help. It'll take a while to get a new law, plus it'll be a phased-in change. Meanwhile, technology is advancing rapidly, which is why Bill Gates,

Barack Obama, Jamie Dimon, Steve Cohen, and others say a four- or three-day week is on its way. (Cohen reports this is why he has invested in golf. See above.)

The way it will likely happen is that the first group will be followed by others that can replicate their successes. Then another group comes online as the pain point of demanding longer hours than their competitors starts to bite. The laggards will be those that are unable to raise their productivity enough. But that group will likely be outpaced on multiple dimensions, not just working hours. If legislation passes, eventually they'll have to comply or figure out that they don't have a realistic business model.

Tracy Smith, the head of HR at Grand Challenges Canada, foresaw this dynamic when we spoke. "I would also say that as an HR person or a people leader . . . the more companies do [offer the four-day week] the ones that don't will appear more archaic, more dusty, not as modern. . . . And so I feel like it's a mark of innovation, it's a mark of a philosophy. And if an organization comes across as old-school, I think they're going to have a harder time in the future attracting folks."

So when people ask me whether all organizations can do it, my short answer is, not necessarily at the moment, but as it spreads, yes, they will (and will have to) figure it out. After all, that's what happened with the five-day week.

MAKING IT HAPPEN

I've been arguing that the four-day week is coming, but that doesn't mean it will happen automatically. Yes, the forces I've written about are coming into play. But it's individuals who create change. And while there are names history will remember (Henry Ford, Bernie Sanders, Shawn Fain), the world is ultimately transformed by people who don't make it into the history books. The CEOs I've written about. The HR directors who take the idea to senior management. The middle managers who bring a book on the topic to their bosses. The rank-and-file union members who ask their shop stewards to look into it. The entry-level employees who raise the idea at a staff meeting. Social change happens when many people make moves big and small where they live. That's already happening to some degree. Now it's time to send the four-day week viral, not just online, but in real life. Every one of us can be a part of this movement.

If you are in senior management, this book should help to get you started, and there are more resources online. You might look for people in your industry or geographic area who have successfully gone to four and have had their organizations written up in the media. I've found that even though they are busy people, many are big supporters of this concept and happy to help others. (This includes some of the people I've profiled in this book.) If you are in middle management, do the reading and then approach the people above you in the organizational hierarchy. If you are in a unionized workplace, start with your union. If you are not in management but want to get this conversation going where you work, google "how to talk to your boss about a four-day week," where you'll find advice for individual schedule changes and help transitioning a whole organization. This is a rapidly growing field. The OG NGO— 4 Day Week Global—has been joined by others (workfour.org in the United States, worktimereduction.com in Canada) as well as many consultancies with plenty of expertise.

There's a lot of gloom and doom these days and many reasons to feel as if the world is falling apart. The four-day week can help us put it back together. As participants in our trials say over and over again, it's a life changer.

CONCLUSION

By a stroke of good luck, I was invited to a writing retreat in a coastal New England town just as I was reaching the conclusion of this book. As I sit on my balcony overlooking the ocean, the beauty and peacefulness of the scene is mesmerizing. But it belies the state of the world.

It's the summer of 2024. Heat waves are killing scores of people, and animals too. Dead howler monkeys are falling out of trees in Mexico; dehydrated birds are dropping in Delhi. If we can't stop the fossil fuel interests very soon, climate destabilization will render large swaths of the planet uninhabitable. The concentration of wealth in the hands of a tiny sliver of the population is not only impoverishing people worldwide; it's threatening democracy, as billionaires dictate outcomes to governments. Artificial intelligence offers the potential to reduce human labor, but an increasing chorus of AI creators speak out in fear that it will become an uncontrollable, malicious actor. Racist backlash is on the rise. The MAGA movement is threatening civil war, and a group of Christian theocrats are planning to take over the U.S. government. The pandemic continues to catch us in its wake, and that in turn fuels an unprecedented level of emotional and mental distress, in the United States and globally.

The academic word for what we are experiencing is "polycrisis"— from the ancient Greek word *poly*, for many. We have multiple simultaneous and interlocking crises. Wealth concentration fuels political discontent. Climate destabilization makes people fearful and inward looking.

I've spent most of the past four years studying and advocating for a reduction in working time. In the face of these truly existential threats my efforts often feel inadequate. After all, most of the people in our trials have steady, well-paying jobs. They mainly live in wealthy countries.

I know that work-time reduction won't solve the polycrisis. That obviously requires concerted effort to its multiple dimensions. But I have come to believe that it's a vital part of getting us started on a new path to healing a troubled world.

One reason is that it's a hopeful intervention. We desperately need ways forward that solve problems, not create them. When I started this project, I had the sense that people would find the four-day week to be an uplifting, optimistic, and unifying issue that they could get behind. I think I've been right about that. Many people have expressed those sentiments to me. I hope this book has made you feel that way. I also believe that even though the shift has started among more privileged workers, it will spread. We're already seeing that, with uptake by social service agencies, health-care organizations, local governments, and the like. Unions are now advocating for work-time reduction. As governments get involved, and give incentives and legislate, they will be looking to make this schedule available to lower-wage workers.

But mainly I'm committed to the four-day week because it's a solution at the scale of the polycrisis, and addresses so many of the problems we face. One reason is that it's a 360-degree reform, meaning it touches everyone. It obviously benefits the people who get an additional day off. I've offered a good deal of evidence about how it can be life-changing. And even if it's not that level of transformative, it makes the employees who get it better off. That in turn affects their families in positive ways. Partners have more time for each other. Children get more attention from parents. People can be there for extended families and friends. And it's not just about amounts of time. The four-day week makes people healthier and happier, which improves their interactions with others.

That dynamic affects many kinds of relationships. Caregivers are some of the most burned-out people in our society. When they get more time off, it improves the quality of their care, whether that's within the family or in paid caregiving relationships. We saw that with nurses and patient outcomes. By the same logic, customers are better served in many settings. At M'tucci's, the restaurant chain, they credit the four-day week with taking their service to the next level.

Within the workplace, the four-day week aligns with a more humane, less hierarchical and rigid management style. That's better for everyone and reduces ill-treatment. The idea that employees can get their jobs done in fewer hours entails a level of respect and degree of trust from management that is affirming to everyone's integrity. Many of the organizations in our trials show that trust by empowering employees to figure out how to make the shorter schedule work.

The four-day week also strengthens the economy by making businesses more financially sustainable. Where productivity is maintained or increased, it boosts morale and quality. By reducing turnover and expanding the number of applicants for jobs, it cuts labor costs. The companies in our trials are doing well.

Reducing work time is a proactive measure to address the coming tsunami of artificial intelligence. Where work time is stuck at either five days or forty hours, the labor-saving innovations of AI will likely lead to one of two wasteful developments. Either Parkinson's law will kick in, or employers will lay people off. Given realistic growth projections, the latter will result in unemployment.

The four-day week recognizes the diversity of individuals'

capabilities and needs. It is especially beneficial for people with disabilities. And while we don't find differences in terms of how much improvement in welfare occurs across categories such as gender, race, and parental status, we do know there are baseline differences in well-being for those groups. Helping those who start out at lower levels of well-being is especially important, and the four-day week does that.

The four-day week gives people more time to participate in their communities, get involved in politics, and work on the manifestations of the polycrisis. Decarbonizing the economy, countering racial injustice, strengthening democracy, and building resilient communities are all time-intensive activities.

We find that the four-day week may have a small but positive impact on reducing carbon emissions. As a first step in a longer process of translating productivity growth into free time, rather than just using it to produce more and more, it can jump-start an important, ongoing contribution to stabilizing the climate. It's a tailwind for sustainability.

We're in for some rocky times ahead as global heating intensifies and the climate is destabilized. We need to decarbonize as rapidly as possible. We also need to prepare for what's coming down the pike. The most important thing we can do is to commit to each other. To near neighbors as well as those across the globe. We need to dig deep to develop the most humane versions of ourselves. Capitalism accelerated everything. Now we've got to decelerate the pace of daily life, in order to give ourselves time to think, connect, and act. We need to slow down and focus on what really matters, which is thriving and surviving. We have a planet and people to protect.

ACKNOWLEDGMENTS

A research effort of this magnitude is first and foremost a team effort, and I am most indebted to my partners. In 2021, I began collaborating with Orla Kelly, who took the lead in the Irish trial, including for the first version of our employee survey. She has been a pure pleasure to work with. Soon after, I signed on to lead the research efforts for 4 Day Week Global and recruited my phenomenal colleague Wen Fan. Guolin Gu, a PhD candidate in our department, joined us, and we three constituted the Boston College team. We worked with Orla on the Irish trial and then took responsibility for subsequent trials. Both Wen and Guolin have been amazing partners and my biggest debt is to them. Wen and I worked on every part of the project together. Guolin handled all the logistics of surveying and collecting data as well as running all our statistical models. She has been truly exceptional.

In 2023, we were able to add Ami Campbell, who is also a PhD candidate in our department, to the team. Ami took over much of the survey administration as well as responsibility for the qualitative data collection. She has done a fantastic job, and I love working with her. Two additional PhD students joined to work on specific aspects of the research and have done excellent work. Jiayu Huang took responsibility for the company data, and Hassan El Tinay is helping to analyze climate impacts. In 2022, we were fortunate to be joined on the team by Phyllis Moen of the University of Minnesota, who is a distinguished scholar of work and the life course, and her PhD student Youngmin Chu. Their presence allowed us to add qualitative data collection, and we have been focusing on the U.S. and Canadian companies. It has been a privilege to work with Phyllis and Youngmin. I am also grateful to two other members of the research team—Niamh Bridson Hubbard of Cambridge University and Tatiana Bezdenezhnykh of University College Dublin. I have learned so much from all these colleagues, and in addition to their excellent work they are all wonderful to collaborate with.

Of course, none of this research would have been possible without the pioneering efforts of 4 Day Week Global. As I noted in the text, Joe O'Connor originally reached out to me. I will be forever grateful to him for that, and for our collaboration and friendship. Joe introduced me to Andrew Barnes and Charlotte Lockhart. Their vision and support have made this movement possible. I am inspired by their leadership and tremendously appreciative of their willingness to invite me into the work. I owe them a lot. I am also thankful for the entire team at 4 Day Week Global—Alex Soojung-Kim Pang, Dale Whelehan, Hazel Gavigan, Rebecca Roberts, Charlotte Dixon, Jack Lockhart, Gabriela Brasil, Karen Lowe, Victoria Scalise, and Debbie Bailey. We worked with great researchers in countries where trials were being conducted. In the U.K. we partnered with the Autonomy Institute, and especially Kyle Lewis and Will Stronge. We also collaborated with the amazing research team at Cambridge University. That group was led by Brendan Burchell and included David Frayne, Daiga Kamerade, Francisca Mullens, and Niamh Bridson Hubbard. It has been a privilege to work with them. Similarly for the South African team of Caroline Halton, Mark Smith, and Angus Bowmaker-Falconer. I am also grateful to have had the opportunity to collaborate with Pedro Gomes and Rita Fontinha on the Portuguese trial, Julia Backmann on the German, and in the United States, Jon Leland, John Sterman, Vishal Reddy, Daisy Morin, and the WorkFour team.

I have a huge debt to the many organizations that have led the way by taking part in these trials and making their stories known, as well as the thousands of employees who responded to our surveys and requests for interviews. I am particularly grateful to all the company liaisons, and especially to those people who were willing to spend time with me over these years, and those who were interviewed for this book. They are identified in the text, but I want to particularly thank Adam Husney, Matt Juniper, Tessa Ohlendorf, Howie Kaibel, Liz Powers, and Sam Smith for going above and beyond.

We had a fantastic group of undergraduate research assistants who did many things, including interview transcription and coding. They have contributed so much and they are also fun to work with. Thank you Meriel Zhao, Jacob Chappelear, Sarah Ix, Anika Obrecht, Nnenna Okorie, Charlotte Andress, Catherine McAnally, Jiaqi Zhang, and Francesca Chirco. I want to especially thank Francesca for her tireless work on preparing the manuscript, tables, and figures.

I am also grateful to a number of people who contributed to the book in other ways. Senator Sanders, thank you for your decades-long commitment to this issue and for inviting me to testify before the Senate. And Tiffany Haas, thank you for months of work to make that appearance possible. Whitney Pennington, you are the best TED curator a speaker could imagine, and Chris Anderson, your excellent questions and suggestions at my rehearsal made a real difference. I also want to thank everyone who invited me to give talks about this research over the past few years. I benefited from all your comments and questions. There are too many to name, but I am especially appreciative of Joan Sanchis, who asked me to give a keynote at the first International Summit on the four-day week in Valencia.

Over the last two decades, Boston College has been a productive and supportive place for me to work, and at no time has this been more true than during the years I have been doing this research. I want to thank the provost, David Quigley; my dean, Greg Kalscheur; my department chair, Sara Moorman; and especially Vice-Provost Tom Chiles and Guillermo Nuñez of the Office of the VP for Research. Tom and Guillermo provided funds at the beginning, to get us started, and have been especially supportive of this work. I am grateful to a number of other people at Boston College. Rani Dalgin and her team provided crucial assistance for the surveying. Siri Nilsson deftly handled the complex legal agreements we had with some of the companies. Erin Sibley and Jay Cortellini at the Institutional Review Board have been wonderful to work with. On the financial and grants side, I thank Jack Lane, Stephen Prophet, Joanne Nesdekidis, Angelica Wilshire, Bryce Kelley, Megan Welch, Ann-Margaret Caljouw, and Maureen Renehan. I also want to thank Burt Howell and Jack Butler for inviting me to the Intersections Villa as I was finishing the book, as well as the other participants in that magical week.

I am grateful to our generous funders. Beginning in 2023, this work was funded by the National Science Foundation, under award No. 2241840, titled "Assessing the Impacts of a Four-Day Workweek." We have also received support from the Russell Sage Foundation, the Better Tomorrow Fund of the Maine Community Foundation, and the Schiller Institute of Boston College. I am particularly grateful to Elizabeth Taylor, for her many years of support and for finding funding when I needed it most.

A few people were especially helpful as I wrote this book. Alex Soojung-Kim Pang has always been generous with his expertise and gave references and suggestions at a few crucial points. Joe O'Connor did as well. Andy Boynton gave me excellent advice early on. Ezra Zuckerman generously shared his sources and findings on the five-day week. Francis Coppola arranged for me to interview staff at his Inglenook winery. Prasannan Parthasarathi, Krishna Dasaratha, Wen Fan, and Guolin Gu read the manuscript and offered excellent comments. Thanks to you all. I owe my biggest debt to Guolin, who took time out from her own research to provide me with specific data and results that I needed for the book. Guolin, I could not have done this without you.

I am fortunate to be represented by Melanie Jackson. Melanie has been brilliant throughout the process of writing the proposal, finding a publisher, and getting this book into print. She is a dream to work with. Thank you, Melanie. Hollis Heimbouch has been a phenomenal editor—everything an author could hope for. I am also grateful to the team at Harper Business: Rachel Kambury, my wonderful associate editor; Ingrid Sterner, who did a meticulous job on the copyedit; Joanne O'Neill, for the cover design, and Rachel Elinsky and Amanda Pritzker for publicity and marketing, respectively. I published my first book with HarperCollins. It is a special pleasure to be back at this storied house.

My children and their partners fill me with love and hope and are an endless font of support. Thank you Krishna, Sulakshana, Lucas, and Mitu. Prasannan, you taught me a new way to think not just about time but about life. I am so privileged to be spending mine with you.

APPENDIX

DESCRIPTION OF THE FOUR-DAY-WEEK GLOBAL TRIALS AND OUR RESEARCH DESIGN AND PROCESS

The trials began in February 2022 and are continuing. Details on timing, location, and numbers for the trials we have researched are in table A.1. The third (U.K.) trial was the largest and was co-organized by 4DWG, the 4 Day Week Campaign (U.K.), and the Autonomy Institute. We have collected data only in Anglophone countries. In other countries (Portugal, Brazil, Germany) we have collaborated with local researchers who have followed our methodology and translated our surveys.

Trials began with recruitment by 4 Day Week Global. Recruitment was done via information sessions, word of mouth, and media attention. To join, companies were required to maintain pay and cut working hours by a "meaningful" amount. In practice that meant at least four hours. However, almost all opted for a full eight-hour reduction. The early trials were free of charge; then a suggested donation and eventually a modest fee were added. Trials lasted six months. Before a trial started, 4DWG offered two months of onboarding sessions to help participants plan for the change. These were weekly sessions with people who had expertise. Many had shifted to four days in their own organizations. They included Andrew Barnes, Joe O'Connor, Alex Soojung-Kim Pang, Banks

Benitez, and others. The sessions included presentations from people who had unique approaches or software to share, and a community of like-minded participants. They covered big-picture advice such as the importance of bottom-up processes of work reorganization and the need for individualized approaches, as well as details on how to handle legal and regulatory structures and what to do about holidays. Participants were assigned peer mentors from companies that had already instituted four-day weeks. Members of the research team joined to explain our process to the company liaisons.

The research design involved a before and after, "within subjects" methodology, with an initial survey at baseline that was repeated in six months, when the trial period ended. Table A.2 has information on the employee participants. We also did a three-month midpoint survey with a small subset of survey questions, plus a time diary for the most recent off day. At twelve and twenty-four months from the start date we resurveyed anyone who had taken prior surveys in order to test the durability of the results. As noted in the text, some companies dropped out at this point, especially at twenty-four months, and employee response rates also fell for those two survey waves.

Our instrument is described in table A.3. It has approximately 150 questions about work experiences, plans for the new schedule, time-use patterns, demographics, energy use, and twenty well-being outcomes. Wherever possible, we relied on existing, well-validated scales from the academic literature. The instrument included two opportunities for open-ended comments, one for comments about employees' experiences, the second for comments about the survey itself. Thousands of respondents left comments. Over time we have revised the survey, mostly by adding new items on work experiences and dropping variables that were less informative. Where our findings are based on a small amount of data because they rely on recently added questions, I have noted this in the text. We also collaborated with local researchers in the Irish, U.K., and South African trials, and they did interviews with participants. Our team began interviewing U.S. and Canadian participants in late 2023; however, those data are not included in this book. In 2023, I began interviewing CEOs and other key people at participating companies to get more detail on what motivated them to join the trial, their implementation strategies, how and why things worked—or didn't—and anything else they could tell me. I draw on those interviews in chapters 3 through 5.

While most of the data I report on here are from the 4 Day Week Global trials, we have also administered surveys for a few other NGOs and with individual companies that are going to four days outside formal trials. Those data are included in what is reported in this book.

We collected administrative data from the companies. Some of these data are included in table A.4. We began with an onboarding survey of basic information about the company such as size, industry, location, and their plans for the schedule change. Many of these variables are used in our statistical models as controls. We identified a small number of performance metrics: revenue, absenteeism, resignations, new hires, and energy use. We also gave companies the opportunity to supply two individualized metrics. In the onboarding survey we asked for six months of data on these metrics from before the trial began. (During the early trials, when COVID was still a major factor, we gave companies the opportunity to choose a normal baseline period. Eventually we asked everyone for the same six months of the trial in the prior year.) About half the companies supplied these data, with variation among some of the variables. For example, we did not get enough energy use data to be useful. (Many of the companies are small and do not track energy use or pay for it directly.) We also did not get many optional metrics, and we have not reported on them. In the third (U.K.) trial we began asking companies to rate the trial. We asked for their overall opinion, and on productivity and performance. Later we added a question on ability to attract employees. At the end of the trial, we also asked companies about the status of the new schedule: Was it becoming permanent, continuing until further notice, leaning toward continuing, undecided, leaning against, reverting to five days?

At twelve and twenty-four months, when we asked companies' permission for additional employee surveying, we again asked them to update us on the status of the trial. In 2024, as we were developing our statistical model to predict whether they'd stick with the four-day schedule, we asked for information on changes at the company, and for any details they could share about how things were going.

As noted in chapter 1, we set up our team as an independent research entity. The Fórsa trade union supported the original Irish trial financially, and in the United States seed funding was provided by Boston College. We were then able to secure research funding from national sources, in particular the Russell Sage Foundation and the National Science Foundation.

Employee data presented in the book are current as of August 1, 2024. They are from our global sample and include all employees we have data from. For companies, data can lag a few months, because they are slower to report and cleaning their data is more time-consuming. As noted in the text, we added questions along the way, so the number of respondents is not identical for all questions. Over time, we also omitted questions to manage survey length. Significance levels reported in all tables are based on paired-sample t tests to determine whether baseline and end-point values are significantly different: $+p < 0.1$, $*p < 0.05$, $**p < 0.01$, $***p < 0.001$.

Throughout the book I draw on quotations and stories from my interviews as well as the open-ended comments from the surveys. Unsourced quotations introduced as "one participant," "one respondent," or similarly are taken from these open-ended comments. I did not use company names when reporting these comments from individuals, to maintain their anonymity. Where people and companies are named, they were interviewed specifically for the book. All open-ended comments are verbatim, including grammatical mistakes, punctuation, and the like. When using quotations from my own interviews, I often took out filler words such as "like," "you know," "um," and in some cases made very small, non-substantive edits for readability.

APPENDIX TABLES

Appendix Table A.1 Cohorts and countries

Trial Number	Timing	Main countries	Participants at baseline	Number of companies	Completed surveys
1	Feb 2022–July 2022	Ireland, US	618	16	326
2	Apr 2022–Sept 2022	US, Canada	300	18	187
3	Jun 2022–Nov 2022	UK	2548	58	1264
4	Aug 2022–Jan 2023	Australia, New Zealand	758	27	405
5	Oct 2022–Mar 2023	US, Canada	698	25	441
6	Feb 2023–July 2023	Europe, US, Canada	739	13	369
7	Mar 2023–Aug 2023	South Africa	575	33	311
8	2023 (self-paced)	US, Canada, UK	849	18	482
9	Oct 2023–Mar 2024	US, Canada	1264	27	1216
10	Mar 2024-Sept 2024	Anglophone	382	10	in process
Totals			**8731**	**245**	**4442**

Table A.2 Describing the employees

	Percent of Sample
Gender	
Male	34
Female	64
Other/non-binary	2
Race	
White	72
Non-white	28
Country of residence	
US and Canada	32
Australia and NZ	13
UK and Ireland	42
South Africa	5
Other	8
Age	
18-34	43
35-44	28.5
45+	28.5
Occupation	
Chief executives, senior officials and legislators	6
Managers	10
Science and engineering professionals	5
Health professionals	5
Teaching professionals	2
Business and administration professionals	18
Information and communications technology professionals	13
Legal, social and cultural professions	15
Technical, clerical, service, craft and other workers	9
"Other"	19
Educational attainment	
Less than college degree	26
Bachelor's degree	43
Postgraduate degree	31
Whether in a relationship	
No	33
Yes	67
Whether a parent	
No	53
Yes	47
Whether a parent and live with children under 18 years old	
No	66
Yes	34
Annual gross salary (US)	
Less than 30,000	6
30,001-45,000	13
45,001-60,000	21
60,001-75,000	19

75,001-100,000	18
100,001-135,000	12
135,001-175,000	7
175,001-250,000	3
More than 250,000	1

Annual total household income (US)

Less than 30,000	5
30,001-50,000	10
50,001-75,000	16
75,001-120,000	26
120,001-180,000	21
180,001-250,000	13
250,001-350,000	5
More than 350,000	3

Disability

Yes, I have a disability, or have had one in the past.	15
No, I do not have a disability and have not had one in the past.	79
I do not want to answer.	6

Union membership

Yes	3
No, we have a union but I'm not a member.	8.5
No, we don't have a union.	89

Table A.3 The employee survey

Scheduling	current schedule, plans for the new schedule
Work experiences	hours of work, productivity, efficiency and workload, work ability, schedule control, social connections, creativity, turnover intentions, willingness to pay for four day schedule, second jobholding, absenteeism
Well-being outcomes	stress, burnout, anxiety, positive and negative emotions, general health status, sleep, exercise, fatigue
Satisfaction and work-life balance	life, job, time and other satisfaction metrics; work-family and work-life conflict and balance
Time use and time adequacy	time spent in various activities, perceptions of time adequacy, distribution of household work
Carbon use and environmental outcomes	commuting, travel, household energy use, pro-environmental actions
Demographic status	age, gender, parental status, race/ethnicity, education, income, disability, occupation, and others
Endpoint survey	all baseline questions minus demographic questions plus a small number of retrospective questions on workload and productivity, trial rating
Twelve and twenty-four month surveys	subset of work experiences and well-being outcomes

Table A.4 Company characteristics and results

Company rating of trial	Average rating (1-10)
Overall	8.2
Impact on productivity	7.3
Impact on company performance	7.3
Impact on ability to attract employees	8.5

Plans for trial at endpoint	Count	Percentage
Definitely going to continue	80	37%
Planning on continuing but no final decision	88	40%
Leaning towards continuing	17	8%
Undecided	6	3%
Leaning against continuing	4	2%
Definitely not going to continue	11	5%
Missing	12	6%
Total	218	100%

	Weighted change	Unweighted change	% Increased	% No change	% Decreased
Revenue: from start of trial to endpoint	9.8%	19.8%	55%	2%	43%
Change in total employees from start of trial to endpoint	2.4%	4.8%	54%	19%	27%

NOTES

Introduction

xi   a distinguished scholar's (faulty) argument: The scholar was G. A. Cohen, the Oxford philosopher, and the book was *Karl Marx's Theory of History.* Cohen was an "analytical Marxist," and most of his book was very logical. But one short section caught my attention. It was about why capitalism has a bias against taking productivity growth in the form of leisure, rather than more output. His answer lacked what economists call a micro-foundation, that is, an argument about the incentives for individual agents (in this case, companies) to behave in this way. My contribution was to identify those incentives. I discuss them in chapters 4 and 6.

xi   working hours were not declining: My conclusions provoked controversy. Some sociologists were analyzing time-use diaries, and focusing on the whole population, rather than workers, and arguing that leisure time was increasing. Others argued that hours were rising for the higher educated, but not for the lower educated. (In part my findings differed because I corrected for under- and unemployment.) I wrote about these issues in Schor (2000).

xi   Richard Nixon's 1956 promise: Blair (1956).

xi   "most people were working harder for less": This phrase was common during the campaign and was included in Clinton's inaugural address. See Berke (1992). Inaugural address at www.presidency.ucsb.edu/documents/inaugural-address-51.

xii   one of the country's most influential: Hallett, Stapleton, and Sauder (2019).

xiii   Gallup's 2024 report on the global workplace: Gallup (2024). Struggling (58 percent) and suffering (8 percent) are defined by scores on a 1–10 "life evaluation" scale.

xiii   In the United States and Canada: Ibid. U.S. and Canadian stress level is 49 percent. U.S. and Canadian engagement levels are 33 percent engaged, 51 percent not engaged, and 16 percent actively disengaged. Intention to leave (49 percent) is defined as either "actively looking for another job or watching for opportunities but not actively looking." Rates of struggling and disengagement are about 10 percent higher globally than in the United States and Canada, but stress is lower globally and active disengagement is the same.

xiii   Microsoft's 2024 global survey: Microsoft Work Lab (2024), 9.

xiii   Americans log ten or more weeks: Average annual hours data from the Conference Board (2024), Total Economy Database.

xiii government's 2021 annual economic policy guidelines: Westfall (2021). The government's guidelines do not require five days' pay for four days' work, as in our trials.

xiv Keynes predicted: Keynes originally published this essay in 1930. A recent version is Keynes (2010).

xv He got the idea: For Andrew's story and the experience at Perpetual Guardian, see his book, *The 4 Day Week* (2020). He discusses the studies on page 2. The U.K. study is discussed by Curtin (2016).

xv The results were outstanding: In addition to the book, 4 Day Week Global published a widely read white paper on the Perpetual Guardian experience: Coulthard Barnes and Perpetual Guardian (2019).

xv a reassessment of priorities: "Half of U.S. Workers Say the Pandemic Triggered a Change in Personal Priorities, While 83 Percent Say a Four-Day Work Week Would Alleviate Burnout," Eagle Hill, Nov. 11, 2021, www.eaglehillconsulting .com/news/pandemic-triggered-change-in-personal-priorities/.

xvii 245 organizations and more than eighty-seven hundred employees: These numbers include all the companies in the 4 Day Week Global trials, plus a few other companies we've been able to collect data from using the same surveys and methods. Throughout the book, unless otherwise noted, I reference the most recent data we have collected, which are current as of August 2024 and include the trials done in Anglophone countries. Data from non-English-language trials were not yet available to us at the time of writing.

xvii twelve, and twenty-four months: To keep response rates high, the three-month and final two surveys are shorter, with a subset of well-being metrics.

xviii one figure stands out: This figure is up to date as of June 2024. As more companies hit the twelve-month mark, it will likely go up as an absolute number. Of the 203 companies that had completed one year by June 2024, we have information from 197. Twenty overstates the discontinue rate a bit because it includes seven companies that never really got going with the four-day week. I discuss these findings in chapter 5.

xix Bolt and Wanderlust: Roula Amire, "Bolt's 4-Day Workweek Boosts Employee Happiness and Well-Being," Great Place to Work, May 5, 2022, www .greatplacetowork.com/resources/blog/bolt%E2%80%99s-4-day-workweek -boosts-employee-happiness-and-well-being; Mike Melillo, "A Year Ago We Dropped to a Four-Day-Work Week, Here's What Has Happened Since," Wanderlust Group, Medium, July 1, 2021, medium.com/the-wanderlust-group/a -year-ago-today-we-dropped-to-a-four-day-work-week-heres-what-has-happened -since-be9616e82e0e.

xix almost all the industries: We have a few retail organizations that have a higher than average rate of reverting to five days. However, there are only seven of them.

xx also true of 99.9 percent of U.S. businesses: Data on small businesses and their employment share are available at Small Business Data Center, U.S. Chamber of Commerce, www.uschamber.com/small-business/small-business-data-center.

xx Simpro: Simpro had an excellent experience with the four-day week and was successfully using it to recruit employees. However, soon after the trial it was taken over by a private equity firm that ended its program.

xxi Our results are consistent: In our well-being models, we test these differences and find they do not affect well-being outcomes. In our model of whether companies continue with the four-day week after one year, we test for these kinds of differences and, with a few exceptions, find they do not predict discontinuation.

xxii Christian Lindner, the German finance minister: Hetzner (2023).

xxii fifty German companies signed up: Private communication from Julia Backmann, University of Münster, lead researcher for 4 Day Week Global's German trial. As this book was going to press, findings from the German trial were released. The trial was a success, as most companies opted to continue. Results can be found here: https://www.4dayweek.com/germany-2024-pilot-results.

xxii workweek of just twenty-six hours: I calculated the average workweek in Germany in 2023 by taking total annual hours (1,342) divided by 52. Weekly hours are typically higher because Germans have many weeks of vacation. German hourly productivity ($79 US per hour in 2022) is roughly tied with France for the highest among large economies in Europe. (A few small countries such as the Nordics have higher productivity, but they also have the benefit of less diverse economies and populations.) Only the United States, with its historic post–World War II advantage, has higher productivity than Germany's. Data from the Conference Board (2024), Total Economy Database.

xxiii an amendment to the New Deal–era Fair Labor Standards Act: The act was passed in 1938 with a forty-four-hour standard workweek. It was amended in 1940 to reduce the standard workweek to forty.

xxiii productivity of the American worker: In 1950, per hour productivity was $22; in 2022, it was $83 (in constant 2021 dollars). Data from the Conference Board (2024), Total Economy Database.

Chapter 1: Two Days Is Not Enough

3 "pour from an empty cup": This and the previous two quotes are from a memo Tessa provided.

4 the "second shift": Hochschild (2012).

4 two-thirds of U.S. women workers: Bureau of Labor Statistics, *TED: The Economics Daily*, Feb. 2024, www.bls.gov/opub/ted/2024/the-share-of-workers-who-worked-full-time-year-round-rose-to-71-0-percent-in-2022.htm.

5 Think nurses or restaurant workers: Burnout rates by occupation available at "Highest Burnout Jobs: Examining Professions with the Most Burnout," Acheloa Wellness, www.acheloawellness.com/post/jobs-with-highest-burnout-rates.

6 "time crunch," "time poverty," and "overwhelm": "Time crunch" and "time poverty" are generic terms. "Overwhelm" is from Brigid Schulte (2014).

6 an additional month of work each year: From Schor (1992).

6   work time rose from 1,783 hours: Economic Policy Institute (2022). The EPI series begins in 1973. The increase from 1973 to 2016 is 204 (with some ups and downs). I haven't updated my original calculations.

7   half of households with married couples: U.S. Bureau of Labor Statistics, "Employment Characteristics of Families," news release, April 24, 2024, www.bls .gov/news.release/famee.htm.

7   a combined schedule of 3,446 hours: Sawhill and Guyot (2020), 2.

7   weekly hours of paid work were 41.2: St. Louis Fed, "Average Hours of Work per Week, Total, Household Survey for United States," FRED Economic Data, fred. stlouisfed.org/series/M08354USM310NNBR#.

7   had fallen to 38.5: The 2023 figures for all workers and full-timers is from Current Population Survey, www.bls.gov/cps/cpsaat21.htm.

7   such as those in western Europe: Annual hours figures in this paragraph and the next are all from the Conference Board (2024), Total Economy Database. These data differ from the estimates given above because they come from business establishments, rather than individual household surveys. Establishment data tend to be lower, because they don't include second jobs or hours that people work without pay, which are included in household surveys such as the Current Population Survey.

9   France and Germany: In 1950, output per hour worked (in 2021 USD) was $10 in France, $9 in Germany, and $22 in the United States. In 2022, it was $78 in France, $79 in Germany, and $83 in the United States. Data from Conference Board (2024), Total Economy Database.

9   "ideal worker norm": See Williams (2001) and Kelly et al. (2010).

9   Nancy Folbre's analysis: Folbre (2025), chap. 2, fig. 1 and table 2.1.

10   paid and unpaid work are just about equal: Addati et al. (2018), p. 56, fig. 2.8.

10   a combined 139 hours a week: Sawhill and Guyot (2020), 22.

10   a daily reduction of twenty-nine minutes: Pailhé, Solaz, and Stanfors (2021), p. 199, table 4. Men's housework increased six minutes a day.

11   childcare hours doubled: Bianchi et al. (2012), pp. 57–58, table 1. Hours increased from 7.3 to 13.7 from 1975 to 2010. See also Pailhé, Solaz, and Stanfors (2021), p. 203, table 5, who find that between 1985 and 2010, childcare time rose 45 minutes a day for female and 48 for male labor force participants.

11   Men tripled their time in childcare: Bianchi et al. (2012), pp. 57–58, table 1A. Men's hours increased from 2.4 to 7.2.

11   in conjunction with something else: See Folbre (2023).

11   less likely to use out-of-home care: Pailhé, Solaz, and Stanfors (2021), p. 188, table 1. The proportion of children 0–2 in childcare and preschool services in the United States was 28 percent in 2014. Only Italy was below the United States (24.2 percent), while France, the Netherlands, the U.K., and Sweden ranged from 33.6 percent to 55.9 percent. The United States is also below Europe for ages 3–5 (66.8 percent versus more than 90 percent).

11   "intensive mothering": The term was coined by Hays in her influential book *The Cultural Contradictions of Motherhood* (1996).

12   More than fifteen million people: The BLS estimated an increase of sixteen million temporary layoffs in April 2020. "Temporary Layoffs Remain High Following Unprecedented Surge in Early 2020," *TED: The Economics Daily,* Feb. 10, 2021, www.bls.gov/opub/ted/2021/temporary-layoffs-remain-high-following -unprecedented-surge-in-early-2020.htm.

12   suddenly relocated to their homes: U.S. Census Bureau, "The Number of People Primarily Working from Home Tripled Between 2019 and 2021," press release, Sept. 15, 2022, www.census.gov/newsroom/press-releases/2022/people-working -from-home.html.

12   42 percent of U.S. employees: Bloom (2020).

12   third shift to their day: On the "third shift" during the pandemic, see Zanhour and Sumpter (2024).

12   women exited the labor force: Lim and Zabek (2021).

12   eventually gaining 2.8 million subscribers: https://www.reddit.com/r/antiwork /comments/ol5gk3/antiwork_subreddit_stats_wow_look_since_2019/.

13   Cal Newport dubbed this moment: Newport (2023).

13   The pandemic put them over the edge: See Newport (2024), especially chap. 3.

13   a global study by Microsoft: Microsoft Work Lab (2021).

13   11 million unfilled vacancies: St. Louis Fed, "Job Openings: Total Private," FRED Economic Data, fred.stlouisfed.org/series/JTS1000JOL. A 2024 analysis argues that the unfilled vacancies series has become less reliable. See Ferguson and Storm (2024).

13   Gallup reports that in 2022: Harter (2023).

14   The Microsoft study: Microsoft Work Lab (2021). The report does not break its data down by race and ethnicity.

14   Interview studies: Zanhour and Sumpter (2024); Harry et al. (2022); Martucci (2023); Obeng, Slaughter, and Obeng-Gyasi (2022).

14   fifty-three mothers in one study: Zanhour and Sumpter (2024), 13.

14   pandemic-related burnout: Preston (2021).

14   41 percent of all Americans: Czeisler et al. (2020).

14   collapse of the boundary between work and home: Igielnik (2021).

15   traditional gender roles: Aslam and Adams (2022). See also Martucci (2023); Obeng, Slaughter, and Obeng-Gyasi (2022); and Zanhour and Sumpter (2024).

15   housecleaners were no longer on-site: Johansen (2022).

15   A McKinsey study: "The Pandemic's Gender Effect," *McKinsey Quarterly,* www .mckinsey.com/featured-insights/diversity-and-inclusion/five-fifty-the- pandemics-gender-effect.

15   difficult to balance remote and household work: Igielnik (2021).

15   existing gender and racial inequalities: Yavorsky, Qian, and Sargent (2021).

15   12 percent of respondents: Qian and Fan (2024), 4.

15   In a second paper: Fan and Qian (2023).

15   companies paid lip service: Zanhour and Sumpter (2024).

15   Hours of work plummeted: St. Louis Fed, "Average Weekly Hours of All Employees, Total Private," FRED Economic Data, fred.stlouisfed.org/series/AWHAETP.

16   people logged onto Microsoft Teams: Microsoft Work Lab (2022).

16   a marked decline in hours: Lee, Park, and Shin (2023).

16   reduction has been voluntary: Faberman, Mueller, and Şahin (2022).

16   people's attitudes to work had changed: Aratani (2021); Liu (2022).

17   how average work time changed: Fan and Moen's (2022) survey of working hours changes among remote workers in October 2020 found more stability than change in comparison to pre-pandemic hours.

17   245 organizations and eighty-seven hundred employees: Whenever I don't include a note to a source, the information comes from our own research.

18   all but a handful implemented: Some companies offered shorter days or a choice between shorter days and a four-day week. A handful started with a four-hour reduction.

18   approximately 150 questions: In 2023, we began to phase out the midpoint survey in order to improve the response rate at the end point and because three- and six-month results didn't vary by much.

21   had an alternative arrangement: In late 2003, we began surveying at a few firms that were starting their work-time reduction path with alternate Fridays off.

23   recruit some control companies: From the beginning, we tried to set up control groups whenever a large organization signed on, but for various reasons those efforts weren't successful.

23   Portuguese government–sponsored trial: Gomes and Fontinha (2024).

Chapter 2: A Life-Changing Innovation

26   A recent analysis: Fleming (2024). Phyllis Moen and her colleagues did find positive impacts of organizational and comprehensive team- or division-wide interventions they have studied, but these programs were discontinued. See their book *Overload* (Kelly and Moen 2021); Moen et al. (2011); Moen et al. (2016); and Kelly et al. (2010).

26   echoing previous findings: See Fox et al. (2022).

27   I kept seeing words: Unless otherwise noted, unattributed quotes from participants in the trials came from the comments on our surveys.

29   The "Sunday scaries": The Sunday scaries are reported to have entered the *Urban Dictionary* in 2009. See Pinsker (2020).

31   study of a custom manufacturing company: Moen and Chu (2023b). Quotation from p. 16.

36   11.5 percent are in unionized workplaces: Only 3 percent are in unions. Nine percent have unions at their workplaces, but they are not members. This could be because only part of their workforce is unionized or they have chosen not to join.

44   men did eventually take on second jobs: Hunnicutt (1992).

48   They were mostly organizations: We were also able to recruit from companies
     that contacted us directly because they were interested in our research.

51   We did this in a paper: The paper is Fan et al. (2024).

52   we added company variables too: We estimated a hierarchical linear model with
     company variables as the second level.

53   outsized jump in work ability: We had also added a "work smart" scale developed
     by Erin Kelly, our team member Phyllis Moen, and their colleagues. Work smart
     also mattered, although we didn't have a baseline measurement for it in the early
     trials. Source for work smart is here: projects.iq.harvard.edu/files/wfhn
     /files/20160126_em_measures_book.pdf?m=1453851091%20%20p%20416.

Chapter 3: Getting Five in Four

55   Revenue rose 20 percent: These results are informative, but have certain
     drawbacks. Many companies didn't report results, or reported only some. About
     half of the sample send monthly data. A second issue is that the revenue findings
     are for six months only, and many businesses are seasonal. While a majority (54
     percent) did experience revenue growth, we also found that 2 percent recorded no
     change and 44 percent registered a decline.

55   Employee retention improved: Resignations and new hire data are monthly
     averages for the six months preceding the trial and the six months of the trial.

62   fifty-five million meetings: Elise Keith, "How Many Meetings Are There per Day in
     2022? (and Should You Care?)," Lucid Meetings, blog.lucidmeetings.com/blog
     /how-many-meetings-are-there-per-day-in-2022.

62   Half of all meeting time: "Time Wasted in Meetings: 30 Meeting Statistics,"
     Golden Steps ABA, Oct. 5, 2023, www.goldenstepsaba.com/resources/time
     -wasted-in-meetings#:~:text=Meetings%20are%20a%20necessary
     %20part,that%20time%20is%20considered%20wasted.

62   A 2015 Harris poll: Marketwired, "Clarizen Survey: Workers Consider Status
     Meetings a Productivity-Killing Waste of Time," Yahoo Finance, Jan. 22, 2015,
     www.yahoo.com/finance/news/clarizen-survey-workers-consider
     -status-130000258.html.

62   His 2022 study with Otter.ai: Rogelberg (2022). Available at Otter.ai. otter.ai
     /meetings.

62   A 2023 global survey: Microsoft Work Lab (2023).

63   Management researchers at Harvard: Perlow, Hadley, and Eun (2017).

63   Interruptions lead to negative mood states: Zijlstra et al. (1999).

63   increase anxiety and depression: Rogelberg et al. (2006).

63   increase fatigue and subjective workload: Luong and Rogelberg (2005).

63   put EEG (electroencephalogram) caps on: Spataro (2020).

63   A real-world study: Kauffeld and Lehmann-Willenbrock (2012).

63   Benjamin Laker and his colleagues: Laker et al. (2022).

64   Productivity increased by 40 percent: Paul (2019).

66 Microsoft global survey: Microsoft Work Lab (2023).
67 According to one shop floor worker: Moen and Chu (2023a), 3.
68 In his book *Rest*: Pang (2016). In his subsequent book *Shorter* (2020), Pang applies these findings to companies that are reducing working hours. See especially pp. 196–210, on four-day weeks and creativity.
69 Cal Newport in his 2024 book: Newport (2024).
71 Matt says that: Quotations in this section come from Matt's podcast with the Toronto Star. See Saba Eitizaz, "What Did We Learn from the Four-Day Work Week Experiment?" This Matters, March 14, 2023, www.thestar.com/podcasts /this-matters/what-did-we-learn-from-the-four-day-work-week-experiment /article_678717ae-1002-568b-ad3e-92256eeef698.html.
71 Tyler Grange: Tyler Grange experience is from Bersin, Bersin, and O'Connor (2023), 9.
73 Our collaborators at Cambridge University: I am grateful to the Cambridge team, and David Frayne particularly, for sharing the transcripts of their interviews. All the quotations in this section came from my conversations with Sam and Ben, but some of the background is from the Cambridge team's transcripts. Write-ups of their findings can be found in Lewis et al. (2023) and Pignon, Lewis, and Mullally (2024).
76 often doing five of them at once: This example comes from an interview done by David Frayne.
78 two questions: The questions came from Q49 of the sixth European Working Conditions Survey, www.eurofound.europa.eu/en/surveys/european-working -conditions-surveys-ewcs.

Chapter 4: When Less Is More
93 reduced nurses' shifts in the Svartedalens retirement home: Lorentzon (2017).
96 epidemic level before the pandemic: Wei et al. (2022).
96 a third (31.5 percent) of nurses: Shah et al. (2023).
96 one study of East Coast nurses: Wei et al. (2022).
96 American Nurses Association's 2023 annual survey: American Nurses Foundation (2023), 5.
96 the Glebe in Virginia: Regan (2018).
96 a waiting list for this position: McKnights.com (2018).
96 Capri Communities in Wisconsin: Andrews (2023).
96 mental health counseling provider 4C Health: Announcement on its website at www.4chealthin.org/news-events/4c-health-announces-4-day-32-hour-work -week.
97 Temple University Hospital: Venditti, Cottrell, and Hanson (2023).
99 Heather used a range of $132,000–$228,000: Heather's assumptions were from Lyle-Edrosolo (2023).
103 great evidence from a local U.K. government: Pink, Kamerade, and Burchell (2024).

103 local (Conservative) MP: The former MP is Anthony Browne. "MP Criticises South Cambridgeshire Council's Four-Day Week Plans," BBC, Sept. 8, 2022, www.bbc .com/news/uk-england-cambridgeshire-62833023.

112 Studies of stock market returns: Dellavigna and Pollet (2009).

113 Responses to business surveys: Hennrich and Wohlrabe (2024).

113 A classic paper on munitions workers: Pencavel (2015).

113 data from a Dutch call center: Collewet and Sauermann (2017).

113 A Belgian study: Delmez and Vandenberghe (2018).

113 Alison Booth and Martin Ravallion cite empirical evidence: Booth and Ravallion (1993), 430. See also Calvasina and Boxx (1975).

113 National Industrial Conference Board: National Industrial Conference Board Report (1929), p. 41, table 9.

114 When the French workweek: Bosch and Lehndorff (2001), 223.

114 One review of the economic impacts: Ibid.

114 white-collar, service sector settings: Ibid., 224.

114 the cost of work-time reduction: Ibid., 231, quoting Cette and Taddei.

119 economy-wide measure of the cost of job loss: Schor and Bowles (1987).

119 connection to wage growth: Schor (1985).

119 Jerry Epstein and I even used it: Epstein and Schor (1990).

119 a rare dataset from the U.K.: Schor (1988).

Chapter 5: Challenges, False Starts, Pauses, and Failures

130 consume a fifth of all toilet paper: Skene (2019), 3.

133 "a privilege, not a right": Pignon, Lewis, and Mullally (2024), 34–35.

134 "trust cultures": From O'Connor's presentation at the Society for the Advancement of Socio-Economics Annual Meeting, mini-conference on work-time reduction, Limerick, June 2024.

138 dissertation research at Harvard Business School: Yen (2023).

141 it will lower wage growth going forward: I am grateful to Malcolm Bidwell for raising this point.

143 trade income for time: It's important to distinguish an individual who works four days in a five-day-a-week company and company-wide conversions to four. Typically, the former will have to take lower wages. When a whole company shifts, it is possible to reap much higher productivity gains because of the collaborative nature of work.

143 Mismatches between desired and actual hours: Reynolds and McKinzie (2019).

Chapter 6: Will AI Give Us a Four-Day Week?

145 the Writers Guild of America organized a strike: Anguiano and Beckett (2023).

148 Voth discovered that: Voth (1998). Adjusting for compositional change due to the decline in agricultural work reduces this increase to either 585 or 738, depending on assumptions.

148 But E. P. Thompson: Thompson (1967).

148 "When the framework knitters": Ibid., 72.

152 one of his slides: My fellow panelist was Robert Seamans, from New York University, a leading economist on the impact of AI on the labor market. Slide provided to author.

152 the balance among three effects: Acemoglu and Restrepo (2019).

152 David Autor reflected the shift: Autor (2022). Since he wrote that paper, Autor's views have become more optimistic.

152 2017 poll of leading U.S. economists: "Robots and Artificial Intelligence," Kent A. Clark Center for Global Markets, Chicago Booth, Sept. 12, 2017, www .kentclarkcenter.org/surveys/robots-and-artificial-intelligence-2/.

153 Tracking the installation of robots: Acemoglu and Restrepo (2020a). See also Acemoglu and Restrepo (2020b) and Acemoglu et al. (2022).

153 that 47 percent of U.S. employment: Frey and Osborne (2017).

153 A McKinsey report estimated: Bughin et al. (2017), p. 38, exhibit 9.

153 AI pioneers have been warning: Roose (2023).

153 An AI-powered search: De Vries (2023), 2191.

154 the consensus figure for annual hours: Huberman (2004). Huberman makes the point that earlier estimates by Angus Maddison incorrectly assumed all countries were at 3,000 hours in 1870. Huberman's calculations, in table 6, show a high of 3,483 in Belgium to a low of 2,755 in Great Britain. However, 3,000 is reasonable as a round number given that Huberman's averages for the Old and New World are 3,191 and 2,911, respectively.

155 American hours were lower: Ibid., table 6. Great Britain and Spain had significantly lower hours than the United States. Subsequently, some European countries began to reduce hours more rapidly than the United States.

155 all had longer hours: Conference Board (2024), Total Economy Database.

155 As one influential paper: Alesina, Glaeser, and Sacerdote (2005). High taxes are assumed to reduce the supply of labor. That's why Alesina and colleagues' paper was a challenge to standard economic models: It found that taxes didn't explain the differences.

156 "tied wage-hours" offers: Altonji and Paxson (1988).

157 44 percent of U.S. employees: Hourly workers are 55.6 percent; salaried are 44.4 percent. Data from U.S. Bureau of Labor Statistics, "Characteristics of Minimum Wage Workers, 2022," BLS Reports, Aug. 2023, www.bls.gov/opub/reports /minimum-wage/2022/home.htm.

157 the growth of inequality: Bowles and Park (2005); Oh, Park, and Bowles (2012).

158 three to four times that amount: These are my calculations from the TED data, from 1973 to 2019. The U.K. has taken only 13 percent and is a bit of an outlier. Germany, the Netherlands, Italy, and France have taken between 25 and 38 percent.

158 Daron Acemoglu and Simon Johnson: Acemoglu and Johnson (2023), 13.

158 Our U.K. collaborators: Garcia, Kikuchi, and Stronge (2023b), 6. This analysis is based on a 1.5 percent annual increase, BLS employment projections, and Felten,

Raj, and Seamans's (2021) AI exposure calculations, based on O*NET data. A similar analysis for Great Britain (Garcia, Kikuchi, and Stronge [2023a]), 6, finds that 88 percent could have a 10 percent work-time reduction and 28 percent could transition to the four-day week.

160 the first reported system of "clocking in": Thompson (1967), 83.

Chapter 7: Powering Down for People and Planet

162 an increase in speeding on the roads: "Speeding and Speed Management," National Highway and Traffic Safety Administration, www.nhtsa.gov/book /countermeasures-that-work/speeding-and-speed-management.

163 "the Great Acceleration": McNeill (2014).

163 nine planetary boundaries: Richardson et al. (2023).

164 Climate destabilization: The National Climate Assessment is an excellent source for climate information. See nca2023.globalchange.gov/.

164 a special report: Masson-Delmotte et al. (2018).

164 a whopping 427 parts per million: "Carbon Dioxide," NASA, climate.nasa.gov /vital-signs/carbon-dioxide/?intent=121.

165 We need about seven times: PricewaterhouseCoopers (2023).

165 Globally the current average: "Per Capita Greenhouse Gas Emissions," Our World in Data, April 8, 2024, ourworldindata.org/grapher/per-capita-ghg -emissions?tab=table.

165 We need to get to 5 tons: Kharas, Fengler, and Vashold (2023).

165 the rate of decarbonization: I focus on carbon emissions, rather than all greenhouse gases, because they are the largest category, and they're most closely related to overall activity, rather than to specific kinds of production.

166 That has been the experience of wealthy countries: Haberl et al. (2020).

166 GDP growth has been hovering: OECD, "Economic Outlook: Steady Global Growth Expected for 2024 and 2025," press release, May 2, 2024, www.oecd.org /en/about/news/press-releases/2024/05/economic-outlook-steady-global-growth -expected-for-2024-and-2025.html.

166 "consumption is oriented": A brief description of the low-consumption scenario (SSP1) is given here: sos.noaa.gov/catalog/datasets/climate-model-surface -temperature-change-ssp1-sustainability-2015-2100/.

166 IPCC raised the issue: Shukla et al. (2022), 263.

167 I published my first paper: Schor (1991).

167 I began modeling the connection: Knight, Rosa, and Schor (2013).

168 the richest 10 percent of the global population: Chancel (2022).

169 A California study: Ho and Stewart (1992), p. 1346, tables 2 and 3. A speculative study by King and van den Burgh (2017) on five types of working time reduction estimated a 15 percent reduction in GHGs for a 17.5 percent working time reduction. They found that increased vacation time and shorter working days were less beneficial in terms of emissions reductions than the four-day week.

169 A widely publicized experiment in Utah: Percoco (2018).

170 10 percent less energy use: Davis (2023).

170 household electricity use went up: Cicala (2023).

173 One of the best studies: Nässén and Larsson (2015).

174 The most popular activities: For an analysis of the carbon intensity of household activities in the U.K., see Druckman et al. (2012).

176 longer hours are associated: This relationship has been shown by Knight, Rosa, and Schor (2013); Fitzgerald, Jorgenson, and Clark (2015); and others. Contrary findings are from Shao and Rodriguez-Labajos (2016).

176 found that it holds across states: Fitzgerald, Schor, and Jorgenson (2018).

176 A recent European one: Cieplinski, D'Alessandro, and Guarnieri (2021).

177 the link between hours and emissions: Fitzgerald (2022).

177 the three richest men: Collins and Hoxie (2017), 2.

177 top 1 percent of Americans: Congressional Budget Office (2022).

178 Julia Steinberger and her colleagues: O'Neill et al. (2018).

Chapter 8: Achieving Four for Everyone

179 A GOP witness: The witness was Liberty Vittert. She claimed that Japanese GDP fell by 20 percent when the workweek was reduced from forty-eight to forty hours, which is preposterous. (Japanese GDP rose over that period.) She also said causality can be shown only in a lab setting, which is false. (There was a recent Nobel Prize awarded for real-world ways of establishing causality.) She did have one valid point, which is that the results I was presenting at that time lacked controls, an issue I discuss in chapter 1. We now have those results, and they support our conclusions. The hearing can be seen here: www.help.senate. gov/hearings/workers-should-benefit-from-new-technology-and-increased-productivity-the-need-for-a-32-hour-work-week-with-no-loss-in-pay.

180 people prefer a four-day week: Here is a sampling of polls; most reference four ten-hour days. *Newsweek*, April 2024, 63 percent overall, varies by generation. Aliss Higham, "Millennials Are Ready for a Four-Day Week," *Newsweek*, April 22, 2024, www.newsweek.com/millennials-ready-four-day-work-week-1892191 (data tables available here: redfieldandwiltonstrategies.com/media-research/).
Qualtrics: February 2022, 92 percent support. "The Numbers Behind Four-Day Work Weeks and Paid Mental Health Days," Qualtrics, February 24, 2022, www .qualtrics.com/blog/four-day-work-week/.
Bankrate: July 2023, 89 percent support. Lane Gillespie, "Survey: 89% of American Workforce Prefer 4-Day Workweeks, Remote Work, or Hybrid Work," Bankrate, Aug. 23, 2023, www.bankrate.com/personal-finance/hybrid-remote-and-4-day -workweek-survey/#support-for-4-day-workweek.
Morning Consult: August 2023, 87 percent support (so long as remote work is not taken away). Jennifer Liu, "Workers Overwhelmingly Want a 4-Day Workweek—on One Condition," CNBC Make It, Aug. 22, 2023, www.cnbc .com/2023/08/22/workers-overwhelmingly-want-a-4-day-workweekon-one -condition.html.

180 Three-quarters or more: The Qualtrics survey finds 74 percent: "Numbers Behind Four-Day Work Weeks and Paid Mental Health Days." Eighty-two percent said it would make them more productive. In the *Newsweek* poll, 46 percent said they would be "more productive," and 23 percent said they'd be "as productive." See Higham, "Millennials Are Ready for a Four-Day Week."

180 "how many hours a week": "41% of U.S. Workers Say They Are Most Productive Outside of 9–5 Work Hours, According to Research from Fiverr," Fiverr, Sept. 20, 2023, www.fiverr.com/news/workstyle-research.

180 A 2024 KPMG survey: "KPMG Study: CEOs Tackling Risks to Growth Including Geopolitics, Cyber, and Structural Changes Such as Tight Labor Market, New Regulations," KPMG, April 11, 2024, kpmg.com/us/en/media/news/us-ceo -outlook-pulse-survey-2024.html.

181 the normal workweek: Author's calculation from National Industrial Conference Board (1929), p. 11, table 1.

181 how did the five-day week come about?: I am grateful to Professor Ezra Zuckerman for generously sharing his sources and findings on the five-day week. His assistance was invaluable.

181 "in the short space": National Industrial Conference Board (1929), 7.

181 Henry Feuerstein: The Feuerstein family made headlines in the 1990s when their civic-mindedness was again on display. After a devastating fire, the CEO, Aaron Feuerstein, protected all his workers and rebuilt the factory. Sadly, the company went bankrupt, unable to compete with low-cost foreign labor.

181 A Jewish Sabbatarian movement: Hunnicutt (1979).

182 New York department stores: De Vyver (1930), 224.

182 a majority of firms: Ibid., 225, quoting a BLS report.

182 give workers more free time: National Industrial Conference Board (1929), chap. 3.

182 Productivity findings: Ibid., p. 41, table 9.

183 "Days off are not given": Feiss (1920).

183 Barnes required his employees: Coulthard Barnes and Perpetual Guardian (2019). The contract is included as app. B.

183 Amalgamated Clothing Workers of America: De Vyver (1930).

184 Edsel Ford originally signaled: Special to the *New York Times* (1922).

184 "the 30-hour week": Hunnicutt (1988), 147. My discussion of the 1930s relies on Hunnicutt's pathbreaking account.

185 a net twenty-eight million jobs: Author's calculations from BLS, Employees on nonfarm payrolls. Historical data available here: www.bls.gov/webapps/legacy /cesbtab1.htm.

185 The fraction of the population: The fraction of the population of working age fell from 67.3 percent in 2007 to 64.8 percent in 2022. From OECD Data Explorer, data-explorer.oecd.org/ vis?lc=en&pg=0&snb=1&vw=tb&df[ds]=dsDisseminateFinalDMZ&df[id]=DSD _POPULATION%40DF_POP_HIST&df[ag]=OECD.ELS.SAE&df[vs]=&pd=2007 %2C2022&dq=USA.POP.PT_POP._T.Y15T64.&to[TIME_PERIOD]=false.

185 fell to a historic low: CDC National Center for Health Statistics, "U.S. Fertility Rate Drops to Another Historic Low," press release, April 25, 2024, www.cdc.gov /nchs/pressroom/nchs_press_releases/2024/20240525.htm. The current rate is 1.66, considerably below replacement. U.S. population growth is at 0.4 percent a year: "Population Growth (Annual %)—United States," World Bank Group, data .worldbank.org/indicator/SP.POP.GROW?locations=US.

186 "mass disabling event": Bonuck et al. (2024). Estimates from the Census Bureau in 2022 suggest up to four million were kept out of work by long COVID (Bach 2022), but that number is likely lower now.

186 nation's labor force participation rate: St. Louis Fed, "Labor Force Participation Rate," FRED Economic Data, fred.stlouisfed.org/series/CIVPART.

186 Bureau of Labor Statistics projects: Dubina (2023).

187 The results were predictable: Abril (2023).

187 Gallup–Bentley University report: "2024 Bentley-Gallup Business in Society Report," p. 30, figure 13, www.gallup.com/analytics/512066/bentley-business-in-society.aspx.

187 childcare responsibilities: On the higher incidence of parents with children at home working four days, see Hamermesh and Biddle (2023), 12.

187 A review of research: Bolino, Kelemen, and Matthews (2021), p. 192, table 2.

188 suffer a sleep deficit: Di et al. (2022).

188 "recovery" sleep doesn't reverse: Depner et al. (2019).

188 The Belgian government: Hurst (2022). The law requires employees to ask for this schedule and employers can refuse for compelling reasons.

188 researched trends in days worked: Hamermesh and Biddle (2023), 7.

189 A piece about Fridays: Krueger (2022).

189 ClassPass: "2023 ClassPass Look Back Report," ClassPass, Dec. 13, 2023, classpass.com/blog/2023-classpass-look-back-report/. ClassPass finding originally reported by Vanessa Fuhrmans of *The Wall Street Journal*.

189 one study found that 55 percent: Gartner, "More Than Half of Organizations Are Offering 'Summer Fridays' This Year, According to Gartner," press release, June 6, 2019, www.gartner.com/en/newsroom/press-releases/2019-06-06-more-than -half-of-organizations-are-offering--summer-.

190 That number has fallen: Sahadi (2024).

190 most common work-from-home day: Barrero et al (2024), 23.

190 Nicholas Bloom and colleagues' research: Bloom, Han, and Liang (2024).

190 A study of computer performance: Roh et al. (2023).

190 Microsoft Teams data: Microsoft Work Lab (n.d.).

190 large increase in Wednesday golfing: Finan and Bloom (2023).

190 difficulties staying productive: Jennings (2024), reporting that 54 percent of knowledge workers in a Quickbase survey said it's "harder than ever to be productive in day-to-day work."

191 Spanish were the first to act: Kassam (2021).

191 Scottish government organized a pilot: The Scottish trial has been slow to enroll companies.

191 The Belgians: The Belgian pilot has also had a slow start, with a small number of companies participating (personal communication with Damaris Castro, researcher for the pilot).

191 Spanish government announced its intention: European Public Service Union (2024a).

191 movement in eastern Europe: European Public Service Union (2024b).

192 activity at state and local levels: WorkFour maintains a listing of federal, state, and local efforts at workfour.org/policy-developments.

192 The city of Golden: Detailed information on Golden's experience is at "The Best for Golden," City of Golden, www.guidinggolden.com/the-best-for-golden.

193 without squeezing profits: There is an additional issue with manufacturing, which is that it faces strong global competition. This may make it necessary to use productivity growth to reduce prices rather than channel that added value to workers or to profits. This is a larger problem, however, that requires other interventions.

195 Cohen reports: Burton (2024).

Conclusion

197 Heat waves are killing: Dash and Mehta (2024).

197 Dead howler monkeys: Stevenson (2024).

197 birds are dropping in Delhi: Chauhan (2023).

Appendix

209 collaborated with local researchers: The local teams did great work collecting qualitative data. The U.K. data collection was coordinated by Brendan Burchell at Cambridge University. It was a large and complex effort due to the size of the trial. Their findings are included in the first U.K. report (Lewis et al. [2023]). They also did one-year follow-up interviews, which are included in a second report (Pignon, Lewis, and Mullally [2024]). The South African team was coordinated by Mark Smith at Stellenbosch Business School. Their findings are included in the report from that trial (4 Day Week Global [2023]), which is available on the 4 Day Week Global website at www.4dayweek.com/sa-2023-pilot-results. Our U.S. team has also been interviewing, but we have not yet completed data collection.

REFERENCES

Abril, Danielle. 2023. "Workers Want a Four-Day Week. Why Hasn't It Happened?" *Washington Post*, May 24.

Acemoglu, Daron, et al. 2022. "Artificial Intelligence and Jobs: Evidence from Online Vacancies." *Journal of Labor Economics* 40 (S1): S293–340. doi.org/10.1086/718327.

Acemoglu, Daron, and Simon Johnson. 2023. *Power and Progress: Our Thousand-Year Struggle over Technology and Prosperity*. New York: PublicAffairs.

Acemoglu, Daron, and Pascual Restrepo. 2019. "Automation and New Tasks: How Technology Displaces and Reinstates Labor." *Journal of Economic Perspectives* 33 (2): 3–30. doi.org/10.1257/jep.33.2.3.

———. 2020a. "Robots and Jobs: Evidence from US Labor Markets." *Journal of Political Economy* 128 (6): 2188–244.

———. 2020b. "The Wrong Kind of AI? Artificial Intelligence and the Future of Labour Demand." *Cambridge Journal of Regions, Economy, and Society* 13 (1): 25–35. doi.org/10.1093/cjres/rsz022.

Addati, Laura, et al. 2018. *Care Work and Care Jobs for the Future of Decent Work*. Geneva: International Labour Office.

Alesina, Alberto, Edward Glaeser, and Bruce Sacerdote. 2005. "Work and Leisure in the United States and Europe: Why So Different?" *NBER Macroeconomics Annual*, 1–64.

Altonji, Joseph G., and Christina H. Paxson. 1988. "Labor Supply Preferences, Hours Constraints, and Hours-Wage Trade-Offs." *Journal of Labor Economics* 6 (2): 254–76.

American Nurses Foundation. 2023. "Annual Assessment Survey— the Third Year." Pulse on the Nation's Nurses. American Nurses Foundation. www.nursingworld.org/~48fb88/contentassets /23d4f79cea6b4f67ae24714de11783e9/anf-impact-assessment-third -year_v5.pdf.

Andrews, Nick. 2023. "Capri Communities Tests 4-Day Work Week with Promising Early Results." *Senior Housing News*, Jan. 31. seniorhousingnews.com/2023/01/31/capri-communities-tests-4-day-work-week-with-promising-early-results/.

Anguiano, Dani, and Lois Beckett. 2023. "How Hollywood Writers Triumphed over AI—and Why It Matters." *Guardian*, October 1. www.theguardian.com/culture/2023/oct/01/hollywood-writers-strike-artificial-intelligence.

Aratani, Lauren. 2021. "Goodbye to the Job: How the Pandemic Changed Americans' Attitude to Work." *Guardian*, November 28. www.theguardian.com/money/2021/nov/28/goodbye-to-job-how-the-pandemic-changed-americans-attitude-to-work.

Aslam, Awish, and Tracey L. Adams. 2022. "'The Workload Is Staggering': Changing Working Conditions of Stay-at-Home Mothers Under COVID-19 Lockdowns." *Gender, Work, and Organization* 29 (6): 1764–78. doi.org/10.1111/gwao.12870.

Autor, David. 2022. "The Labor Market Impacts of Technological Change: From Unbridled Enthusiasm to Qualified Optimism to Vast Uncertainty." NBER Working Paper no. 30074, July. doi.org/10.3386/w30074.

Bach, Katie. 2022. "New Data Shows Long Covid Is Keeping as Many as 4 Million People out of Work." Washington, D.C.: Brookings. www.brookings.edu/articles/new-data-shows-long-covid-is-keeping-as-many-as-4-million-people-out-of-work/.

Barnes, Andrew. 2020. *The 4 Day Week: How the Flexible Work Revolution Can Increase Productivity, Profitability, and Well-Being, and Create a Sustainable Future*. With Stephanie Jones. London: Piatkus.

Barrero, José María, et al. 2024. "SWAA April 2024 Updates." WFH Research. Palo Alto, Calif.: Stanford University. wfhresearch.com/wp-content/uploads/2024/04/WFHResearch_updates_April2024.pdf.

BBC. 2022. "MP Criticises South Cambridgeshire Council's Four-Day Week Plans." *BBC News*, Sept. 8. www.bbc.com/news/uk-england-cambridgeshire-62833023.

Berke, Richard L. 1992. "The 1992 Campaign: The Ad Campaign; Clinton: Criticizing the President." *New York Times*, September 21. www.nytimes.com/1992/09/21/us/the-1992-campaign-the-ad-campaign-clinton-criticizing-the-president.html.

Bersin, Josh, Julia Bersin, and Joe O'Connor. 2023. "The Four-Day Work Week: Learnings from Companies at the Forefront of Work-Time Reduction." Toronto: Josh Bersin Company. joshbersin.com/the-four-day-work-week/.

Bianchi, Suzanne M., et al. 2012. "Housework: Who Did, Does, or Will Do It, and How Much Does It Matter?" *Social Forces* 91 (1): 55–63. doi .org/10.1093/sf/sos120.

Blair, William M. 1956. "Nixon Foresees 4-Day Work Week." *New York Times*, September 22. timesmachine.nytimes.com /timesmachine/1956/09/23/95810374.html?pageNumber=1.

Bloom, Nicholas. 2020. "How Working from Home Works Out." Stanford Institute for Policy Research, June. siepr.stanford.edu/publications /policy-brief/how-working-home-works-out.

Bloom, Nicholas, Ruobing Han, and James Liang. 2024. "Hybrid Working from Home Improves Retention Without Damaging Performance." *Nature*, June. doi.org/10.1038/s41586-024-07500-2.

Bolino, Mark C., Thomas K. Kelemen, and Samuel H. Matthews. 2021. "Working 9-to-5? A Review of Research on Nonstandard Work Schedules." *Journal of Organizational Behavior* 42 (2): 188–211. doi .org/10.1002/job.2440.

Bonuck, Karen, et al. 2024. "Long COVID Disability Burden in US Adults: YLDs and NIH Funding Relative to Other Conditions." medRxiv, January 10. doi.org/10.1101/2024.01.09.24301057.

Booth, Allison, and Martin Ravallion. 1993. "Employment and Length of the Working Week in a Unionized Economy in Which Hours of Work Influence Productivity." *Economic Record* 69 (207): 428–36.

Bosch, Gerhard, and Steffen Lehndorff. 2001. "Working-Time Reduction and Employment: Experiences in Europe and Economic Policy Recommendations." *Cambridge Journal of Economics* 25 (2): 209–43.

Bowles, Samuel, and Yongjin Park. 2005. "Emulation, Inequality, and Work Hours: Was Thorsten Veblen Right?" *Economic Journal* 115 (507): F397–412. doi.org/10.1111/j.1468-0297.2005.01042.x.

Bughin, Jacques, et al. 2017. "Artificial Intelligence: The Next Digital Frontier?" Discussion Paper. McKinsey Global Institute.

Burton, Katherine. 2024. "Billionaire Steve Cohen Sees Four-Day Work Week Coming." *Bloomberg News*, April 3. www.bloomberg.com/news /articles/2024-04-03/billionaire-steve-cohen-sees-four-day-work -week-coming.

Calvasina, Eugene J., and W. Randy Boxx. 1975. "Efficiency of Workers on the Four-Day Workweek." *Academy of Management Journal* 18 (3): 604–10.

Chancel, Lucas. 2022. "Global Carbon Inequality over 1990–2019." *Nature Sustainability* 5 (11): 931–38. doi.org/10.1038/s41893-022-00955-z.

Chauhan, Rohan. 2023. "Delhi Too Hot for Animals." *Patriot*, June 6. thepatriot.in/environment/delhi-too-hot-for-animals-36825.

Cicala, Steve. 2023. "JUE Insight: Powering Work from Home." *Journal of Urban Economics* 133:103474.

Cieplinski, André, Simone D'Alessandro, and Pietro Guarnieri. 2021. "Environmental Impacts of Productivity-Led Working Time Reduction." *Ecological Economics* 179 (Jan.): 106822. doi.org/10.1016/j.ecolecon.2020.106822.

Collewet, Marion, and Jan Sauermann. 2017. "Working Hours and Productivity." *Labour Economics* 47 (Aug.): 96–106. doi.org/10.1016/j.labeco.2017.03.006.

Collins, Chuck, and Josh Hoxie. 2017. "Billionaire Bonanza: The Forbes 400 and the Rest of Us." Washington, D.C.: Institute for Policy Studies. ips-dc.org/billionaire-bonanza/.

Conference Board. 2024. Total Economy Database (TED). data-central. conference-board.org/.

Congressional Budget Office. 2022. *Trends in the Distribution of Family Wealth, 1989 to 2019*. Washington, D.C.: Congressional Budget Office. www.cbo.gov/publication/57598.

Coulthard Barnes and Perpetual Guardian. 2019. "Guidelines for an Outcome-Based Trial—Raising Productivity and Engagement." White paper. Auckland: Perpetual Guardian, University of Auckland, Auckland University of Technology, and MinterEllisonRuddWatts. www.4dayweek.com/access-white-paper.

Curtin, Melanie. 2016. "In an 8-Hour Day, the Average Worker Is Productive for This Many Hours." *Inc.*, July 16. www.inc.com/melanie-curtin/in-an-8-hour-day-the-average-worker-is-productive-for-this-many-hours.html.

Czeisler, Mark É., et al. 2020. "Mental Health, Substance Use, and Suicidal Ideation During the COVID-19 Pandemic—United States, June 24–30." *Morbidity and Mortality Weekly Report*, August 14. www.cdc.gov/mmwr/volumes/69/wr/mm6932a1.htm.

Dash, Jatindra, and Tanvi Mehta. 2024. "Indian Heatwave Kills Dozens over Summer, Media Says Nearly 25,000 Fall Ill." Reuters, June 3. www.reuters.com/world/india/heat-wave-kills-least-56-india-nearly-25000-heat-stroke-cases-march-may-2024-06-03/.

Davis, Lucas. 2023. "Weekends Are No Free Lunch Anymore." *Energy Institute Blog*, Sept. 5. energyathaas.wordpress.com/2023/09/05/weekends-are-no-free-lunch-anymore/.

Dellavigna, Stefano, and Joshua M. Pollet. 2009. "Investor Inattention and Friday Earnings Announcements." *Journal of Finance* 64 (2): 709–49. doi.org/10.1111/j.1540-6261.2009.01447.x.

Delmez, Francoise, and Vincent Vandenberghe. 2018. "Long Working Hours Make Us Less Productive but Also Less Costly." *Labour* 32 (4): 259–87. doi.org/10.1111/labr.12128.

Depner, Christopher M., et al. 2019. "*Ad Libitum* Weekend Recovery Sleep Fails to Prevent Metabolic Dysregulation During a Repeating Pattern of Insufficient Sleep and Weekend Recovery Sleep." *Current Biology* 29 (6): 957–67.e4. doi.org/10.1016/j.cub.2019.01.069.

De Vries, Alex. 2023. "The Growing Energy Footprint of Artificial Intelligence." *Joule* 7 (10): 2191–94. doi.org/10.1016/j.joule.2023.09.004.

De Vyver, Frank T. 1930. "The Five-Day Week." *Current History (1916–1940)* 33 (2): 223–27.

Di, Hongkun, et al. 2022. "Evaluation of Sleep Habits and Disturbances Among US Adults, 2017–2020." *JAMA Network Open* 5 (11): e2240788. doi.org/10.1001/jamanetworkopen.2022.40788.

Druckman, Angela, et al. 2012. "Time, Gender, and Carbon: A Study of the Carbon Implications of British Adults' Use of Time." *Ecological Economics* 84 (Dec.): 153–63. doi.org/10.1016/j.ecolecon.2012.09.008.

Dubina, Kevin S. 2023. "Labor Force and Macroeconomic Projections Overview and Highlights, 2022–32." *Monthly Labor Review*, Sept. doi.org/10.21916/mlr.2023.21.

Economic Policy Institute. 2022. "Annual Hours of Work." State of Working America Data Library. www.epi.org/data/#?subject=hours.

Epstein, Gerald, and Juliet B. Schor. 1990. "Corporate Profitability as a Determinant of Restrictive Monetary Policy: Estimates for the Postwar United States." In *The Political Economy of American Monetary Policy*, edited by Thomas Mayer, 51–64. Cambridge, U.K.: Cambridge University Press.

European Public Service Union. 2024a. "Reducing Working Time Case Studies: Spain and Portugal." Brussels: European Public Service Union. www.epsu.org/sites/default/files/article/files/04%20-%20SPAIN%20AND%20PORTUGAL.pdf.

———. 2024b. "Reducing Working Time Case Studies: Poland, Czechia, Slovakia, and Hungary." Brussels: European Public Service Union. www.epsu.org/sites/default/files/article/files/06%20-%20Poland%2C%20Czechia%2C%20Slovakia%20and%20Hungary.pdf.

Faberman, R. Jason, Andreas I. Mueller, and Ayşegül Şahin. 2022. "Has the Willingness to Work Fallen During the Covid Pandemic?" *Labour Economics* 79 (Dec.): 102275. doi.org/10.1016/j.labeco.2022.102275.

Fan, Wen, and Phyllis Moen. 2022. "Working More, Less, or the Same During COVID-19? A Mixed Method, Intersectional Analysis of Remote Workers." *Work and Occupations* 49 (2): 143–86. doi.org/10.1177/07308884211047208.

Fan, Wen, and Yue Qian. 2023. "State Contexts, Job Insecurity, and Subjective Well-Being in the Time of COVID-19." *Journal of Happiness Studies* 24 (6): 2039–59. doi.org/10.1007/s10902-023-00669-9.

Fan, Wen, et al. 2024. "Does Work Time Reduction Improve Workers' Well-Being? Evidence from Global Four-Day Workweek Trials." Preprint. SocArXiv. doi.org/10.31235/osf.io/7ucy9.

Feiss, Richard A. 1920. "Why It Paid Us to Adopt the Five-Day Week." *Factory: The Magazine of Management* 25 (4): 523–26.

Felten, Edward, Manav Raj, and Robert Seamans. 2021. "Occupational, Industry, and Geographic Exposure to Artificial Intelligence: A Novel Dataset and Its Potential Uses." *Strategic Management Journal* 41 (12): 2195–217.

Ferguson, Thomas, and Servaas Storm. 2024. "A New Era of Endless Labor Shortages? A Critical Analysis of McKinsey's New Report." Institute for New Economic Thinking, July 15. www.ineteconomics.org/perspectives/blog/a-new-era-of-endless-labor-shortages-a-critical-analysis-of-mckinseys-new-report.

Finan, Alex, and Nick Bloom. 2023. "How Working from Home Boosted Golf." March. Palo Alto, Calif.: Stanford University. nbloom.people.stanford.edu/sites/g/files/sbiybj24291/files/media/file/golfingfromhome.pdf.

Fitzgerald, Jared B. 2022. "Working Time, Inequality, and Carbon Emissions in the United States: A Multi-Dividend Approach to Climate Change Mitigation." *Energy Research and Social Science* 84 (Feb.): 102385. doi.org/10.1016/j.erss.2021.102385.

Fitzgerald, Jared B., Andrew K. Jorgenson, and Brett Clark. 2015. "Energy Consumption and Working Hours: A Longitudinal Study of Developed and Developing Nations, 1990–2008." *Environmental Sociology* 1 (3): 213–23. doi.org/10.1080/23251042.2015.1046584.

Fitzgerald, Jared B., Juliet B. Schor, and Andrew K. Jorgenson. 2018. "Working Hours and Carbon Dioxide Emissions in the United States, 2007–2013." *Social Forces* 96 (4): 1851–74. doi.org/10.1093/sf/soy014.

Fleming, William J. 2024. "Employee Well-Being Outcomes from Individual-Level Mental Health Interventions: Cross-Sectional Evidence from the United Kingdom." *Industrial Relations Journal* 55 (2): 162–82. doi.org/10.1111/irj.12418.

Folbre, Nancy. 2023. "The Responsibilities of Parental Childcare: Evidence from the American Time Use Survey." Unpublished manuscript. University of Massachusetts.

———. 2025. *Accounting for Care.* Berkeley: University of California Press.

4 Day Week Global. 2023. Research Results. www.4dayweek.com /research.

Fox, Kimberly, et al. 2022. "Organisational- and Group-Level Workplace Interventions and Their Effect on Multiple Domains of Worker Well-Being: A Systematic Review." *Work and Stress* 36 (1): 30–59. doi.org/10 .1080/02678373.2021.1969476.

Frey, Carl Benedikt, and Michael A. Osborne. 2017. "The Future of Employment: How Susceptible Are Jobs to Computerisation?" *Technological Forecasting and Social Change* 114 (Jan.): 254–80. doi .org/10.1016/j.techfore.2016.08.019.

Gallup. 2022. "State of the Global Workplace: 2022 Report." Washington, D.C.: Gallup.

———. 2023. "State of the Global Workplace: 2023 Report." Washington, D.C.: Gallup.

———. 2024. "State of the Global Workplace: 2024 Report." Washington, D.C.: Gallup. www.gallup.com/workplace/349484/state-of-the-global -workplace.aspx.

Garcia, Luiz, Lukas Kikuchi, and Will Stronge. 2023a. "GPT-4 (Day Week): Great Britain Edition." London: Autonomy Institute. autonomy.work /portfolio/gpt-4-day-week-gb-edition/.

———. 2023b. "GPT-4 (Day Week): U.S. Edition." London: Autonomy Institute. autonomy.work/portfolio/gpt-4-day-week-us/.

Gomes, Pedro. 2021. *Friday Is the New Saturday: How a Four-Day Week Can Save Capitalism.* London: Flint.

Gomes, Pedro, and Rita Fontinha. 2024. "Four-Day Week: Results from Portuguese Trial." Policy Commons, July 17. policycommons.net /artifacts/13373666/portugal20420day20week20pilot20results20 -20420day20week20global/14271453/.

Haberl, Helmut, et al. 2020. "A Systematic Review of the Evidence on Decoupling of GDP, Resource Use, and GHG Emissions, Part II: Synthesizing the Insights." *Environmental Research Letters* 15 (6): 065003. doi.org/10.1088/1748-9326/ab842a.

Hallett, Tim, Orla Stapleton, and Michael Sauder. 2019. "Public Ideas: Their Varieties and Careers." *American Sociological Review* 84 (3): 545–76. doi.org/10.1177/0003122419846628.

Hamermesh, Daniel S., and Jeff E. Biddle. 2023. "Days of Work over a Half Century: The Rise of the Four-Day Workweek." *ILR Review*, Nov. doi .org/10.1177/00197939231209965.

Harry, Elizabeth M., et al. 2022. "Childcare Stress, Burnout, and Intent to Reduce Hours or Leave the Job During the COVID-19 Pandemic Among US Health Care Workers." *JAMA Network Open* 5 (7): e2221776. doi .org/10.1001/jamanetworkopen.2022.21776.

Harter, Jim. 2023. "Is Quiet Quitting Real?" *Gallup Workplace* (blog), Sept. 6. www.gallup.com/workplace/398306/quiet-quitting-real.aspx.

Hays, Sharon. 1996. *The Cultural Contradictions of Motherhood.* New Haven, Conn.: Yale University Press.

Hennrich, J., and K. Wohlrabe. 2024. "From 'I Don't Like Mondays' to 'Friday I'm in Love'—Day-of-the-Week Effects in Business Surveys." *Applied Economics Letters*, June, 1–5. doi.org/10.1080/13504851.2024 .2363320.

Hetzner, Christiaan. 2023. "Top German Politician Warns Against Adopting a 4-Day Workweek: 'Never in History Has a Society Increased Its Prosperity by Working Less.'" *Fortune*, Nov. 6.

Ho, Ami, and Akki Stewart. 1992. "Case Study on Impact of 4/40 Compressed Workweek Program on Trip Reduction." *Transportation Research Record* 1346:25–32.

Hochschild, Arlie. 2012. *The Second Shift: Working Families and the Revolution at Home.* New York: Penguin Books.

Huberman, Michael. 2004. "Working Hours of the World Unite? New International Evidence of Worktime, 1870–1913." *Journal of Economic History* 64 (4): 964–1001. doi.org/10.1017/S0022050704043050.

Hunnicutt, Benjamin Kline. 1979. "The Jewish Sabbath Movement in the Early Twentieth Century." *American Jewish History* 69 (2): 196–225.

———. 1988. *Work Without End: Abandoning Shorter Hours for the Right to Work.* Philadelphia: Temple University Press.

———. 1992. "Kellogg's Six-Hour Day: A Capitalist Vision of Liberation Through Managed Work Reduction." *Business History Review* 66 (3): 475–522. doi.org/10.2307/3116979.

Hurst, Luke. 2022. "Workers in Belgium Can Now Switch to a Four-Day Week—but They Won't Be Working Fewer Hours." *Euronews*, Feb. 11. www.euronews.com/next/2022/11/21/workers-in-belgium-can-now-switch-to-a-four-day-week-but-they-wont-be-working-fewer-hours.

Igielnik, Ruth. 2021. "A Rising Share of Working Parents in the U.S. Say It's Been Difficult to Handle Child Care During the Pandemic." Pew Research Center, Jan. 26. www.pewresearch.org/short-reads/2021/01/26/a-rising-share-of-working-parents-in-the-u-s-say-its-been-difficult-to-handle-child-care-during-the-pandemic/.

Jennings, Ed. 2024. "How to Implement a 4-Day Workweek, According to a CEO." *Fast Company*, April 16. www.fastcompany.com/91106578/how-to-implement-a-four-day-work-week-according-to-a-ceo.

Johansen, Kara. 2022. "Cleaning During COVID: Navigating Working Arrangements for House Cleaners and Their Employers in Boston and Dallas." Undergraduate thesis, Boston College. osf.io/jm7bz/.

Kassam, Ashifa. 2021. "Spain to Launch Trial of Four-Day Working Week." *Guardian*, March 15. www.theguardian.com/world/2021/mar/15/spain-to-launch-trial-of-four-day-working-week.

Kauffeld, Simone, and Nale Lehmann-Willenbrock. 2012. "Meetings Matter: Effects of Team Meetings on Team and Organizational Success." *Small Group Research* 43 (2): 130–58.

Kelly, Erin L., et al. 2010. "Gendered Challenge, Gendered Response: Confronting the Ideal Worker Norm in a White-Collar Organization." *Gender and Society* 24 (3): 281–303. doi.org/10.1177/0891243210372073.

Kelly, Erin L., and Phyllis Moen. 2021. *Overload: How Good Jobs Went Bad and What We Can Do About It.* Princeton, N.J.: Princeton University Press.

Keynes, John Maynard. 2010. *Essays in Persuasion.* London: Palgrave Macmillan.

Kharas, Homi, Wolfgang Fengler, and Lukas Vashold. 2023. "Have We Reached Peak Emissions?" Brookings Institution, Nov. 30. www.brookings.edu/articles/have-we-reached-peak-greenhouse-gas-emissions/.

King, Lewis C., and Jeroen C. J. M. van den Bergh. 2017. "Worktime Reduction as a Solution to Climate Change: Five Scenarios Compared for the UK." *Ecological Economics* 132 (February): 124–34. doi.org/10.1016/j.ecolecon.2016.10.011.

Knight, Kyle W., Eugene A. Rosa, and Juliet B. Schor. 2013. "Could Working Less Reduce Pressures on the Environment? A Cross-National Panel Analysis of OECD Countries, 1970–2007." *Global Environmental Change* 23 (4): 691–700.

Krueger, Alyson. 2022. "Endless Summer Fridays." *New York Times*, April 1. www.nytimes.com/2022/04/01/style/four-day-workweek-friday.html.

Laker, Ben, et al. 2022. "The Surprising Impact of Meeting-Free Days." *MIT Sloan Management Review*, Jan. 18. sloanreview.mit.edu/article/the-surprising-impact-of-meeting-free-days/.

Lee, Dain, Jinhyeok Park, and Yongseok Shin. 2023. "Where Are the Workers? From Great Resignation to Quiet Quitting." NBER Working Paper no. 30833, (January). www.nber.org/papers/w30833.

Lewis, Kyle, et al. 2023. "The Results Are In: The UK's Four-Day Week Pilot." London: Autonomy Institute. autonomy.work/portfolio/uk4dwpilotresults/.

Lim, Katherine, and Mike Zabek. 2021. "Women's Labor Force Exits During COVID-19: Differences by Motherhood, Race, and Ethnicity." *Finance and Economics Discussion Series*, October, 1–39. doi.org/10.17016/FEDS.2021.067.

Liu, Jennifer. 2022. "How People Have Changed the Way They Think About Work, According to Their Therapists." CNBC.com, March 16.

www.cnbc.com/2022/03/16/how-people-have-changed-the-way-they
-think-about-work-according-to-their-therapists.html.

Lorentzon, Bengt. 2017. *23 månader med 6 timmar. Följeforskning
om forsok med reducerad arbetstld.* Aarhus: Scandinavian Book.
olivierpintelon.wordpress.com/wp-content/uploads/2017/04
/evaluatierapport-experiment-svartedaelen-23-maanden.pdf.

Luong, Alexandra, and Steven G. Rogelberg. 2005. "Meetings and More
Meetings: The Relationship Between Meeting Load and the Daily Well-
Being of Employees." *Group Dynamics: Theory, Research, and Practice* 9
(1): 58–67. doi.org/10.1037/1089-2699.9.1.58.

Lyle-Edrosolo, Giancarlo. 2023. "The Business Case for Addressing
Burnout in Frontline Leaders: A Toolkit of Interventions from Nurse
Executives Around the United States." *Nursing Administration
Quarterly* 47 (1): 94–99. doi.org/10.1097/NAQ.0000000000000558.

Martucci, Sara. 2023. "He's Working from Home and I'm at Home Trying
to Work: Experiences of Childcare and the Work-Family Balance
Among Mothers During COVID-19." *Journal of Family Issues* 44 (2):
291–314. doi.org/10.1177/0192513X211048476.

Masson-Delmotte, Valérie, et al. 2018. "IPCC, 2018: Summary for
Policymakers." In *Global Warming of 1.5°C*. Cambridge, U.K.:
Cambridge University Press. www.ipcc.ch/sr15/chapter/spm/.

McKeown, Greg. 2014. *Essentialism: The Disciplined Pursuit of Less.* New
York: Crown Currency.

McKnights.com. 2018. "The 30/40 Club." *McKnights Long-Term Care News*,
June. www.mcknights.com/wp-content/uploads/sites/5/2018/07
/mltcn_june2018_execdec_85638.pdf.

McNeill, J. R. 2014. *The Great Acceleration: An Environmental History of
the Anthropocene Since 1945.* Cambridge, Mass.: Harvard University
Press.

Microsoft Work Lab. 2021. "The Next Great Disruption Is Hybrid Work:
Are We Ready?" Work Trend Index Annual Report, March 22.
www.microsoft.com/en-us/worklab/work-trend-index/hybrid
-work.

———. 2022. "Great Expectations: Making Hybrid Work Work." Work
Trend Index Annual Report, March 16. www.microsoft.com/en-us
/worklab/work-trend-index/great-expectations-making-hybrid-work
-work.

———. 2023. "Will AI Fix Work?" Work Trend Index Annual Report, May 9. www.microsoft.com/en-us/worklab/work-trend-index/will-ai-fix -work.

———. 2024. "AI at Work Is Here. Now Comes the Hard Part." Work Trend Index Annual Report, May 8. www.microsoft.com/en-us/worklab /work-trend-index/ai-at-work-is-here-now-comes-the-hard-part?apcid =0064ee6a9372063ff8cc0600.

———. n.d. "The Rise of the Triple Peak Day." www.microsoft.com/en-us /worklab/triple-peak-day.

Moen, Phyllis, et al. 2011. "Changing Work, Changing Health." *Journal of Health and Social Behavior* 52 (4): 402–29.

Moen, Phyllis, et al. 2016. "Does a Flexibility/Support Organizational Initiative Improve High-Tech Employees' Well-Being? Evidence from the Work, Family, and Health Network." *American Sociological Review* 81 (1): 134–64. doi.org/10.1177/0003122415622391.

Moen, Phyllis, and Youngmin Chu. 2023a. Changing Time Study Final Report. University of Minnesota, May.

———. 2023b. "Time Work in the Office and Shop: Workers' Strategic Adaptations to the 4-Day Week." *Work and Occupations*, September. doi.org/10.1177/07308884231203317.

Nässén, Jonas, and Jörgen Larsson. 2015. "Would Shorter Working Time Reduce Greenhouse Gas Emissions? An Analysis of Time Use and Consumption in Swedish Households." *Environment and Planning C: Government and Policy* 33 (4): 726–45.

National Industrial Conference Board. 1929. "The Five-Day Week in Manufacturing Industries." New York: National Industrial Conference Board.

Newport, Cal. 2023. "An Exhausting Year in (and out of) the Office." *New Yorker*, Dec. 27. www.newyorker.com/culture/2023-in-review/an -exhausting-year-in-and-out-of-the-office.

———. 2024. *Slow Productivity: The Lost Art of Accomplishment Without Burnout.* New York: Portfolio/Penguin.

Obeng, Cecilia, Mary Slaughter, and Emmanuel Obeng-Gyasi. 2022. "Childcare Issues and the Pandemic: Working Women's Experiences in the Face of COVID-19." *Societies* 12 (4): 103. doi.org/10.3390 /soc12040103.

Oh, Seung-Yun, Yongjin Park, and Samuel Bowles. 2012. "Veblen Effects, Political Representation, and the Reduction in Working Time over the 20th Century." *Journal of Economic Behavior and Organization* 83 (2): 218–42. doi.org/10.1016/j.jebo.2012.05.006.

O'Neill, Daniel W., et al. 2018. "A Good Life for All Within Planetary Boundaries." *Nature Sustainability* 1 (2): 88–95. doi.org/10.1038/s41893 -018-0021-4.

Pailhé, Ariane, Anne Solaz, and Maria Stanfors. 2021. "The Great Convergence: Gender and Unpaid Work in Europe and the United States." *Population and Development Review* 47 (1): 181–217. doi .org/10.1111/padr.12385.

Pang, Alex Soojung-Kim. 2016. *Rest: Why You Get More Done When You Work Less*. New York: Basic Books.

———. 2020. *Shorter: Work Better, Smarter, and Less—Here's How*. New York: PublicAffairs.

Paul, Kari. 2019. "Microsoft Japan Tested a Four-Day Work Week and Productivity Jumped by 40%." *Guardian*, Nov. 4. www.theguardian .com/technology/2019/nov/04/microsoft-japan-four-day-work-week -productivity.

Pencavel, John. 2015. "The Productivity of Working Hours." *Economic Journal* 125 (589): 2052–76. doi.org/10.1111/ecoj.12166.

Percoco, Marco. 2018. "The Impact of Working Time on Fuel Consumption and CO2 Emissions of Public Fleets: Evidence from a Policy Experiment." *Transport Policy* 71 (November): 126–29. doi .org/10.1016/j.tranpol.2018.08.003.

Perlow, Leslie A., Constance Noonan Hadley, and Eunice Eun. 2017. "Stop the Meeting Madness." *Harvard Business Review*, August.

Pignon, Tatiana, Kyle Lewis, and Liam Mullally. 2024. "Making It Stick: The UK Four-Day Week Pilot One Year On." London: Autonomy Institute. autonomy.work/portfolio/making-it-stick/.

Pink, Joshua, Daiga Kamerade, and Brendan Burchell. 2024. "Four Day Week Trial South Cambridgeshire's Council Key Performance Indicator Evaluation." Cambridge University and Salford University Manchester, July. scambs.moderngov.co.uk/documents/g9810 /Public%20reports%20pack%20Monday%2015-Jul-2024%2010.30 %20Employment%20and%20Staffing%20Committee.pdf?T=10.

Pinsker, Joe. 2020. "Why People Get the 'Sunday Scaries.'" *Atlantic*, Feb. 9. www.theatlantic.com/family/archive/2020/02/sunday-scaries-anxiety -workweek/606289/.

Preston, Camille. 2021. "Pandemic-Related Burnout." *Psychology Today*, January. www.psychologytoday.com/us/blog/mental-health-in-the -workplace/202101/pandemic-related-burnout.

PricewaterhouseCoopers. 2023. "Net Zero Economy Index 2023." www .pwc.co.uk/services/sustainability-climate-change/insights/net-zero -economy-index.html.

Qian, Yue, and Wen Fan. 2024. "Stressful Life Events and Depressive Symptoms During COVID-19: A Gender Comparison." *British Journal of Sociology* 75 (1): 38–47. doi.org/10.1111/1468-4446.13067.

Regan, Tim. 2018. "CCRC to Pay Full-Time for 30 Hours of Work for CNAs." *Senior Housing News*, March 30.

Reynolds, Jeremy, and Ashleigh Elain McKinzie. 2019. "Riding the Waves of Work and Life: Explaining Long-Term Experiences with Work Hour Mismatches." *Social Forces* 98 (1): 427–60. doi.org/10.1093/sf/soy112.

Richardson, Katherine, et al. 2023. "Earth Beyond Six of Nine Planetary Boundaries." *Science Advances* 9 (37). doi.org/10.1126/sciadv.adh2458.

Rogelberg, Steven G. 2022. "The Cost of Unnecessary Meeting Attendance." Otter.ai. otter.ai/meetings.

Rogelberg, Steven G., et al. 2006. "'Not Another Meeting!': Are Meeting Time Demands Related to Employee Well-Being?" *Journal of Applied Psychology* 91 (1): 83–96.

Roh, Taehyun, et al. 2023. "Examining Workweek Variations in Computer Usage Patterns: An Application of Ergonomic Monitoring Software." Edited by Radoslaw Wolniak. *PLoS ONE* 18 (7): e0287976. doi. org/10.1371/journal.pone.0287976.

Roose, Kevin. 2023. "A.I. Poses 'Risk of Extinction,' Industry Leaders Warn." *New York Times*, May 30. www.nytimes.com/2023/05/30 /technology/ai-threat-warning.html.

Sahadi, Jean. 2024. "What's to Become of Summer Fridays in the Age of Hybrid Work?" *CNN Business*, June 21. www.cnn.com/2024/06/21 /business/summer-fridays-hybrid-work/index.html.

Sanok, Joe. 2021. *Thursday Is the New Friday: How to Work Fewer Hours, Make More Money, and Spend Time Doing What You Want.* New York: HarperCollins Leadership.

Sawhill, Isabel V., and Katherine Guyot. 2020. "The Middle Class Time Squeeze." *Economic Studies at Brookings*, Aug. www.brookings.edu /wp-content/uploads/2020/08/The-Middle-Class-Time -Squeeze_08.18.2020.pdf.

Schor, Juliet B. 1985. "Wage Flexibility, Social Welfare Expenditures, and Monetary Restrictiveness." In *Money and Macro Policy*, edited by Marc Jarsulic. Boston: Kluwer-Nijhoff.

———. 1988. "Does Work Intensity Respond to Macroeconomic Variables? Evidence from British Manufacturing, 1970–1986." Harvard Institute for Economic Research. Discussion Paper No. 1379, April.

———. 1991. "Global Inequality and Environmental Crisis: An Argument for Reducing Working Hours in the North." *World Development* 19 (1): 73–84.

———. 1992. *The Overworked American: The Unexpected Decline of Leisure*. New York: Basic Books.

———. 2000. "Working Hours and Time Pressure: The Controversy About Trends in Time Use." In *Working Time: International Trends, Theory, and Policy*, edited by Deb Figart and Lonnie Golden, 73–87. London: Routledge.

Schor, Juliet B., and Samuel Bowles. 1987. "Employment Rents and the Incidence of Strikes." *Review of Economics and Statistics* 69 (4): 584–92.

Schulte, Brigid. 2014. *Overwhelmed: Work, Love, and Play When No One Has the Time*. New York: Sarah Crichton Books.

Shah, Megha K., et al. 2023. "Prevalence of and Factors Associated with Nurse Burnout in the US." *JAMA Network Open* 4 (2): e2036469. doi. org/10.1001/jamanetworkopen.2020.36469.

Shao, Qinglong, and Beatriz Rodriguez-Labajos. 2016. "Does Decreasing Working Time Reduce Environmental Pressures? New Evidence Based on Dynamic Panel Approach." *Journal of Cleaner Production* 125:227– 35. www.sciencedirect.com/science/article/pii/S0959652616301044.

Shukla, P. R., et al. 2022. *IPCC 2022: Climate Change 2022: Mitigation of Climate Change. Contribution of Working Group III to the Sixth Assessment Report of the Intergovernmental Panel on Climate Change*. Cambridge, U.K.: Cambridge University Press.

Skene, Jennifer. 2019. "The Issue with Tissue." Washington, D.C.: National Resources Defense Council. www.nrdc.org/sites/default/files/issue -tissue-how-americans-are-flushing-forests-down-toilet-report.pdf.

Spataro, Jared. 2020. "The Future of Work. The Good, the Challenging & the Unknown." *Microsoft 365* (blog), July 8. www.microsoft.com /en-us/microsoft-365/blog/2020/07/08/future-work-good-challenging -unknown/.

Special to the *New York Times*. 1922. "5-Day, 40-Hour Week for Ford Employees." *New York Times*, March 25.

Stevenson, Mark. 2024. "It's So Hot in Mexico That Howler Monkeys Are Falling Dead from the Trees." AP News, May 22. apnews.com/article /mexico-heat-wave-howler-monkeys-dying-b99e0570dfb53a2fb7ebe6 63acecde78#.

Thompson, E. P. 1967. "Time, Work-Discipline, and Industrial Capitalism." *Past and Present* 38:56–97.

U.S. Bureau of Labor Statistics. 2022. "Average Weekly Hours of All Employees, Total Private." Current Employment Statistics (Establishment Survey). FRED, Federal Reserve Bank of St. Louis. fred .stlouisfed.org/series/AWHAETP.

Venditti, Angelo, Barbara Cottrell, and Kimberly Hanson. 2023. "Designing Structures to Support a 4-Day Workweek for Nurse Leaders." *Nursing Management* 54 (10): 28–32. doi.org/10.1097/nmg .0000000000000057.

Voth, Hans-Joachim. 1998. "Time and Work in Eighteenth-Century London." *Journal of Economic History* 58 (1): 29–58. doi.org/10.1017 /S0022050700019872.

Wei, Holly, et al. 2022. "The Prevalence of Nurse Burnout and Its Association with Telomere Length Pre and During the COVID-19 Pandemic." *PLoS ONE* 17 (3): e0263603. doi.org/10.1371/journal .pone.0263603.

Westfall, Sammy. 2021. "Japan Proposes Four-Day Workweek as Idea Gains Purchase amid Pandemic." *Washington Post*, June 24. www .washingtonpost.com/world/2021/06/24/japan-four-day-work-week/.

Williams, Joan C. 2001. *Unbending Gender: Why Family and Work Conflict and What to Do About It*. New York: Oxford University Press.

Yavorsky, Jill E., Yue Qian, and Amanda C. Sargent. 2021. "The Gendered Pandemic: The Implications of COVID-19 for Work and Family." *Sociology Compass* 15 (6): e12881. doi.org/10.1111/soc4.12881.

Yen, Julie. 2023. "Navigating Tensions Between Well-Being and Productivity: How Win-Win Framing Contributed to the End of a

4-Day Workweek Trial." Unpublished manuscript. Harvard Business School.

Zanhour, Mona, and Dana McDaniel Sumpter. 2024. "The Entrenchment of the Ideal Worker Norm During the COVID-19 Pandemic: Evidence from Working Mothers in the United States." *Gender, Work, and Organization* 31 (2): 625–43. doi.org/10.1111/gwao.12885.

Zijlstra, Fred R. H., et al. 1999. "Temporal Factors in Mental Work: Effects of Interrupted Activities." *Journal of Occupational and Organizational Psychology* 72 (2): 163–85.

INDEX

ABOUT THE AUTHOR

Juliet Schor is an economist and a professor of sociology at Boston College and the bestselling author of numerous books, including *The Overworked American, After the Gig,* and *The Overspent American.* She is a fellow of the American Association for the Advancement of Science and has been featured across national and international media, including the *New York Times,* the *Wall Street Journal, Newsweek, People, 60 Minutes,* the *Today* show, and *Good Morning America.* Her 2022 TED Talk, *The Case for a 4-Day Work Week,* has been viewed more than three million times.